Come What May

The Autobiography

DÓNAL ÓG CUSACK

PENGUIN BOOKS

PENGUIN BOOKS

Published by the Penguin Group
Penguin Books Ltd, 80 Strand, London WC2R ORL, England
Penguin Group (USA) Inc., 375 Hudson Street, New York, New York 10014, USA
Penguin Group (Canada), 90 Eglinton Avenue East, Suite 700, Toronto, Ontario, Canada M4P 2Y3
(a division of Pearson Penguin Canada Inc.)
Penguin Ireland, 25 St Stephen's Green, Dublin 2, Ireland (a division of Penguin Books Ltd)
Penguin Group (Australia), 250 Camberwell Road, Camberwell, Victoria 3124, Australia
(a division of Pearson Australia Group Pty Ltd)
Penguin Books India Pvt Ltd, 11 Community Centre, Panchsheel Park, New Delhi – 110 017, India
Penguin Group (NZ), 67 Apollo Drive, Rosedale, North Shore 0632, New Zealand
(a division of Pearson New Zealand Ltd)
Penguin Books (South Africa) (Pty) Ltd, 24 Sturdee Avenue, Rosebank, Johannesburg 2196, South Africa

Penguin Books Ltd, Registered Offices: 80 Strand, London WC2R ORL, England

www.penguin.com

First published by Penguin Ireland 2009
Published in Penguin Books 2010
3

Typeset by Palimpsest Book Production Limited, Grangemouth, Stirlingshire
Printed in England by Clays Ltd, St Ives plc

ISBN: 978-0-141-04451-4

www.greenpenguin.co.uk

Penguin Books is committed to a sustainable future
for our business, our readers and our planet.
The book in your hands is made from paper
certified by the Forest Stewardship Council.

Acknowledgements

I grew up in Cloyne, a town where hurling is a part of life. There are lots of towns and villages that get tagged with that old cliché. A community that expresses itself through hurling. A place where the game is life and death. A village where religion comes second. And so on.

Each line is true, I suppose. Hurling is in our culture and in our history and in our daily lives. It is our sport and our entertainment and the game courses through our conversations like blood through our veins. It unites us and sometimes it divides us, and when people talk about places like Cloyne, hurling is often the prism through which they view us.

Like most clichés, the one about Cloyne and hurling fits broadly enough but it's lazy too and a little patronizing in the way it bestows a broad simplicity of mind on us all. Life is more complicated than that. We don't live in Cloyne or in Killeagh or in Midleton as a generic tribe of happy folk, content once we have ash to swing and leather or rivals to strike.

We have the usual trials and tribulations. We lose our jobs. Our marriages bust up. Our friendships break. Alcohol ruins some of us. Depression follows others like a black dog. We fight. We love. We scar. We heal. We die.

And when we die, somebody will always say piously that death or illness puts all the hurling into perspective, as if our departed comrade had given his life to something trivial and wasteful. Nobody says it puts it all into perspective when they are walking behind the coffin of a dead musician or a dead poet.

This is my story, the story of Cloyne and the Cork hurling team, and a story about perspective.

I believe hurling is the best of us, one of the greatest and most beautiful expressions of what we can be. For me that is the perspective that death and loss cast on the game. If you could live again you would hurl more, because that is living. You'd pay less attention to the rows and the mortgage and the car and all the daily drudge. Hurling is our song and our verse, and when I walk in the graveyard in Cloyne and look at the familiar names on the headstones I know that their owners would want us to hurl with more joy and more exuberance and more (as Frank Murphy used to tell us) abandon than before, because life is shorter than the second half of a tournament game that starts at dusk.

This is my story and the story of a town and a county where people feel much the same. The game deserves a certain reverence. And where that is absent, most of the people in this book have strived to create it.

The Cork team of which I am privileged to be a part has been on strike three times in the years between 2002 and 2009. The thought of amateur players withdrawing from the county team ran against the grain for many traditionalists. Feelings still run high and I know there are many people who won't buy this book because my name and my face appear on the cover. So it goes.

We are people who share the same sort of daily lives as those who pay in to watch us, and as a team we have experienced extraordinary support and amazing hostility as a result of those strikes. In the end I believe that those who bless us and those who blame us aren't divided by much. If there is a reverence and a respect for the history of the Cork jersey and all the men who wore it once, there is a duty to provide the men who wear the jersey now and those who will wear it in the future with the best possible support. It denigrates the entire history and culture of Cork hurling to send teams out to do their best without having given them the chance to prepare to their best.

Asking for things to change and then fighting for change was always an act of love for the game and for the jersey and for Cork. There are many around the country and in Cork and in Cloyne who felt that what was good enough for previous generations should be good enough for now and for all times.

And yet I see people who opposed us fiercely and who, in our clubs, in Cloyne and elsewhere, work tirelessly to improve everything, from under-age competitions to senior training. They don't say that cold showers were always good enough for the men of the past. Or that the absence of floodlights was always good enough when they played. Or that teams shouldn't warm up and stretch.

All that energy to progress and move on is a part of the character of the GAA clubs everywhere, of the organization which built Croke Park and a network of massive grounds as cathedrals to amateur games. And that energy went missing in Cork. We stagnated.

For the love of the jersey we fought back. This is my part of our story.

There are so many people who helped, from my first steps as a hurler and as a person through to those strikes and beyond, who need to be written about, acknowledged and thanked.

Firstly my parents, Dónal and Bonnie, who put their all into making me what I am, for better or worse. To my brothers, Conor and Victor, and my sister, Treasa, for putting up with me most of the time and supporting me the rest of the time. Not always easy to do either. (I never told you, Conor, but I felt so proud to have my younger brother on the field with me in an All-Ireland final, especially knowing where you had come from to get there. From 19 stone 13 pounds in the bad days to 13 stone that day is a long journey.)

To my uncles and aunts, twenty-five of them, and to my Grand-father Mick who lives by his own word: 'Live while you can and die when you can't help it.'

To all my friends. There are few things as important to me in life as friendship and I have been blessed to have great friends. You know who you are. At times I'm an odd fish, I know, but your friendship and support mean more to me than I could ever express.

To the people of Cloyne. Ye made me mad and ye keep me sane. And to the master, Michael O'Brien, for nurturing the love of the game in me.

To all my teammates in the red jersey of Cork and in the red-and-black of Cloyne down the years. We soldiered together and had good days and bad together. On the bad days I wasn't always the easiest to share a dressing-room with. In my defence I can only quote Willie 'Alien' Beamen from *Any Given Sunday*: 'I'm trying to win, coach. I ain't trying to disrespect nobody, but winning is the only thing I respect.' It's not quite the only thing I respect, but the bond will always be there, boys.

Through the strikes and troubles lots of people, too many to list, came to help us and guide us. My friend Diarmaid Falvey has always been there for me and for Cork. In this last strike (to end all strikes!) we had the help of some wonderful people. Thanks to the Duhallow Five, Denis Withers of Banteer, Donie Mahony of Kilbrin, John O'Flynn of Freemount, Jim Sullivan of Castlemagner and Bridie Murphy from Meelin. Ye hit the pitch at just the right time in the game. On Saturday mornings when we trained alone as a team, we would be fed and tended to royally afterwards by the women of Na Piarsaigh, Eleanor Gardiner, Ca Martin, Ann Cooke, Mary Kelleher, Ann Coade, Joan Guest, Pauline Burke. To Clyda Rovers and their chairman John Roche, Cathriona O'Callaghan and Don McEvoy. One night Don came to me with money that people in a local pub had collected for us; the money mightn't have lasted long but the memory of the kindness will. To Kieran Miller and Mallow GAA club for the use of their facilities. To all of ye, your warmth at a time when we were out in the cold was something special for us.

To Paddy Healy for valiant deeds too various to mention, to Ray O'Mahony, to the Bomber Roche and his friend Paul, and Pa the Piper, for being on the front line with us.

To the people who followed and encouraged us the times we needed it most, Gerry O'Sullivan, Fanahan O'Leary, Mary Cahill, Con O'Keefe, Rory O'Driscoll, Tomás Ryan, Carmel Hackett, Niamh Hackett, Anthony Duggan, Claire Duggan, Tim Crowley, Val Dempsey, Paul Kiely, Jo Anne O'Sullivan, Willie Coleman, Jer the Chief, Barry O'Sullivan, Jillian Kiely, Ken Kiely, John Dunne, Ronan Sheehan, John Buckley and James Cadogan.

To Brian Corcoran for, well, just being the man he is and not sitting on the fence.

To Opel and Richard in Johnson and Perrott, to Catherine Tiernan of O2, to Eddie McGrath of C&C, to Louise in the washeteria, to May Motherway for the biscuits, and to Eddie O'Donnell for your guidance. You have all made my journey easier.

To the lads in the Alley Bar, Cathal, Billy and Mos, what a craic and experience.

To the friends I lost due to the demands of the game along the way, including Fran, Tosh, Dax and Bounce.

To all my work colleagues in DePuy, a place I always think of as a little piece of America put down in Ringaskiddy, a land of opportunity for anybody willing to work. And to Sean Ahern for putting me on the right path at the start.

To Dessie Farrell, a Dub and a comrade who became my friend, and to all the colleagues in the GPA.

To Tom Humphries. Sometimes you know you are in the presence of someone special. More rarely you get the chance to work closely with them and get a glimpse inside of their heart. I was privileged to do all of these things. Thanks, Tom.

In putting this book together Michael McLoughlin and Brendan Barrington of Penguin Ireland were indispensable. Thanks to Martina McGilloway and George Hatchell for their wonderful photographs and to Louise Dumbrell for all her work.

And that's it.

This story begins with an infamous defeat and a bad day. Part of life is picking yourself up after days like that. It takes drive and sometimes it takes a certain selfishness if you are to get there.

I'm no angel, never claimed to be and never want to be – but this place, this book, this is the corner I'm coming from. I didn't write this book to gain friend or foe. This is just my story and how I saw things. I know well that the way I viewed things and felt things might be different from the way a lot of people mentioned in these pages saw things, and I respect that, especially if they viewed them with passion and fight in their hearts.

I read something a long time ago about moderation being 'lukewarm tea, the devil's own brew'. It stuck with me . . .

Moderation? It's neither doing nor not doing. It's the wobbling compromise that makes no one happy. Moderation is for the bland, the apologetic, for the fence-sitters of the world, afraid to take a stand. It's for those afraid to laugh or cry, for those afraid to live or die. And, I would add, for those afraid to love or hate.

Mostly these pages are filled, I hope, with love for the place I come from and for the game which holds us in its grasp. We spend all our lives mastering it and at some point we stop and realize that the game has mastered us. Friend and foe, we are hurling people, all driven by our passions.

And if not? Sure, enjoy your lukewarm tea.

A room. Four walls lined with pale faces. Lads with their backs pressed against the cold walls behind them. No air. No chat. We're almost dead and this room is our vault. How do we like it?

It's OK. We could sit in this silence for ever. The door is shut. The unforgiving world is outside. We're in here. It's warm enough and safe enough and we have little or nothing to say to each other. Almost nothing.

We have just retreated and barred the world behind us. In the next few minutes we need to find a miracle in this dressing-room because outside we are getting hammered. It's worse than that: we are being laid bare. We are being made fun of. We are having strips torn off us and handed back to us. By Kilkenny.

We can barely begrudge them their fun though, can we? They are cold and ruthless about it, but it's fun just the same.

And it's business.

And it's personal.

I've been playing against Kilkenny teams since I was a young fella, starting with the minor final, back in 1995 (Cork 2-10, Kilkenny 1-2), and I know that if the boot was on the other foot I'd be doing exactly what they are doing. I'd be tramping down the dirt on their graves and I'd be wearing a smile.

I play for Cork. This thing for me over the last few years has been more personal than just wearing a red jersey, though. It's been us against them. Sully against Comerford, Seán Óg against Shefflin, Joe Deane against Hickey, and so on. We play for Cork but there is more to it than that for us. And for a lot of them there is more to it as well. Under those stripey jerseys beat hearts with a genuine disdain for us and what we stand for. Cold as it may sound, it *is* us and it *is* them.

If we lose today, any day, it is Kilkenny beating Cork. Not just that, though: it's also those fuckers beating us. And a lot of people will be pleased.

It's funny. We were born as a team, in the public's mind anyway, ten years ago in an All-Ireland final against Kilkenny. We were a bunch of kids who came out of nowhere. Cork hadn't even been in an All-Ireland final for nine years. And on a greasy day we beat the odds and we beat Kilkenny and won the All-Ireland championship of 1999. Everybody said we were a fine thing to happen to the game of hurling.

And we have grown up in the rivalry with these fellas and their county and their black-and-amber colours and their tradition which they hold up against ours every now and then to measure their worth. We've grown up and grown apart from them. Now? We are the trouble-makers, the unforgiven, the outlaws. They are the men you'd want your daughters to marry.

We went our separate ways, I suppose, back in 2002. They have seen themselves as another species since then, something more evolved perhaps. The differences between the two sides define the teams on and off the field now, but we first noticed that gap on the day of the league final of 2002, when we played Kilkenny in Thurles.

That winter and spring in Cork we were having a particularly bad time as players. Every time we tried to open our wings and take flight again, the County Board seemed to grip us tighter and tighter. Morale hit bottom when we were asked by the County Board one Tuesday evening to take half a day off work on the Friday of that same week. We were to get a bus the length of the country to Derry. On previous trips to Derry we had always flown. Now we were to sit in a bus for 220 miles while we were supposed to be at work.

The players met that Tuesday night and talked about getting ourselves organized within the Gaelic Players' Association. Management didn't like it, but the need for something to be done was underlined for us after the game with Derry.

Niall McCarthy received a bad gash to the face. Our team doctor, Dr Con Murphy, hadn't been able to travel with us and Niall got a few perfunctory stitches from the Derry doctor. The gash was so bad that it bled all the way home. Niall sat on the bus for hour after hour, pressing handkerchiefs against his wound to staunch the bleeding.

When we got home Niall was finally brought to a hospital for more stitches.

The GPA was looking around that spring for a way to make a symbolic gesture on the issue of players' rights and welfare. After much debate it was suggested (and this sounds so naïve, looking back, that it is almost embarrassing to remember) that we, both Cork and Kilkenny, would wear our jerseys hanging outside our shorts and our socks down around our ankles in the pre-match parade in Semple Stadium before the league final. It wouldn't be anarchy but it would be a small, good thing to do along the road to making things better for all players.

The night before the game Andy Comerford, the Kilkenny captain, rang me as arranged at nine o'clock. I was driving out from Midleton in my Micra.

'Look, you're in trouble for tomorrow.'

They'd had some internal debate up in Kilkenny, but their manager, Brian Cody, had buried the issue. Their big men, the likes of D. J. Carey and Charlie Carter, were out for that game. Andy was alone on this.

'I got no backing.'

He didn't think anybody from Kilkenny was going to protest the next day but he said that he would go through with it himself. He impressed me, but there wasn't much to say.

'Andy, we've had our own troubles as well but there will be more than one of us doing it.'

I could tell he felt he was letting us down but that he had done what he could.

'Anyway, Andy, look sure we'll drive on, whatever happens in the game happens and so be it, but fair play to you. At least you stood up.'

Sure enough, Andy Comerford had the socks down the next day. That might seem childish now but that small gesture stood for something. Especially if you were a county player struggling to find the right support for your career. Especially if you had been on that bus journey from Derry. Especially after what we had to go through before the game.

We Cork players were called into a room and Bertie Óg Murphy, our manager at the time, gave a loud and passionate speech about history and tradition. Some of the names that he dusted down were abducted from the annals of Cork hurling, some of them legends, some of them men who had either had their day or who were spinning in their graves at the thought of our protest. They were dragged into it, though, enlisted against us! But in our hearts we felt that this was our time. As well as the responsibility that the Cork jersey carries, we had the right to make our own path.

I remember Jimmy McEvoy, the team's masseur – who became a very good friend afterwards – came to me and said, 'I'm going to ask you a favour – call off the thing today, will you?'

I looked at Jimmy. Either someone had got to him or he was cracking under the pressure. I said, 'That ain't going to happen, Jimmy, whatever this ends up in let it be.'

The pressure and the melodrama was incredible over such a small gesture, but the issue of players' rights was a genie that could never be let out of the bottle. There would be no getting the lid on again. Especially in Cork!

There were actual tears shed that day because of the pressure and the sense of guilt that came with being told you were committing an atrocity against the world's greatest amateur sporting organization. The fabric of the nation was going to crumble and decay if we wore our socks around our ankles. All for making a modest point about player welfare.

In the end there were seven or eight of us from Cork who went through with our harmless protest, and Comerford who did it for Kilkenny.

Our problem was that we went and got beaten then. Jesus Christ, it was tough being beaten by them, having been isolated when it came to making the protest. Any of the critics who wanted to pile in and kick us to death for what we had done, they had a licence now.

We didn't change the world that day, but for us the whole business left a sour taste about Kilkenny. We were disappointed in them and in things that were said in the papers the following week. I remember Peter Barry of Kilkenny was on the *Examiner* the next day, saying that all he wanted to do was play for Kilkenny, thank you. Peter, in fairness, has since cleared it up and said he was being misquoted, out of context, etc., which, from what I've since come to understand about the media, is very plausible.

But I remember thinking at the time, Thanks, Peter, we're down and now you're burying us.

Now. Some of the biggest kicks I have got out of the GPA involvement have been in the response you'd get from other counties, weaker counties, players writing and saying that things had changed for them because of what has happened in Cork over the years and because of what Cork and the GPA had done. I always think that Kilkenny could have driven it on as much as we did, but maybe they just genuinely were happy with their own lot. That's their choice, but even they have benefited along the road.

Some of them benefited individually. Big time. A couple of them have won cars and stuff like that out of the GPA being there and they have gone and done television ads. Best of luck to them. That's how it should be. But I have no problem saying that the GPA would not have survived at one stage were it not for the Cork hurlers, and that all players have benefited from that.

(One of the prime pieces of abuse that gets flung at us as a group in Cork is that because of our association with the GPA we must be obsessively greedy. Everyone has some twisted myth to back this up.

But I know that Seán Óg turned down very serious money to appear in an ad for a certain sports drink but stuck with Club Energise because C&C actually put something back into the GPA. And who is the player who starred in an expensive Club Energise campaign and now appears shilling on behalf of Lucozade? A Kilkenny star who had done well out of the GPA.)

We have made different journeys. We struggled and Kilkenny left us out there to walk our path alone.

Through all the troubles we have had we have often thought how much easier and how much more effective for all players this would be if Kilkenny and Cork were marching together. Fine, let's flake each other on the pitch but let's pull together off it.

It hasn't happened like that, though. The more strife we have in Cork, the more pointedly 'of the establishment' Kilkenny seem to become. The more disorder there is in Cork, the more Kilkenny likes to be thought of fondly as the land of milk, honey and contentment. The GAA's version of the Stepford Wives.

They went their way, I suppose, and we went ours. They are a great team but I wouldn't be gone on them bar, say, Eddie Brennan, who I know stands up for the GPA in a tough dressing-room environment. I do understand that they have their different ways and who am I to say which way is the best or right? We all have to take our journeys and do what we have to do, but Kilkenny? I wouldn't be gone on them.

I'd imagine the feeling runs both ways.

A few minutes ago, for instance, I got showers of abuse as we were coming into the tunnel for half-time. Gatchy (Martin Walsh, our logistics man) knew what was going on. He had heard Kilkenny supporters chanting, 'Where's The Nigger Now?' in the first half. He was beside himself with hurt and rage for Seán Óg. The abuse kept coming down as we entered the tunnel: 'Cusack, you fucker, ye are still on strike!' – and worse, of course. When I was warming up, some of their supporters couldn't help but proudly draw attention to a banner they had draped over the hoardings. It said, 'We'll Strike To Keep Liam McCarthy!'

Coming in at half-time, Gatchy couldn't resist looking for the source of the comments. I just stared straight ahead. I think he would have gone into the crowd and fought.

I appreciated Gatchy's company and support, but I said to him after that if we ever found ourselves in that situation again he shouldn't acknowledge the guys who are shouting. Don't be staring at them or looking at them. Either ignore them or just go up into the stand or terrace or wherever and fight them! Anything in between seems pointless to me.

This is their day, though. Here we are, rehabilitating ourselves as a team after a long and bitter strike, and they are beating us by thirteen points at half-time in a league game in their back garden. Through almost all of this league campaign they have been overpowering teams, but today they are mowing us down for the sheer joy of it. Their crowd are cheering every wound they inflict on us. The abuse coming down to me from the terraces is among the worst I can remember. It's poison but there is such glee in it. We are the unforgiven. They don't just want us beaten, they want us torn limb from limb. When the Cork team van with all the equipment in it pulled in a few hours ago, a small group of Kilkenny gentlemen came out carrying the Liam McCarthy Cup and posed for their picture in front of our van! Don't know who they were, but they had access to the holy grail. It was like posing with one foot on our chest before they kicked sand in our faces.

And us? We're not structured for a battle at all. As a result of the third players' strike to hit Cork GAA in seven years we have new management today. A new leader and new players, lots of them. It's nobody's fault but we have no system, no idea as to who is doing what. Even among the players we have no clue about who are the guys we can look to and who are the guys just along for the ride. We're coming out of a civil war after all!

So everyone in this silent dressing-room is just wondering what is going to happen next, and some are wondering how the fuck they got to be here in the first place. The seconds are ticking by. We'll have to go out there again soon.

I think to myself that this is some start for Denis Walsh, our new boss. He was given the option of waiting until we had finished our league campaign before taking the appointment. If he had exercised that option he would have spared himself this.

In fairness, our brand-new manager is very calm. There is little to be said, so that's what he does. He says very little, just that there were many people who had been hoping that we would crack over the winter but we hadn't cracked. That's what he says. We are here and we have to walk on from here.

(As we sit here I think back to Gerald McCarthy, our last manager and the central figure in the war we have just fought. I know what he'd be saying to us now. Same old, same old. 'Ye have five fucking minutes now lads to start playing.' And then Gerald would hit us with the cure-all remedy. 'Get down over the ball, boys, down over the ball.' And we'd be sitting there thinking, Fuck getting down over the ball, Gerald, we're trying to find a way out of here, tell us where to start digging.)

Our new management are still unsure as to where the fractures are in this wounded dressing-room. They are looking at us, the older guys, to give a lead and I know a lot of the older guys are looking at me, to see if I'll be the one to speak.

Ben O'Connor says a few words and as he speaks I look around this room and this new mix of faces. There are fellas here who played for Cork while we were on strike. There are faces I scarcely know. There are comrades I've played with all my adult life who are missing.

Generally I don't open my mouth during league games, but Pa Finn, one of our new selectors, whispers to me on the quiet: 'Fucking talk here, will ya. It's too quiet.'

He's right, so I say a few words too.

'Lads, a lot of us don't know each other and even some of us have had differences, but we're in trouble here. They won't stop. They won't. They will try to bury us. Everything that we are not but everything that our enemies say we are is being shown out there today. What these fuckers say we are is how we are looking out there. Like I say, a lot of us don't know each other but we are in trouble here. We need to get out of here. Whatever it takes, we need to change the course of this game.'

And that's it.

It's only half-time. There's some fellas in here who were trying to kill us a few weeks ago. And we were trying to kill them. That was our civil war and this is the aftermath. There is no point in talk or delusions just now. We have no structure to claw our way back to today. No chance left. We'll have to take what is coming to us now and start healing ourselves next week.

On other days, in other places, we have had our backs to the wall too, but even if we were on our last legs, still we had our men, our warriors, our spirit or love or whatever. Still we would say, 'Fuck it, we will find a way out of this.' But to engage with fellas now and talk to them to start the process here in this vault? Stop.

I know that I will be sick to my stomach for a week after this. That I will want to be alone. That I won't be able to speak to my father about hurling for days. That I will go to the gym in Cloyne, turn out the lights in case the boys come looking for me and see the lights glowing. I'll just turn on my music full blast. I'll work it out of myself, letting loose the odd scream, the odd mad roar into the darkness. Losing hurts me like I can't describe.

The Kilkenny fellas are coming up the corridor past our dressing-room now. We can hear their studs on the concrete outside. We're happy with the journey we have made, our three All-Ireland titles, our five Munster wins, the stands we took; but damn, we'd like to be them right now. The best team in the country, at home against their old enemy and winning big in this vicious, partisan atmosphere. They got a standing ovation at half-time when they were coming in. We got the spiteful flipside of it when we came traipsing in after them.

Now they are back out for more sport and adulation. All their big guns are coming out to get a piece of us. They've had a good league campaign but we are the target now. They want to stuff and mount our heads on a wall.

In here after all these years we feel like boys, not men. We haven't our warriors with us. Half of our backs have never played a serious game for Cork before. We have new management. We are tentative. We hardly know each other, let alone trust each other. We listen in silence to Kilkenny as they go past our door.

We have nothing to fall back on. They have everything to look forward to. They are walking back to the battlefield, just picking it up into a run now as they pass us. We listen. We are their prey. Not black sheep any more but lambs, fucking lambs. It's not a hunt. We're fucking kidding ourselves. It's a cull. We hear them passing the door. They aren't shouting and roaring. They are focusing. They know we are inside here and they know we are in trouble. Their studs go click, click, click on the concrete. Click click click.

We stand up eventually and we go back out. It's cold. We are against the wind, leaning into the chill. It's Kilkenny. They will set about us like pathologists, opening us here and opening us there. The championship is nine weeks away.

We are dead.

2

I don't know if it is because Cloyne has its own abbey and a famous old round tower or that we have a bishop patrolling a diocese named after our own village, but my home place used to be a great advertisement for the Catholic Church's view of contraception.

My father grew up next door to my mother in a terrace of small houses which ran around in a little ring. There were eleven children in my father's family. Next door in the Costines', where he found my mother, there were fourteen children, seven boys and seven girls. And just across the ring – twenty yards away – were the O'Sheas. They outbred everyone with fifteen kids.

That's forty kids from three tiny houses. There must have been stampedes when the school bell was ringing. If the bishop had any serious notions though about Cloyne being a genuine centre of the faith, he only had to visit us. The church was a minority interest. Hurling was, and still is, our one true religion. That's a cliché in a lot of places. It's a fact of life in Cloyne. Hurling runs the town. The town runs on hurling. It's our love and our celebration and our identity and our source of community. That's what we talk about. Hurling. That's what we daydream about. Hurling. That's what we do. We hurl.

My Aunt Fay tells a story. Her sister's children ended up playing hurling for Midleton, which is a few short miles up the road. As it happened, one day when we were very small kids, we, Cloyne, ended up playing Midleton.

My aunt, as she always did after my grandfather died, drove my grandmother to the game. Anything involving a Cloyne hurling team was of devout interest to my grandmother. My cousins Liam and Pat Walsh were playing for Midleton that day.

With two grandchildren hurling in the black-and-white of Midleton and one hurling for Cloyne, it would never have occurred to my grandmother to be impartial. She spent the game roaring for Cloyne, and roaring for me in the famous red-and-black jersey. My mother's sister Brenda didn't speak to my grandmother for the longest time afterwards over it. My aunt thought that her mother was favouring one grandchild over the other pair. She was, but my grandmother was just doing what she always did, shouting for Cloyne.

That's how things were. Always. We grew up in a house that backed on to the hurling field. A sacred place once known as Spillane's Field, it had been there since the early 1930s, right in the centre of Cloyne. It served as our back garden.

When I was small I used to go out the field with the big boys. Everybody in Cloyne has a nickname and mine back then was Liga because I'd arrive out the field with my Liga biscuit in my mouth (today, a lot of fellas even on the Cork team call me Boscheen or Bosch). My Aunty Fay, my dad's sister, had cut down a couple of old Cloyne jerseys and stitched them back together to make me a little Cloyne jersey when I was just about still in nappies. I was small but I was ready to go.

Once you were old enough to go out over the back wall of our house and on to the hurling field, you never looked back. You weren't just a kid any more, you were part of the life of Cloyne. You were good or you were a prospect or they thought they could make a hurler of you if only . . . In the evening, especially the long amber summer evenings, we played games that lasted for ever. And the games were life and death to us.

We would have endless competitions and tournaments. Men and boys all playing. We'd pick teams during the day when we younger fellas would be pucking about and messing in the field, just arguing the toss for hours over who could mark who. You heard some fairly frank opinions about your own ability. And you gave some brutally honest opinions about everybody else's. The games would be played in the evenings after the day's work.

My best buddy was this fella we called Casper because he was so pale. Another fella – Ger Lewis, who was a bit of legend in the town – was called Smurf, because of his habit of wearing a funny cap when he played. He was one of the three Lewis brothers who played on the Cloyne team that got promoted from Junior level to Intermediate in 1987, a huge thing in our history. Joe was Bomber, for obvious reasons

(Joe Louis, wake up!), and Johnny was Horse, a midfielder/half-forward and a big powerful man. Smurf was corner-forward, a real goal-poacher and the star who came up with the goals whenever they were needed.

I was only a kid, but I can remember walking up the village one night when we had won and seeing Smurf standing outside the Alley Bar having a drink. He was that much of a hero around the place that you'd remember something small like that from the famous night. Smurf having a drink.

Hurleys were always an issue. We had one of those old Wavin plastic hurleys in the house. It was sort of a sacrilegious item, but we had one anyway. For some reason, when it came to games in the field Smurf more often than not would have no hurley, and though he was a few years older than me I'd always look after that for him. I'd always have the grey Wavin hurley hidden for Smurf just in case he would announce that he had no stick and therefore couldn't play. If I could get the hurley for him he'd make sure he was on my team, and having Smurf with you was always an advantage.

You couldn't count the hours we spent in that field. It wasn't a thing of childhood. If you could play, you came to the field. That's where you found the men of Cloyne as long as there was daylight. The tension! Jesus, from the start I hated losing. I remember one time being picked with a bad team and knowing that it was a waste of time, that we were going to lose. I hadn't the heart for it. Casper was captain of that team, and I had to tell Casper I wasn't going to play and I had to come up with a reason. I had a brainwave: I hid my hurley, then I went and told Casper that I couldn't play because my hurley was missing, tragically lost.

Cloyne has grown since then, but essentially our village is just four streets. The senior hurling team for the past few years generally has ten starters who come from just three families, the Cahills, the Cusacks and the O'Sullivans, and there are other big Cloyne families who would trace their family trees down through the history of Cloyne and the history of our hurling.

I'm thirty-two years old now, my brother Conor is two years behind and Victor is another two years back. I have been playing for Cork for a long time. Conor had a run with the county and came on as a sub in the All-Ireland final in 2006. My friend Diarmuid O'Sullivan became a legend with Cork. Yet Victor, who had one year minor and three years under-21 starting with Cork, is the most talked-about man among management teams. The enigma wrapped up in a riddle and then fogged in some mystique.

I don't know if Victor just resisted falling into line with his two older brothers, but he can take or leave the hurling. This makes him so unusual that we worry about him, and ourselves. How do we get it out of him, how do we get Victor feeling about hurling the same way the rest of us do? How do we interest him again? What's eating Victor Cusack? For the rest of us, hurling is just the bread and water of our days. His indifference, or whatever it is, makes us feel odd. Being born in Cloyne means you hurl, as our club motto says, come what may.

When I was young I had an over-active thyroid gland which stymied me a bit when it came to training. I'd get pains in my chest and my heart would be pumping scarily. I couldn't do much running, and in those days Cloyne's idea of training was basically to go out and about, running the length and breadth of the parish. Dr Con diagnosed the thyroid problem. (I remember one cross-country run through the Rostellan woods near Aghada. We were doing a circuit. I was way behind when I took a short cut and dropped straight into the middle of a ton of briars. As easy to keep going forward as back. By the time I rejoined the group I was covered in blood and scratches.)

Anyway, I came up with a plan one night that would keep me hurling: when the running began I would lag behind and then at the right moment hide myself in some bushes for half an hour till the bunch came back around and then I'd quietly rejoin them. I was a decent hurler. If I could get through this running business with nobody noticing a weakness, I'd be grand. I picked my moment and I picked my spot. I hid out, waiting and waiting, till I heard them come panting back. When the lads came jogging past with their chests heaving and their feet starting to drag I waited another half a minute and slipped out and after them in the slipstream. All good – except I hopped straight into the path of my friend Cathal Cronin. Cathal was a bit on the heavy side and acutely aware of it. He was lagging well behind the pack.

Now we both had a dilemma. Some desperate bargaining followed. Well, not so much bargaining as begging. Would either of us tell? My crime was greater, so my position was weaker.

'Please, Cathal, don't tell. Don't tell the boys. For fuck's sake, please.'

'Right so, Liga.'

What does he do when he comes in to the hall? The one thing that will shift the attention away from his own late arrival.

'Dónal Óg was hiding in the bushes!'

My father, being a practical man who felt he could fix anything, got the idea into his head that steak was the very thing that would sort out my busy thyroid. We weren't on the breadline but we weren't a house that would see a steak on the plate every day either. But this was Cloyne and I was going to be a hurler and action had to be taken. So for a long time my brothers uncomplainingly ate their regular meals while his lordship the hurling prospect would be served steak. Every day!

Before I would leave for Harty Cup matches in secondary school I would have a steak for my breakfast. A big steak! I'd be in school digesting a fine slab of meat while everyone else was half filled with their cornflakes or Coco Pops.

I was the eldest and I was our father's prospect for hurling. If it wasn't a Harty Cup day I'd have porridge for breakfast. Dad – a tough man with a job driving cranes to get to – would bring up the steaming bowl of porridge for me to eat in bed before he left for work. Even then I knew the way of the world: the main thing that was driving the man up the stairs every morning with the porridge was hurling. Not the day's study, not building me up to get a job. Hurling.

And of course, like every other hurler in Cloyne, we Cusacks measured ourselves against the great *laoch* who grew up a couple of doors down from our own house. Our strides and our footprints were smaller than his, but we couldn't stop ourselves comparing and wondering. Ring. Ring. Ring. Christy Ring.

Listen. George Berkeley, the famous philosopher and empiricist, was Bishop of Cloyne for eighteen years from 1734 onwards and there is a monument to him in the cathedral. The city where the University of California's main campus is located is named for him. No such luck in Cloyne. Not even a saloon bar.

His lordship would be pleased to know that as we are unable to see him we don't recognize his existence. He never hurled, so he might as well never have existed. We think about him and talk about him hardly ever – not even to refute him, like Dr Johnson. His monument could disappear overnight and it might be weeks before the alarm was raised.

Berkeley, like all of us, takes his place in the shadow of Christy Ring. No matter how Cloyne grows and expands, it will always be Christy Ring's home place. He came from the house just a door or so up from our own, and if we trace the steps back I am distantly related to him. The Rings can claim their presence here back to the fourteenth century. My father always says that we go back just as far. Probably further, if records allowed us to.

Ring drives us on, even though he died two years after I was born. When myself, Conor and Victor were younger, Dad would bring us out to the hurling field and he'd teach us how to hurl. He wouldn't tolerate us not putting our hands up to catch the sliotar and insisted on us keeping our heads up without ducking, no matter how quickly the thing was hurtling at us. He would throw the ball up between us – there were no helmets at that time – and we would tussle away.

Our instinct, like most kids, was to put up the stick and bat the ball away or duck. If we did that though he would crack. It was a sin. Sensing his fury, whichever of us had committed the mortal sin of refusing to catch would make a run for the house, zig-zagging like a soldier under fire till he got there As he ran for home, Dad would be firing sliotars low and hard at whichever of his sons had become the latest to disappoint him.

I said it to him years later about how he would drive those balls at us as we ran for the kitchen.

'Arrah sure I would only be aiming for yeer legs.'

'We were three feet tall. You were good but you weren't that fucking good!'

That's part of the lineage, though. Dad would fire balls at us when we were young fellas. If you complained too loudly when you got into the house you'd hear the story of how Christy Ring used to hit Dad blows of the hurley to his elbow every Saturday.

My grandmother was first cousin from Christy Ring. Dad would go home as we would later, keen to air his grievances to a mother who was as daft about hurling as the rest of the village.

'My elbows are all sore from Christy Ring hitting them.'

'Ah! Christy! Christy! Sure, don't mind that at all.'

If it was anybody else in Cloyne hitting her son, there'd be trouble. But Christy? That was grand. Almost an honour.

Ring was vicious about winning. He had the killer instinct in him that a guy like Henry Shefflin has or like Ben O'Connor has. He hated losing. He would come home to Cloyne every Saturday – cycling the twenty miles from the city to our village in his early years, driving when he got older – to play a match in the field behind our houses.

The scene has always been easy for us to imagine when we look out the back windows at the hurling pitch. The men and the boys would be waiting on Saturday in the field for Ring to come out from Cork. Next thing, there would be a few balls fired out from over the wall of the Ring house and Christy would be after getting home. Christy himself would come out half an hour or so afterwards and they'd start the match.

My dad was quick and brave, a forward on the Cork minors of 1961, and he could get away with the ball on his stick. Christy Ring was big but he was quick too and he'd give chase, smacking the hurl into his elbows as he went, just to see what Dad was made of.

Now Ring could be playing a Munster final the next day. It might be ten at night by the time they would finish. The local fellas would be big strong men and in Cloyne, though few would say it then or now, there would have been some mixed feelings because Ring had left our club and gone to play with Glen Rovers in the city. It is said that at the time Cloyne people broke the windows in the Ring house.

Imokilly would have been the senior outlet, the divisional team into which small clubs like Cloyne poured their best players for the championship in the days before senior status came our way. One year Imokilly played against the Glen in the Cork county championship. Ring got three goals at the end of the game to save it for the Glen, having been quiet all day. He was being marked by a fella from Killeagh, just up the road, and nothing would do the Killeagh man but to kick and mock Ring while Imokilly were ahead. Ring went and got the three goals for his retaliation.

Anyway, on Saturdays Bunty Cahill, our biggest and toughest man, or one of the Aherne brothers, would be put in to mark Christy Ring, and often on those Saturdays one or other of them would be split open with the blood pouring. Ring might have a game to play for Cork the next day but he would never give in. Bunty (Philip on his birth cert) and the Aherne lads would never have allowed Ring's diary for the following day to inhibit the enjoyment of marking him. Ring would never have asked to be spared.

Every Saturday, Ring would be down. He knew, as we all grew up knowing, that hurling in Cloyne was a religious duty with its own rites and rituals. His sister Mary Agnes was stone mad for the hurling as well. Every two hours or so she would come out to the field with this big tray of ponnys, they used to call them, little tin cups and a big dish of water.

'C'mon now lads, c'mon Christy.'

And the boys would all rush over at top speed because legend has it that the last fella that was drinking from the dish would almost be drinking blood, with all the fellas' cut hands and the spitting and rinsing.

Ring's barrel-chested statue stands high on a plinth in Spittal Street for us to pass under every time we walk into or out of the club. On our club crest there is a star as the centrepiece. It represents Ring. And there is a teardrop on the heart because he did leave Cloyne. It was with Glen Rovers in the city that he won his thirteen county championship medals. The tear expresses the sadness of Cloyne and also the hope that we should be strong enough that no great player would ever have to leave again.

That's Ring. That's Cloyne. That's us.

3

These last few years, when spring comes it brings that feeling of the world suddenly bearing down on us with more momentum than it had the year before. I suppose it's called getting old? Tipperary wait for us at the end of May. Before that we will have club championship business with Cloyne. Another tilt at the windmill.

It's four years since Cork won an All-Ireland. Players are retiring. Most people think our chances of another big win together as a team are seeping away with every season. So is our youth. But I'll keep turning up for every battle. I still believe.

When we were kids, the summer and the championship couldn't come around quick enough. We rushed through the winters of hard preparation, we loved the sudden stretch in the evenings, and we longed for those big days and summer hurling so much that we hardly thought about what it all meant or how brief it would all be. We expected to win. If we didn't there would always be another season coming around the bend. Now the seasons that we have left to us are few. It all goes a bit too fast.

Since we last won an All-Ireland with Cork, appearing in our fourth final in a row and narrowly failing to win our third title in a row, we have watched Kilkenny win three in succession. With Cloyne we climbed the mountain three times but never planted the flag. Three county finals in a row and a pain that grows inside us like a tumour. Still no county title for our club, and the last of those finals was three years ago, in 2006. We are a small village with just over 2,500 souls. I fear that those three defeats could turn out to be what passes as a golden age for us.

And it was two years ago in March that I came to the Alley Bar in Cloyne, a place I run with three friends, and noticed an unusual number of cars parked through the village. An odd thing Smurf had said to me about not being around the following weekend just had time to float through my brain before I walked in to a huge surprise party for my thirtieth birthday. I'm not one for parties or celebrations (never had an eighteenth or a twenty-first) but this was a special night. Cork teammates, Cloyne players, old friends and old Miss O'Shea, matriarch of all the O'Sheas, came up.

The lads took me to Rome that weekend, a gang of us, young and old, from Cloyne. Thirty seemed a young age to be.

We've had two more hurling strikes in Cork since then; and for the second one of those I had to ask myself, had I the belly for it, could I stand and take the hassle and grief that would come with it? Yet once we decided to go for it I knew I would dedicate all the energy I had to it. We don't know yet what toll the last couple of years has taken on us all.

But we believe what we believed at the start: in the red of Cork and the red-and-black of Cloyne. We just believe that this year is our year. Every year. We believe that those colours demand the best from us on the field and off. We fucking rage against the dying of that light.

Fellas are retiring, though, and, like it or not, something is ending. Little bits of the world are breaking away. Lads I grew up with have families and mortgages and worries which they claim are at least as big as hurling.

I can't remember, for instance, when Diarmuid O'Sullivan wasn't part of my life. We hurled together on so many teams from childhood onwards that we lost count. I was a wispy little forward, just ten years old, when we started together on the under-12s in Cloyne. Sully wasn't as strong and tough and tall as you would imagine when he was eight and a half years old. But he was Sully.

We played together for school, club and county and were the first Cloyne players to bring All-Ireland medals back to the parish while still playing for the club.

Sully grew up just outside of town in a house on a hill, and he and his father and his brothers played as much hurling on that hill – which doubled as their front garden – as myself and my brothers played in the field over the wall. They were big tough men and able for anything.

Last summer, when we beat Clare in an epic comeback in Semple Stadium in Thurles, Sully was almost at his end. We'd survived but there was no joy left in it for him. He was feeling the pressure. Every full-forward was coming to pick the old gunslinger clean. Jesus, back in 1997 he put on a Cork senior jersey for the first time on a championship Sunday against Clare and he coursed Niall Gilligan around the pitch in Limerick until Gilly was withdrawn at half-time. Against Clare last summer Gilly had the last laugh, coming back to pick Sully's pockets.

All summer Sully was under so much pressure that we feared for him. He just wanted to get games over with, get his young son Cian into his arms and go home and lock the door.

After the Clare game I was looking across the dressing-room at him. Something struck me. I said it to Sully: 'Don't go home. We'll go down the town for a pint because we will never again do that as players.'

I could see it in him that he was gone. And he knew it too, I think. He said, 'All right.' He went out and told his wife Gráinne he was going. It's a grand feeling, especially if you are after winning a big game, to be strolling down through Thurles an hour or so after the match.

Sully had had enough by that stage of the day, really, but we had to go. The same thought was in both our minds as we walked up Liberty Square.

We'll never again do this. We'll never again do this as players.

Fuck.

We always went down to the same bar, the Castle Tavern. We'd been going in there since 1999. A few people would know our habit, and one or two fellas would be waiting in there for us, to buy us a drink or to slag us. Sully nearly walked into one of them after the Clare game last summer. He was in fierce form and in we go and your man is there, looming with his Dublin accent and up for the crack.

And I hear Sully: 'Aw for fuck's sake.'

His glower shut the Dub's mouth like pressing the mute button on a remote control.

We had a quiet drink and talked about old times. Like a couple of old men. His time at full-back was gone, though. The same playing with Cloyne in the backline last year. It's a high-wire act being a big-name full-back and he was just about holding it together. In the space between the Galway and Clare games the pressure on the man was unbelievable.

Ger Cunningham spent a load of time in the ball alley with Sully. I remember one evening spending about five hours with himself and

Cathal O'Reilly, just trying to get him back to his best. He did well in the All-Ireland semi-final against Kilkenny, but I don't know if he has the belly for full-back play this year. Not full-back. With all the scrutiny it brings.

He has been playing some rugby for Highfield and it's great to see him playing under no pressure. You see the true athlete still in him. He has been operating as a forward with Cloyne. Denis Walsh has told him to play away at club for a few weeks and then they'll talk. Who knows? Maybe this year Sully and myself won't play together for Cork. I won't have him standing in front of me at full-back as he has always done. There is only one pairing of full-back and goalie that have played more championship games than Sully and myself: Brian Lohan and Davy Fitzgerald of Clare. We have double the amount of time together of the next Cork pairing in those spots.

What we've learned, though, is that it passes on, the jersey, the tradition, the duty, whatever the fuck you want to call it. Sully will go. I will go. Not for a few years, I hope, but we will all move on. And we'll hardly be missed. It passes on.

When Cloyne play Bishopstown in the club championship in a few weeks there's a chance that Luke Cahill will start for us. And possibly so will his father, Philip.

We had a match some time back against Glen Rovers. There was a bit of a scuffle with around fifteen minutes left and we thought it wisest to get young Luke off the pitch. He was replaced that night by his father. That's club hurling.

It will be a proud day for our club president and one of our best players ever, Bunty Cahill, if he sees a son and a grandson on the field together in the red-and-black jersey in a championship game. The overlap of the generations will be brief, though. It always passes on.

When I watch Sully sometimes in the red-and-black of our club I am reminded of a famous incident years ago, in 1992 to be exact, when the club got a run to the county Intermediate final. Along the way we played Youghal, in Castlemartyr, and late on the game was on the line.

A Youghal player, Mickey Downey, came running in on to the ball in front of goal. Our nearest defender had lost his stick. lifted and pulled. Our man threw himself in front of the sw took the full belt of it. We survived. That was Jerry O'Sullivan, Sully's dad.

There's a headful of Sully moments like that we could talk about.

That summer of 1997 earned him the reputation of a swashbuckler. He became The Rock. In the All-Ireland under-21 final that year against Galway Sully got split badly after ten minutes. The first blow had left him needing stitches inside his mouth. The second blow busted his temple open and this great fountain of blood erupted from him. He wouldn't come off, and the best that could be done was to staunch the flow until half-time.

At the break I broke into a speech about doing it for Sully. I was getting to the rousing climax when the same Sully walked out of the medical room with a helmet made of white bandage and a hurley in his hand, ready for war again. Indestructible.

That year, 1992, when Sully's dad made the block with his hand, we got beaten in the Intermediate final; but we have three Intermediate titles to reminisce about on winter's nights in the Alley Bar: 1966, 1970 and 1997.

My family has its own tradition too. My Aunt Marie was named full-back on the camogie team of the past millenium and my Aunt Kathleen won All-Irelands playing in goals for Cork senior camogie teams. In 1966 my father was the goalie when the club won its first Intermediate championship. In 1970 my Uncle Pat played, he was the goalie too. In 1997 I played. In goals of course.

That's the thread of our club and our community. The same names speckled through team sheets down the decades. It comes down through us and on to those after us. The love and the madness. All the love and madness.

Myself, I would have played for the top adult team in the club in 1994 when I was fifteen years old and they stuck me in as a quick forward. Most fellas remember the first senior game they ever played for their club, but mine was unforgettable. We had three fellas sent off. My friend and hero, Smurf, committed a fucking crazy act that evening: the keeper caught a ball and Smurf just came in and flaked him! Pow! I remember thinking to myself, What the fuck is Smurf doing? The ref didn't stop to ask the same question. He just sent Smurf off. Jerry Cowhig had already been asked to walk. Then Philip Cahill clocked a fella – Bang! I looked at the referee because the play had gone on in that way it does and the referee hadn't seen it. I looked back and the linesman was waving his flag. Philip got sent off.

There was this one fella that came on as sub that day, his name was Maurice Lynch. He came into the forwards where I was posted and said, 'You stand in there beside me, young fellow.' I remember I was furious. For fuck's sake, there are three of our forwards gone and they've put on Grandpa here to protect me?

But he scored a brilliant goal, he doubled on a fierce ball, straight to the net. You never know what a fella's story is.

We finished the game and on the wrong side of a hiding. Next I remember walking off the field. My Uncle Dede and Timmy O'Sullivan (Sully's uncle) were trying to get over the wire to fight some fella. We went into the dressing-rooms and Willie John Ring, a brother of Christy, was lying down, sick, with a crowd around him. They were feeding Willie John tablets and people were in a panic. I remember thinking this is fucking terrible here, we were after getting hammered, we just had three fellas sent off, they boys are fighting outside and now Willie John could be dying. Perfect. I've brought some kind of curse to the club.

That was a Saturday night. Monday rolled around and I remember coming up from my part-time job with the Cahills to go training with Cork minors. The boys were gathered as usual at the cross. It was a lovely summer's evening and I was dandering along slowly. As I approached them I noticed something odd. There was a disproportionate number of *Echo*s being read. Every fella had an *Echo*.

So I strolled over and the boys were a bit fucking cagey with me. Newspapers being folded and fellas clearing their throats and getting ready to leave. I knew there was something wrong, so finally an *Echo* was handed over. There was a fella on the front page of the *Echo* covered from head to toe in bandages with his leg out and the big quote was 'I thought I was going to die'.

That was the main headline in the *Echo* that Monday. Man almost murdered in Cloyne! Put within inches of his life! Somebody had had an argument with the guy on the Friday.

On Saturday, after the hurling, the blood was still running high in a lot of fellas. It was said around the town afterwards that the posse went to the fella's door armed with hurley sticks and his girlfriend answered.

'Where is he?'

'He's upstairs in the bedroom on the right.'

She might have been nervous, but she didn't really have to add the detail about him being in the room on the right! So the boys went up and nearly killed the guy. Next day everyone in Cloyne knew who it was had done it but everyone was cagey with the *Echo* and the other local media that descended.

(The fella who got beaten up grew up in the town a few years ahead of me. I used to know him when we were young lads. He was always in trouble, but he'd never do anything to me or to the grandmother because, like the rest of us, he was half afraid of my grandmother. On Sunday mornings it was my job to bring my other grandmother the Sunday papers. To get it out of the way because I had no interest I would go to first Mass and sit above in the gallery, leafing through the papers, then I would bring the papers to my grandmother after Mass.

He would join me up in the gallery some weeks. Halfway through the Mass, he'd grow tired of me and he'd make his way downstairs. Off he'd go up the aisle till he was standing in front of the priest. And then he'd start imitating the padre.

I used to think this was great because the priest would be getting all nervous. He didn't know what tack to use and we'd all watch him in beady-eyed silence. He'd begin by trying to ignore him, but the heckling would go on too long and you'd hear these urgent whispers from the congregation, 'For fuck's sake, boy, sit down now, they're all talking about you!'

Great entertainment, and it boosted the numbers at first Mass for quite a while. I'd go over to my grandmother afterwards and the first thing she would ask was if our man had been at the Mass. Everyone would agree that it was a disgrace, but not many could agree the point with a straight face.)

Anyhow, that was the way Cloyne appeared in the paper that Monday, two days after my adult championship debut! On the front, this fella nearly dead having been beaten with hurleys. On the back, Cloyne finishing with twelve fellas in the championship bloodbath on Saturday night.

Come and live in beautiful, tranquil Cloyne!

I love that spirit which runs through Cloyne. It's like electricity. It keeps crackling and lighting our lives up.

Back in 1995 eleven lads repeated the Leaving Certificate in Midleton CBS and one of them was me. Eight of us had lost the Harty in 1994, beaten by a North Mon team with Seán Óg Ó hAilpín in it, and we'd come back to put that right.

In our world, where hurling was religion and everything else was distraction, the fact that we were making an all-out charge on the Harty Cup, Munster's famous schools' hurling championship, was far more important than the requirements of the education system or the whims of future employers.

I was the captain. There was an argument to be made that my first cousin, Pat Walsh, should have been captain. He was a wonderful hurler and made the senior Cork panel before any of the rest of us did, but I was obsessed. I would have run the entire team if I was let by Terry O'Brien and Eamonn O'Neill, who felt that as they were teachers and good hurling men they knew more than me!

We knew we had a good team. Seven of us played minor for Cork later in the year. We had Pat my cousin, Joe Deane, Mickey O'Connell, Dara Cott and Pat Mullaney. A big young fella from Cloyne who I always knew as Sully forced his way on to the team as the year progressed.

We trained from the week that school resumed in September and we were the big men in the school. Teachers would fret if any of us had a cold. We spent that whole year inside in the library, talking hurling and messing about. We drank and smoked in that room – did just about everything except study. We never cracked a book open once, apart from Mickey O'Connell, who had a brain and did a bit of work occasionally to show us up.

In fact that year stands out not just for the games, which were a huge thing, but for how I realized clearly for maybe the first time that hurling was more important than just about any other considerations.

Before that there were no other considerations to compare hurling to.

I hardly did a Leaving Cert at all either year that I was entered for the exam and Seánie Farrell often joked about the place afterwards that on the night the results came out I could have had a pint for every point I got and still not have been drunk. (Not true by the way!) The Leaving Cert just never registered with me as an important stage of life. Everything really vital happened when I was out on the field.

With the Leaving Cert being so marginal in my thoughts, the mock exams to prepare us hardly registered at all. I used to be outside playing hurling the night before major exams. One thing on my mind. We'd lost one Harty Cup campaign. We weren't going to lose another.

When the mock exams rolled around I had decided to skip the hardship and just went and sat inside the hurling dressing-rooms at school. I'd be happy enough in there, daydreaming away, content with my own company. After a while I heard somebody about – it was Liam O'Brien, a man who had run in the Olympics for Ireland and also a teacher and a hurling coach. He'd caught me!

I suppose I was a pupil and he was a teacher, but hurling changed that relationship a little bit. It was like we were both in it together.

'Look you won't tell anybody, will ya?'

'Sure they'd be looking for you.'

'Listen, it'll be OK so long as the boss doesn't hear it.'

So, depending on Liam not to tell the headmaster, I didn't give it another thought. The next day North Mon were playing Lismore in the semi-final on the other side of the draw. We had already qualified for the final and we wanted to get a look at our opposition. It was an exam day, but myself and the father had decided to go and see the game with Pat Mullaney (who would score 1-5 in the Harty final that year) and his father, Jimmy.

I hadn't bothered going in to school that morning. I did notice while I was about the house that the phone was ringing an awful lot. Something wrong. So eventually I picked it up. It was Jimmy Mullaney.

Now Pat had as little interest in school as I had, but his father was worried.

'There's trouble, the boss has been on. If ye don't go in to school today ye are going to be suspended. Ye better get up the school.'

I said to him that I didn't know about this at all. The father came in. I spoke to him. I told him straight up that I was supposed to be inside in the school sitting exams but there was a bit of trouble and the next time the phone rang it was likely to be the school. They were talking about suspensions!

So the father thought it over for a second and said, 'Look, we better head away to the match quickly so.'

Jimmy Mullaney had more sense, I suppose, and in the end we were made to go in anyway. My mother had a rare fit with Dad and me. Pat and I thought we were making the ultimate sacrifice, but there was murder when we got to the school. No gratitude to the two stars for showing up.

By the time we arrived the word had spread like mad. There was going to be a hanging! The vice-principal, Gerard Cott (an uncle of Dara's), met us with his serious face on and ushered us towards the principal's office.

'Listen, lads, go in and say nothing.'

In we went and the boss locked the two sets of doors behind us, so we knew it was serious. He sat us down and gave us his best hard stare.

'Look, I wanted to suspend the pair of ye for two weeks but Eamonn O'Neill says that if ye are on the bank for the Harty final so will he be.'

And that was the end of it. With one bound we were free!

4

Monday morning. Tell me why I don't like Mondays. Ah yes. That's it. Kilkenny beat us by twenty-seven points yesterday. First thing I think of when I wake up. First thing I will think of for a week or two.

Yesterday was our worst day since we played Galway in Thurles, back in 2002. I remember that afternoon going out to Fergal Ryan who was playing wing-back and saying, 'Fergal, we're fucked here.' And there was twenty minutes to go.

But that day against Galway the margin was only nine points and we knew it wasn't personal. Yesterday Kilkenny were putting us away and nailing down the lid. To really bury us meant a lot to them. Just as to do them would have been special to us.

I don't accept it that they are superior – never could, never will. If I did, I would pack up in the morning.

Stupid we may be at this stage, but we believe we can and will beat them. We just won't accept that they are unbeatable. We beat them as kids and we beat them in All-Ireland finals that were one-point games. Bare-knuckle stuff. And we won.

We had great games but we never got close as people. I remember last winter I was the only Cork player on the All-Stars trip to New York. I arrived a day early because of work circumstances. When I checked in I was told that I would be rooming with a Kilkenny player. Great!

Days went by and the others arrived, but my friend never came to share the room. Stripey man missing! Until one night in the early hours I came back to find himself and a teammate of his entertaining company in the room. I left them to their work. Next morning when I went up to the room both of the cheeky bastards had signed one of my hurleys. Meant a lot to me.

So I know beating us yesterday was as sweet for them as it would have been for us.

This morning when I woke up thinking about it, I had to make a decision. Did I want to forget it or remember it? I made up my mind. If I am seventy, if I am eighty, I want to remember yesterday.

It was a result which framed our isolation as a team. We're so far out in the fucking cold in the hurling world that we could reverse global warming. When the scoreline was announced at grounds around the country, there was cheering at the news of our humiliation. People are fatigued and annoyed with us and we are a lightning rod for general discontent.

Kilkenny put the Cork troublemakers in their place! Yahoo!

I feel it worse because four goals went past me and I triggered the avalanche myself, completely misplacing a puck-out after seven minutes. Seconds later I had to pick the ball out of the net. All those people who hate our use of short puck-outs, I could hear their knives being sharpened on whetting stones just behind my back.

The game was torture in two instalments. You think things can't get worse, and then they do. Every few seconds it felt like the ball was flying over my crossbar. Zing! Zing! Zing! Incoming! Flick of the scoreboard. There was a fella behind the goals with a bag full of sliotars. Before the ball is over the crossbar each time he has a ball pulled out of the bag and thrown to me to puck it out quickly. We are against the wind. I'm trying to buy a little delay. A little mercy time. He doesn't want this, though. He wants more scores. And more. And more.

He doesn't even have a proper bag, just an old plastic supermarket carrier thing, but he has his balls ready. He has the weapon of our destruction. He wants me to pass the weapon out to the boys as quickly as possible so he can further enjoy the spectacle of watching us get riddled.

I said to the umpire, 'He shouldn't be there.'

The umpire nodded his head helpfully. Shrugged. 'I know, yeah.'

Nobody knows you when you're down and out. So I took the umpire's indifference to mean that it would be up to me to slow the supply of sliotars down. I went over to the man with the bag. Quiet word.

'You don't really know me at all but I'll tell ya this. Ye are beating us by twenty points or whatever and I'm cracking here. Bad day! Now, I promise you I will make you famous if you throw another fucking ball in front of me like that. I'm telling you I will make you famous.

I'll never play another game again, I'll get such a long suspension – but you'll be famous too.'

The umpire is shouting to me now. He's suddenly full of life. 'Come back, come back, come back.'

Your man with the bag of balls acts the innocent and says, 'What's wrong with ya?'

In fairness to him though, the balls stopped coming. Thank god. What was making matters worse was that the balls he was giving me were awful, the rims were huge on them. It was cold, we were getting hammered, we were missing some of our greatest warriors. And this man was feeding me bad balls to puck out quickly.

And to be fair again, he came over after the game and said, 'Do you want a hand bringing in your hurleys?'

And he did give me a hand. Fair play to him.

We were due a little sympathy by then anyway. In the second half Kilkenny had made fun of us. The crowd wanted goals and any time Henry Shefflin in particular got the ball I could hear them baying at him to go for goal.

There is a killer inside Henry Shefflin. Like Ring. There has to be. You see it in him, that's what makes him. He's a great player, but normally he passes himself off as a happy-go-lucky fella. Yesterday, though, you could see he has that ruthlessness that the great ones have. He'd look you in the eye and fillet you with a knife at the same time if he needed to. He's a winner and he wants to win by as much as possible. That old thing about it not being enough for you to succeed, your enemies have to fail.

Late on, Kilkenny were awarded a 21-yard free and the crowd began chanting for Shefflin to go for goal. He didn't. There was a moment of panic near the end when he hit a shot at me, though. My foot placement was bad. I knew the ball was spinning and that I had to be set up properly. I had one foot in front of the other and the ball nearly spun off my stick away to my left and into the goal. I recovered just in time. There was a gasp of frustration from the crowd. They'd almost had a moment of perfect humiliation to enjoy.

That would have given Kilkenny the perfect day. In terms of fellas they wouldn't like here in Nowlan Park, I know I'm well up there (maybe in the top spot!). It didn't make my day any better to save that shot, but it didn't make Henry's any better either. And if it had gone in, my day would have felt a whole lot worse. And lots of men in stripey jerseys would have been smiling at each other and offering respects to their king.

Henry came in to the square after the final whistle and shook my hand. He looked me in the eye and most of what he was saying to himself was, There you go now, Cusack, twenty-seven points. Take that home with ya.

He knew. I knew. They had put us away. Made their statement. It was his moment. I just had to say to him, 'You're a great team.' And fuck it, they are a great team. Somehow in the last ten years they have got away from us.

You need the right things if you are to keep going as a team. You need the right manager. The right players. When I started out under Jimmy Barry-Murphy in the late 1990s we had the momentum of players who had ideas, management whom we idolized and who had the same ideas. We had supporters. And we had the All-Ireland victory of 1999 following on underage success. We knew that if we kept it going, the next decade could be ours. We had no fear.

Kilkenny came with us as rivals and we kept raising the bar for each other.

In Cork, while we have had a series of managers over the years, we have watched Kilkenny thrive under what seems like the eternal presence of Brian Cody. We have always felt that we could have finished Cody off in 2006 if we had beaten them in the All-Ireland final and completed a three-in-a-row run of titles.

That would have hurt Kilkenny deeply and Cody would have been under pressure to go. Instead we created a monster. We lost that game and, instead of going toe to toe with them, Gerald McCarthy came in and we lost any momentum we should have had. We were just going back into the wilderness after that, while Kilkenny were getting better and better and realizing that their old rivals had just disappeared off the radar.

The last time we played in Croke Park was the All-Ireland semi-final of last year. Kilkenny beat us that day as well. We travelled up as a heavy-hearted team despite having had two big comeback wins in the previous rounds. Things were so bad with our manager that by then we had a professional facilitator, Cathal O'Reilly, working with us to get us all through the season. Cathal was doing good work but a man with a suit and a degree wasn't going to save us against Kilkenny.

I had a new iPhone that weekend and somebody was messing about with it on the journey up to Croke Park. They took a picture of me. They looked at it and handed the phone back. 'Ógie, you look like a man going to his death.' In terms of worry that's not far off how I was feeling.

And what was bothering me was not that we were going up to play a great Kilkenny team. It was that we had no plan. Nothing. No Plan A, no Plan B. Nothing to give us even a chance. The only thing we had to fall back on was our stubborn pride.

A lot of people in Cork would like to think that would be enough. Pride in the Cork jersey, pride in our history. Life would be more simple if that was true, because no group has ever taken more pride in the jersey than us; but pride in the jersey works at all levels, and it includes management and the Board giving the men who wear the jersey the very best preparation and the very best chance of winning.

And then going on to the pitch, the men in the jerseys have to have a plan. That's the way pride in the jersey works most of the time in Kilkenny and Tipperary and places where they don't spend their lives taking short cuts and hoping to win All-Irelands on the cheap.

And even if those counties did do things on the cheap, it is not the way a Cork hurling team should ever do things. We have the proudest sporting history of any county in the country, from Roy Keane to Ronan O'Gara to Sonia and all the great rugby players, soccer men and GAA men in between. There is a debt of honour that we all owe to that tradition. It doesn't come cheap.

On the Saturday night before a big game in Dublin, a gang of us always go out and take a walk. Always the same walk. Before every big game. We walk to Herbert Park, have a puc-around there. One night before an All-Ireland final years ago we walked right through the park and came up to the gates at the other side and found they were locked. We climbed a wall and next thing the whole road was out to confront us. There must have been a Neighbourhood Watch in operation. It turned out we'd been climbing up over some old woman's wall in our track-suits and hoodies.

We pushed Seán Óg to the front to face the mob. Even in Dublin 4 they know Seán Óg.

There's another part to the ritual, too. I have a coin which I left in a tree on Raglan Road many years ago now. And we walk down to that beautiful leafy part of Dublin and find the tree and I take out the coin. 'We're going to be back, boys,' I'll say, and I'll put the coin back in its hiding place once more. This will sound stupid, but I always put it back there again as a sign that we will be returning to Croke Park as a team. And the day we know it is over, in my head anyway, I will throw it away. (It's still there. Kevin Hartnett checked for it a couple of weeks ago on a weekend away with his girlfriend Keara.)

The night before the semi-final against Kilkenny last summer we went and found the coin and for the first time ever I had to take a good look at it. It was Shane O'Neill, Cathal Naughton, Pa Cronin, Anthony Nash, Tom Kenny, Kevin Hartnett, Seán Óg and myself. We were so down over Gerald and the lack of any plan that I had the feeling that I wanted to throw the thing away, but some stubborn part of me said, 'Fuck it, no. We'll fight on.'

From our tree on Raglan Road we can see a postbox up along the way. We always have our hurleys and our sliotars with us and the traditional competition has always been to see who can hit that post-box from a stop sign near our tree. It's the heart of genteel Dublin 4 and lots of people would stick their heads out and take a look because they have never seen sliotars on Raglan Road, let alone sliotars being driven by such a shower of desperados.

This night the spirits aren't as light as usual. I say to Seán Óg, who has been with me in just about every battle I ever fought in a Cork jersey, 'What is happening tomorrow, Seán Óg? What's the plan?'

Seán Óg shakes his head. We have no plan. We should play our short game, but we can't because we have done no work on it. We are going to get killed if we suddenly try to improvise our old style without having weeks of work done. We should play sensibly, keeping the ball and moving it among ourselves quickly. But we can't and we will get doubly savaged by doing that badly.

I said to the lads, 'We need to go to Gerald. We need to get something sorted out.'

It was starting to rain and we were heading back. To say the least, the lads weren't keen on the management by this stage, so I said I would go to Gerald myself. We needed something. These fellas in the stripes were coming for us. All week we'd been waiting for some kind of plan to be handed down to us. None had come.

I found Gerald. We went into his room. We sat together at a table. I was worried about tomorrow, I told him. The team and I. All worried. We were sitting either side of a table, Gerald and I.

'We don't have a plan, Gerald. If we play it short, which is our nature against them, we will get in more trouble. We can't just switch that on tomorrow. It's a high-risk game, you need to spend time on it.'

He nodded.

My thinking was that our only hope was to try to get the ball into their half-forwards and crowd them. If we played for fifty–fifty balls we would lose possession. They were going to destroy us. We would crowd them and try to win second-phase ball. Rather than us playing our correct natural game, which we weren't prepared for, and getting slaughtered forty yards from our goals, we would go for breaks.

Gerald nodded again.

'Grand job so, that's what we will do.'

That's the thing that would drive you mad about Gerald. He would listen and take things on. He wouldn't initiate. You could go to him with something, and he would see the sense of it and go with it. But he hadn't the leadership in him to bring it to us himself. How often had this happened in our time together?

Once at one of our review meetings – John Gardiner, myself and the selectors – I suggested that we get in a mind coach for the team, sort of a more positive, proactive version of a sports psychologist. We needed to do some positive stuff like visualization. Gerald said, 'Yep, grand, I'll contact him.' The guy I had in mind had been snapped up by another county team, though.

Gerald came to me at training with an idea.

'Sure listen Ógie, why don't you do it? They listen to you. You could do that with them.'

And I began to worry that he was agreeing to things but didn't really see the point or didn't want to be telling the County Board about them.

That night before the semi-final, in the Burlington Hotel, we went down and spent some time drawing the game plan all out on the board. We went through it step by step. Gerald was happy. We were a bit happier. The next day we won a lot of breaks in the first twenty minutes, but it couldn't keep going at that pace. Kilkenny were used to performing at that intensity. We had fallen back.

We weren't at the races for the rest of the day.

We left the coin in the tree in Raglan Road, though, and I'm glad we did. I'm thirty-two years old now and I have been doing this a long time. Yesterday in Kilkenny we got the worst beating of our lives. That day last summer Kilkenny beat us pretty comfortably as well. But no way will I accept that that is how things have to be. Of course I believe Cork will beat them again in the championship. I believe still that we are as good as them. If I didn't believe that then I would not keep wearing that jersey. I would walk away.

Today I could hardly speak to anybody. I am just unable to communicate. Myself and my father won't talk for a week after a match. All he wants to do is talk hurling. I can't, especially not this week. Twenty-fucking-seven points!

Denis Walsh, our new boss, said to me this week I should think about being more upbeat and not getting as down as I do after games.

I wish.

In the hotel afterwards yesterday I couldn't sit at a table with the lads. I can't talk to anybody on a day like yesterday. A couple of fellas went off to watch the Manchester United game on the television. That worries me. How can Manchester United matter on a day like this?

Kevin Hartnett, my friend, came to me.

'What's the story. Are we going training in the morning?'

I said we would.

He said something I always say to him.

'All we do now is go step by step.'

I got off the field yesterday after we did our warm-down and it was like an escape. I was glad that we had stuck to what we always do and did our warm-down out there on the pitch. We didn't run away.

A lot of Cork people poured on to the pitch as we were warming down. John Gardiner's dad (John also) and a lot of faces who had supported us during the strike. Letting us know they were still there for us.

When we were on strike we had trained on our own as a team. The sessions kicked off, early one winter morning in Mallow. There was frost on the ground and a bitter, still cold in the air. It was almost symbolic – the landscape, the elements saying to us, This ain't going to be easy, boys. We just had to do it though, and it was a beautiful setting that morning. We were together and that was the way we wanted to do it.

And that first day a fella came down to us with the present of six sliotars. I knew his face from being around the place. His name was Gerry O'Sullivan and he and his young son Paul came to every session after that. It meant so much. There we were, getting hammered every-where – the media, the Board, radio phone-in shows, our own fans – but he believed in us and what we were doing and he brought down the sliotars and gave us his quiet support.

And it grew from there. People would hand us cheques, offers of hospitality. Clubs let us train on their pitches. Don McEvoy from Clyda up in north Cork was so good to us, and the women in Na Piarsaigh on Saturday mornings made sure we were fed properly.

Our old trainer Seánie McGrath came down to give us that first session in Mallow and he made it fun and he made it worthwhile, and his support meant a lot to us. Jerry Wallis, the physical coach, also trained with us, which must have been difficult for him, since he had been working with Gerald for the previous two years.

A couple of lads had problems in work. One of us works in a bank and a client who had taken against the strike said he wouldn't deal with him any more. He let it be known to the player's superiors, too. So another man who did a lot for us turned up at the bank within days and lodged two million euro. And made a call to the player's superiors that he was lodging it precisely because the bank employed the player involved.

Twenty-seven points, but we'll keep going for all those people especially and the closeness there is between the team and those who supported us.

This morning at nine I met Hartnett in the ball alley in Rochestown and we said it again. 'Step by step.'

We have nine weeks to go until the championship starts. Outside our own group, players, family, friends and some supporters, we are as reviled as any team has been in the history of the game. Isolated and alone.

We have lots of steps to take before we feel the warmth of a real championship summer again. In nine weeks Tipperary will be waiting for us and the hurling world will be watching to see if we have been able to climb out of this deep hole we are in. And plenty of people will be waiting to shove us back in and cover us over with earth.

5

Ballynoe, 15 April 2009
Killeagh 2-18 Cloyne 1-9

A routine league match tonight, but we don't have our big players with us or our heads tuned in. Still, it's Killeagh and there's a little local edge to it. They enjoy beating us. We don't like losing to them.

Joe Deane buries us. At one stage he controls a fast ball with just his left hand on the stick as he comes across the square and puts it over the bar before he is fully across the width of the square. So unorthodox. Such a genius. Tonight he still has the full bag of tricks.

Life in the GAA is about where you are from, but certain fellas change the entire perception of that place. Ring is Cloyne, only bigger. Different club names mean different things. Would the name Killeagh mean anything to anybody if Jamesie Kelleher, Joe Deane and Mark Landers hadn't come from here?

Jamesie was one of the great Cork hurlers. He played early in the last century for Dungourney, as they were called, but the games were here in Killeagh. People often draw a straight line between himself and Ring in terms of greatness.

I draw a different line. One hundred and one years ago Jamesie said:

I have seen to my disgust the players draw the crowds, make the money and lose their sweat at many a hard hour's game while those gentlemen at the head of affairs take charge of the bag and jump into their cars again before the match is over . . . they will scoff at the application from injured players for compensation . . . the official never caught a hurley in his hand, never felt the sting of the ash on his shin bones, does not know what it is like to be laid up . . . the governing body has been captured by non-players and the players themselves . . . seem to have no direct representation on it.

Life is much the same as it ever was around here, Jamesie boy.

When I hear the name of Killeagh, those are the words I think of. The two faces I see are Joe Deane, quiet and mature and a man, an independent-minded man, since we were all thirteen or fourteen; and Landers, a few years older but still cocky. Yep. Cocky even by the exalted standards of Cork cockiness.

Joe is tormenting us tonight, and Landers is managing them. He's doing a good job. Myself and Landers, though, I don't know where we stand these days. During the strike he came out with a few sidewinders which weren't helpful, coming from an old comrade.

Joe and I go a long way back. When I started playing on Cork teams as a young fella going out for an under-14 team, I had no choice but to hitch into the city in order to get the training. Now a young fella with hurleys wouldn't have too much trouble getting a lift, but Joe, who was in school with me in Midleton, organized that he and I could get to Cork with that great Killeagh clubman, Tommy Seward.

Joe was always fierce small. No matter what he did for Midleton CBS or Killeagh or Cork underage teams, lads at home would always be saying that Joe would never make it with Cork. More powerful teams like Limerick and Clare were doing well in the mid-'90s and Cork were looking for bigger players, but I always argued that Joe was so good and so skilful he had to make it. Give him good ball and he could do magic. Jimmy Barry-Murphy saw it and brought Joe with him all the way.

This is the first year of Joe's retirement from the county team and we are going to miss him badly. Not just his cool reassuring presence but the impact he had on other players.

In 2003 he was a special influence on Setanta Ó hAilpín, guiding him through games, playing off him, switching spots with him and generally making Setanta an even better player than he had a right to be at that age.

And this year it looks more and more like Setanta's younger brother, Aisake, might be in our full-forward line. Aisake has had four years in Australia trying his hand at the Australian Rules football. He's home and there is no doubt from the early experiments that he would give us something different. He is nearly six foot seven inches tall. That's something different. You can teach a fella how to play hurling but you can't teach him to be six foot seven.

For now, Aisake is not the player Setanta was. He put some weight on his upper body when he was in Australia but still wouldn't be as strong as Setanta was when he burst away for his goal in the 2003 All-Ireland final. He is an Ó hAilpín, though, and no matter how coltish he is he will learn quickly. Having Joe there would accelerate that, but I think Joe has had enough. He was always ahead of us in terms of his maturity and his calmness in dealing with things. We wanted to prolong boyhood as long as we could. Joe just always seemed to operate in the adult world.

We played Harty Cup together. He was a genius. I wouldn't touch a drink the first year, but the second year we played I had a good try at it. Joe wouldn't. Always mature. Always true to himself.

He is a banker and you could almost say he was born to that trade. Sober, mature judgement is what he is all about. Joe works for ACC and he could have been going down for the tea on the South Mall with all the other Cork legends who do that and make deals with each other on the backs of fag boxes and napkins; he could have slipped into that old network, but in 2002 he stood up, and he has stood up for the team any time it was required since. Guys like Joe and Seán Óg and Gardiner and Tom Kenny had more to lose than fellas like me. They could have been the establishment.

In 2006, when Cloyne lost the county final to Erin's Own – our third final defeat in three years and the most painful – I went on a bad bender. It was all over after years of really epic effort for us. I found myself in the pub Wednesday morning when one of my best friends, Diarmaid Falvey, rang me.

'I've bad news for you. I was talking to Joe.'

'Yeah? And?'

'Well, he has cancer.'

I was after a load of drink, but it hit me like a lorry hitting a wall. What would Joe have done in those circumstances? The opposite to what I did. I got into the car in a panic. My co-ordination was gone. I may have been still drunk from the night before, I was shredded with tiredness. The weather was bad and I was terrified, driving through Cork in the lashing rain.

I had to go and see him, though. I was in an awful state.

Joe was in the Bons. I looked worse than he did when I found him. I was wrecked. Overwrought. He was sitting there, still Joe. One testicle lighter, that was all.

'I'm grand. Look at me. Here's the story.'

And he told me the story. How he didn't want to make a thing of it. How it was no big deal. Such calm. And that was it. Not a little bit of fuss.

Jesus, he's a different species to me, I sometimes think. It was one of the first truly adult things to hit somebody on the team, something we couldn't sort with a meeting or in a huddle. And it would be Joe, the man most capable of dealing with it.

He would drive me mad loads of times, the same Joe. He was in charge of the players' fund and it was all in his head. Nothing was a bother even when I'd be complicating things, wondering should we have systems in place for this and for that. Easy-going, but there's also a tough streak inside of him. Well able to look after himself for a small fella in a yellow helmet. We played Killeagh out in Castlemartyr one night a couple of years ago, and my friend Killian Cronin (hereafter referred to as Billy, his Cloyne nickname from childhood when he carried a toy six-shooter everywhere and was known as Billy the Kid) was playing full-back. Joe laid Billy out. One movement. Bam!

The championship is not far away tonight and in Killeagh there would be an edge about it. They came up to intermediate from junior in 1995 and went senior in 2001. They still have that hunger about them. They have this thing on the field, too, calling each other by pet names. Markeen and Joeeen.

Landers is on the line tonight, cocky as ever.

Quick Landers story. We went to a training camp in Lanzarote once. They called out the room assignments. Me, Sully and Landers together. Two Cloyne fellas and one Killeagh fella.

I remember we left the bags up and Sully went away down the town. Landers hadn't packed a bag, just walked out and got on a plane. I came back up to the room. Landers had Sully's shorts and T-shirt on him. Now Sully would be immaculate always. He loves his clothes. I remember thinking, Landers, boy, Sully is going to kill you.

So. Sully came back and, of course, reams of abuse. But no punches thrown. A let-off for Landers, I'm thinking. Sully storms out again. I wander off. An hour later I come back in. Landers is lying on his bed yakking to home on the mobile phone. Sully's mobile phone.

Cocky, I tell you.

During the strike my mother rang me one day. I was involved in a project to create an energy research centre which will eventually be located in Cork. The project takes me to Portlaoise a lot; it involves government, universities and industry. I'm the industry lead and it takes time and it's tough. I noticed the father's mobile phone number flashing up and said hello. It was my mother.

'What's up?'

'Mark Landers is what's up.'

'What has he done?'

'He's in the *Echo* today, saying stuff about you. What's his number?'

Normally I'd tell her to stay away from it but I was busy and it was Landers, so I rattled off the number.

She rings him up.

No answer.

She leaves a big message on the phone and orders him to ring her back.

Mark doesn't get back.

A couple of days later it is still on the mother's mind. She is going on about it. 'Cheek of that Mark Landers not calling me back.'

So now the father rings him up. Gets the message machine again.

'Mark. How are you, boy. Listen, I'm after coming into a good few pounds and I'm in need of some investment advice.'

Ten minutes later the phone rings. Landers's number flashing!

'Hello?'

'Hello! Mark Landers here.'

'Oh, hold on one second, Mark.'

The father passes the phone to my mother, who devours Landers, starting with the fact that he never rang her back. The two of them, both in their mid-sixties, are laughing about it ever since!

Funny, but when I think of the cast list in the Cork dressing-room I think of the fellas who were there when I walked into the dressing-room first. Landers was older and he drifted while we had good years ahead. Now Sully is going and Joe is gone. Those fellas were stayers, they all played for a decade, and it's a fierce change within the group. Take Joe. Anything to do with money, Joe would have been the man for us. He was the bank man and he was experienced and he was trusted.

I was supposed to help him administer the players' fund. I don't even know if I ever did anything. The only thing I know for certain that came out of the situation was an amount I asked him for. I went to Joe and asked him for the money and gave him some story about what it was for. He handed it over with his normal efficiency.

Once I had the money, the boys gave it straight back to him. The money was for himself. It was just after he had the cancer. We'd asked Dr Con how much the whole thing was costing Joe and he reckoned about that.

Joe didn't need it. He was the last fella on the team that would have needed it.

I handed him the cheque and said, 'Look, Joey, I spoke to a couple of the boys here about this, we know you don't want it or you don't need it but as sign of, look, fuck it, we're delighted you got over this, blah, blah, blah, take the money, now.' We'd murder with him trying to get him to accept, but it was just a sign of respect for him because the fellas had such time for him and he had brought way more money into that fund probably than ever got given out.

A couple of weeks ago there I rang him. I said, 'Look, fuck it, Joe, I think you should hold on. Forget the retirement. I think if you give it a chance there's more in you and more in the team.'

I wasn't on a solo run. The selectors had said it to me. I'd be a bit wary about ringing a fella in that situation in case it would be messing with their life, but one of the selectors in particular pressed for me to get on to him.

But Joe said that his belly was gone for it, his mind was gone for it. He'd done his bit and he'd had enough.

We left it there. You'd know with Joe always that he would know his own mind.

I wonder, will I have the clearness in my head to make the decision when the time comes. One day you are playing and you are defined as a Cork hurler, and even if that means being hated because of the strikes and all that it is still a definition of yourself that you held for a long time. And then you are gone and you are an oul fella that used to play, a lad that still tips away with the club maybe but you are into the other half of your life.

Joe had the brain to make that crossover easy for himself. Landers has such self-belief that he has probably always defined himself differently anyway. Just as Landers! Sully might struggle and I wonder if I will too.

6

It's coming down the track. Not afraid of it but I don't like it either.

Embarrassing story. Christmas Day a few years ago. I was out cycling, pushing hard. I'd tipped away up to the city from my house in Ballinacurra and decided I would do a ring of Cloyne – I'd hit a rhythm and it was a beautiful fresh evening and I was recalling great dance tunes in my head.

Christmas Day? I know, I know, but I used to love it. I read a book years ago, *Bad As I Wanna Be* by Dennis Rodman, the famous and controversial forward with the Chicago Bulls (Wayne Sherlock, you still have my book!), and he spoke about training at night and how he loved the feeling that it gave him an edge. I identified with that. You train hard on Christmas Day and you think you are getting that much of an edge over every fella who is sitting on the sofa full of turkey.

So I am out and pumping hard, and next thing I remember is being outside Diarmuid O'Sullivan's family house and the lights went out. Not Sully's. Mine. I collapsed outside Sully's house on Christmas Day on my bike.

I got a weakness and I kicked one foot out of the stirrup on the pedal and then I think I just went to put down my other foot but that was still clicked in to its stirrup, and snap, I was gone.

And I was more afraid of the Sullys taking a peek out the window than anything else. Not a thought for what would cause a blackout. Just panic.

Jesus Christ, one of the O'Sullivans is going to come out and they're going to see me laid out on Christmas Day on the bike and they'd be saying, 'That fucking Cusack, what is the fucker like?' They'd be there St Stephen's Day in the pub saying, 'You're not going to believe what we saw last night, no listen, fucking Cusack laying out on the ground outside the house and he was all cut and bleeding and everything but up he got on the bike and away with him. Mad!'

So Christmas Days since then I'm in the ball alley usually. Sometimes I go to the gym with Seán Óg. Always I do something, though.

I'm a goalkeeper. It's different. There's pressure on every one of us. So getting out on Christmas Day, you think, maybe Cummins isn't doing this. Maybe Fitzy isn't. Is Marty? Is Nasher?

In my house goalkeeping is the family trade. My uncle and my father played in goals for the club. I started playing in goals for the team in Cloyne when I was thirteen, I'd say. I'd say it was thirteen because I remember when I was an under-12, a man called Peter Hegarty asked me to play in goals for one of the older teams and my father wouldn't let me and I went mad with my father. I couldn't believe it, he wouldn't let me play for Cloyne.

At that time in Cloyne, any fella who might be able to hurl, all he had to do was stand in goals and he had the job. Plus obviously I had some sort of aptitude. I was better than most fellas, probably from all those days in the field with the father making me put my hand up to catch.

So you go in goals for one team and what happens is you get put in goals for all the older teams, which would be the natural thing in country clubs. Then I went to Midleton CBS and they put me into goals all the time.

I played out the field every now and then, and that was very good for giving me a perspective. There are certain facets to goalkeeping that are a luxury compared to being out on the hurling field. You don't appreciate that if you didn't play out the field occasionally. Time unfolds differently for a goalie. When you are in goals you have the time to deal with a ball without the danger of a fella coming from behind at one hundred miles an hour. In goals you have a certain amount of protection and you can see any fella that's coming at you.

The downside is that your mistakes weigh more in the public mind. There's a rule in the Cork team: never fuck the goalie out of it. If a goal goes in, whether it's me or Marty or Nasher in goal, you never turn and put your hands on your hips and stare at the keeper. Never. Because the keeper will come out and he will fuck you out of it in front of 50,000 people every time you make a mistake.

I always say to the lads who don't play in goal that all that stuff that happens out the field helps them to focus on the here-and-now. They are getting the adrenalin going. Whereas a lot of stuff that happens to a man standing in the goalkeeping position actually tends to draw him out of his focus. You might warm up for twenty minutes and then the game starts and you don't see the ball for twenty minutes. In latter years I learned how to perform imaginary pucks and saves just to try to keep my brain clicked into gear. In games like that you have time to look at the scoreboard and stuff like that, which is not where you want to go in your head. In Croke Park now I use the big screen: I am calm enough that if the ball is down the other side I'm watching the screen to see what's going on. It doesn't distract me, but that's because you evolve as a player and learn. I was lucky enough too that Cork had fellas that stuck with me and let me evolve.

After 2002, say, I was getting a lot of criticism and to be honest I wasn't playing as well as I should have been. There would have been a case for Dónal O'Grady to drop me. Now he says there was never a possibility and maybe I'm being too self-critical, but at the time I felt his belief in me and I felt I had to repay it by improving.

That's one of the things about the GAA that needs changing: coaching and development. Any player who is working and being coached well should start from level A and should get to level D in a season. He shouldn't go back to level A at the end of the year. What happens in most GAA teams, though, is that a new manager comes in and there is no established structure so more often than not they actually take everyone back to level A and then they only go from A to D.

Some players spend virtually all of their career going from A to D. I would aspire to a system where you might go back to C in the winter but maintain yourself there and then you progress to F the following year. There should be programmes to develop the person and the player, but the GAA has always seen the player as a transient, here one year, gone the next year, and the competitions are structured so that for everybody it is shit or bust every year. Teams don't have long-term plans for players; sure you're only here this year, you mightn't be here next year.

(Dealing with the County Board over the years, we used to get that handed to us a lot as an official attitude. They'd say, 'Sure ye will be gone.' We'd say, 'Look, we're here representing the boys, but the young fellas coming after us are exactly the same way and we're willing to take that chance that you will be looking across the table at us next year.' It was a new way of thinking for them.)

On the playing field I was lucky that guys had belief in me over the years, because it would be a shame if you went before you reached what you could be. Especially for a keeper. I often watch Iker Casillas for Real Madrid. He's a great goalkeeper now for Real but he wasn't like that when he was a young fella. They let him grow. Your goalkeeper is your long-term investment.

Great saves are a bonus, even for top keepers. Goalkeepers judge each other on safety, positioning and dealing with high balls as much as on saves. The more simple it can be made to look, usually, the better the goalkeeper is.

I'd always go out with the hand; you know a hurling keeper is under pressure when he goes with the hurley. If he's batting away the ball he is in trouble. Maybe it actually does go back to the father's training and being afraid of getting a belt of the ball from him, all those days of keeping my head up, eye on the ball and catching the ball. There is a saying in American football: 'You might as well catch it, it's going to hurt anyway', and that's often the case in hurling: forwards coming in on you and you have to be prepared to take the belt, but better to catch and take the belt than drop and take the belt.

I try to practise different situations. The reason I catch the ball down low a lot of the time is that my hand is out of the contact zone there. If you're going up with flailing hurleys your hand is in the contact area. A smart forward is watching your hand and using his stick to make sure you don't catch the ball. The defenders make a path for the ball to drop to you if possible. You call the ball as yours and they let it come to you. More than half the skill is the unseen – having your defenders coached towards a system of how you want the game to be played in there.

I always say that in goals it's easier to do the right thing. If you're nervous in goals, if you are hesitant, you mightn't get involved in the high ball at all. The full-back will deal with it nine times out of ten anyway and nobody will notice, but it creates a worse situation for you that you'll be forced to deal with eventually. A ball will come dropping through with a player just in front of you batting at it and you having to try and catch it then – nearly impossible. Or the ball is breaking, dropping short, and now you're going for a fifty–fifty ball. You and the big full-forward.

The easiest thing to do is have proper procedures in place, call the ball early, have the defenders well coached. The right thing is the easiest thing. Keep telling yourself that and you'll be all right, in goals. And elsewhere.

I was lucky. From childhood I had Paddy Joe Ring telling me that I would keep goals for Cork some day. And when I got to the Cork panel the hand that shook mine and welcomed me belonged to Ger Cunningham.

(Ahead of me the year before, there was a guy called Brian Hurley. Brian was earmarked to become Ger's replacement and was a fine goalie. In 1994 he was the Cork minor keeper and I was his understudy. He was very good to me. I leapfrogged him next year to get a place on the under-21s, but he remained a great keeper.)

Ger had eighteen years as Cork's Number One. He saw off twelve different reserve keepers in that time. He won three All-Irelands, seven Munster Championships and four All-Stars awards, and for a lot of people he is probably the best goalkeeper ever to have played. The length of his puck-outs was legendary. He won the Poc Fada competition through the Cooley Mountains seven times in a row.

He was my idol, but I'd always have been feisty enough about competing with Ger and wanting to take his place. I played a game for the seniors in the Oireachtas competition back in 1996, against Tipperary. I'd say, looking back, I definitely wasn't ready. I remember Declan Ryan was full-forward and he seemed so big and imposing I was surprised that there was any sunlight hitting the goal area at all. John Leahy was playing as well. I remember Leahy going down the steps and thinking to myself, That's fucking John Leahy there. I was distracted enough to be noticing these fellas, but I used to be thinking I was as good as them too.

Same with Ger. Even if you are as cocky as some of us were in the early days training with the county seniors, you mind yourself. One night early on I went running with Cunningham because I thought the goalie maybe should be training with the other goalie. The rest of the team had gone ahead and I was hanging back with Ger, the two goalies together.

We're tipping along and Ger says to me, 'Listen, you want to be running away up there with the other fellas, I'm too fucking old.'

At that time anybody over the age of thirty in the GAA was like the Ancient Mariner. So I got to thinking, Yeah, this looks bad, I'm going to keep up with the young fellas. What I didn't know was that Ger was getting rid of me because he wasn't running the full circuit!

Jimmy Barry-Murphy and Teddy Owens used to send us off out around the Marina, and we'd all go running around by the Tedcastles coal place, but Ger and all these older fellas took a short cut. I didn't find that out until JBM came up to me one evening and said, 'Dónal Óg, don't mind that fucking run, you're a goalkeeper, this is what you do, run up there, cut out there and just come back down around!' JBM thought just the goalies were taking this short cut, but it was sort of the official way home for anybody old enough in GAA terms to qualify for a bus pass.

I got little looks-in, bit parts to play. Management knew that some-time soon Cork was going to have to face up to life without Ger Cunningham. They held discreet auditions.

I played my National League debut away to Meath. I still mess with Ger about that, telling him that it wasn't by chance he wasn't playing that day. The rain came lashing out of the heavens and I remember we were losing at half-time. That was a sensation. Cork behind at half-time to Meath!

At half-time that day Brian Corcoran went bananas. Corcoran is not usually that type of fella at all but the man went mad. He's not the type of fella that ever saw himself on a Cork team losing to Meath either, I suppose.

I thought he was going to beat some of us up. I remember JBM was freaked too. And I remember saying to myself, 'Oh Jesus Christ, I'm going to be on this fucking infamous team. Corcoran is going to go insane and stay that way and we'll have driven him to it. We're going to get beaten, we'll be all hung and we'll be remembered for

ever as the Cork team that lost a hurling game to Meath. Why didn't
I hide my hurley and say I couldn't play! I'll be forgotten for everything
except today. Pub quiz question: Who was in goal the day Meath beat
Cork? Eh, was it the great Ger Cunningham? No, in fact it was somebody called Dónal Óg Cusack.'

We only won by a goal that day.

The next morning I was working on a building site in Cork and I
remember going in and the radio was on loud. Dessie Cahill was doing
the sports bulletin. It was the funniest thing in the history of the world,
apparently, Meath nearly beating us. I heard them making a joke about
it and I remember saying to myself, I'm telling you, Dessie, that will
change, we'll be back.

I believed we would because as young fellas we had won the under-
21s, we'd won minor, we were winning everything all the way and
then you were coming in with Cork seniors and, I'd hate to say it, but
Cork were nearly half afraid of Clare at that time. Clare had this aura
about them that they built up deliberately. And that Cork team gave
them too much respect.

Cunningham was a seriously competitive fella. He still is. Get him
in the ball alley and you know all about it. We used to play this competition in training, a slogging match we used to call it. A really simple
goalie's thing. We put down two sets of goals about twenty-five yards
apart and we would flake the ball at each other full force. If you stopped
the ball and it went out for a 65, you'd strike the next ball off your
left. It was the first to five, then you'd swap sides.

With Ger there was no stopping, no pausing. I thought I was feisty
and competitive but I was nothing compared to him. He could hit the
ball at one hundred miles an hour, literally puck it the length of the
field sometimes if he wanted to or needed to. Sometimes in this training game the ball would come at me so fast that I would stop it with
my body and the effect was like getting hit with a large rubber bullet.
But he wouldn't stop. He would drive on with the game, driving balls
at me. I remember him hitting my thumb one night and me going
down and him telling me to get up.

And he was right. I couldn't beat him and I used to be fucking mad
to get the better of him but I hadn't a hope. At the start he would

hammer me, absolutely hammer me; 10–0 every time. I wouldn't give up, though. I got closer all the time. I'd score the odd point at first. Then two or three a game. But I never beat him.

Ger retired after the championship in 1998, but he trained away with me the next season to help me. Which was an unreal thing to do after eighteen years. He might have sat on the bench so fellas could say to him, 'Ah Ger, you should be in there.' But he retired so I wouldn't have that pressure. And then he helped me.

I made my championship debut against Waterford, and I well remember the last Friday evening before the game. Ger came and he trained away with me as usual, but that night was a big thing for me. Ger had kept goal for Cork for eighteen years, eighteen championships. Always the first name on the teamsheet.

Now I was taking over from him on Sunday and I remember we had our usual little game and I couldn't get over the fucker! He was fucking flaking the ball at me still, the Friday before the game when I wanted to be wrapped in cotton wool. But he went away a little early and obviously it was emotional for everyone because some fellas had been with him a long time and Jimmy Barry-Murphy had played with him. Even me – I'd been with him for a couple of years and now this was it, the boy was going to be flying himself, flying the nest.

I watched him leave. An era walking out the gate.

When I got back to the dressing-room he had put a good-luck card into my kitbag. It said: To The Number 1. Keep Your Eye On The Ball.

Aw fuck. I had that card stuck up along with a picture of my grandmother in front of the mirror as long as I lived at home. Every morning for years I saw that card and my grandmother Costine looking back at me.

We beat Waterford that Sunday. Six of us made our debuts for Cork. Mickey O'Connell, my old school friend, started in midfield in his first game and gave an exhibition. Paul Flynn put a goal past me from a free but we were off the blocks and into a Munster final. Gerald McCarthy was in charge of Waterford. JBM, Gerald's old clubmate at St Finbarr's, had told us he would never, ever coach any team other than Cork and asked us to do it for him that day. At the end JBM sprinted out on to the field almost in a caper.

He had gambled big-time on us. In the run-up to that championship we had played Tipperary in two challenge games and they had humiliated us. We were boys against men. But JBM had stuck with the boys.

In the Munster final we played Clare. We caught a break along the way: their best forward, Jamesie O'Connor, broke his arm playing against Tipperary in a tough semi-final on the other side of the draw. Still, Clare carried a fierce reputation. We were a little bit in awe of them.

Before the game we watched a video of them playing us in 1998. They were swatting us like flies, they were so tough. The great Anthony Daly was in one clip defiantly showing the ball to the camera, having won a free early. The tape was stopped on that image. Clare had motivated themselves for years against Tipperary with the memory of Nicky English smiling to himself after a soft point was given to him on a plate after he had come in as a sub on a day when Tipp dismembered Clare. We took the same out of Daly's gesture, and in the parade before the game we were so keyed up the lads were shouting across at Daly.

(It was mainly me shouting the abuse. Perhaps only me. I was very wound up. I had to sit at the dinner table with him at the All-Stars later that year, and he made me really welcome at the table. Somebody asked me did I want some wine; I declined, and they said, 'Ah go on, it would be good for the heart.' Daly interrupted and said, 'There is nothing wrong with this fellow's heart.' I often wondered, was he referring to that Munster final. We were wired.)

Joe Deane scored his first championship goal that day. I kept a clean sheet. We were Munster champions. We were free.

We beat Offaly, the reigning champions, in the All-Ireland semifinal, a game that was immediately declared a classic.

And so to the final. Versus Kilkenny.

Expectation never takes the back seat in Cork. We had beaten the All-Ireland champions of the previous two years. We were in an All-Ireland final against the bookies' favourites and the previous year's beaten finalists, but it never struck us that we might lose. Not the team. Not the Cork public. We were raging underdogs, and we didn't care.

That day! Jimmy presented me with the famous red-and-white

hooped goalkeeper's jersey. He went around the dressing-room and presented each of us with our jersey. Talk about pride and hair standing on the back of your neck.

(Afterwards Teddy Owens produced a picture from 1996: JBM, Tony O'Sullivan and Tom Cashman in the dugout against Limerick looking lost and helpless. They had come in as a managerial dream team and that day was a nightmare for them. We had gone full circle.)

I look back at who Kilkenny had in their forward lines that day – D. J. Carey, Henry Shefflin, Charlie Carter and John Power – and I don't know where we got our arrogance from, but Corcoran was inspirational to our backs, and the sight of John Power being called to the bench with ten minutes left drove us on.

Ronan Dwane, who was looking after the sticks that day, told me afterwards that Noel Skehan, the former Kilkenny goalie, had been behind the Kilkenny goal and told James McGarry, the Kilkenny goalie, to drop an early ball right down on top of Brian Corcoran, 'and we'll see what he's like with John Power on him'. Corcoran caught it brilliantly and returned it. The crowd rose to him. He'd set the tone yet again. We finished with another clean sheet. The goal against Waterford was the only one we had conceded all year.

I got an All-Star in 1999, and recognition like that in your first season is great, even though I think Davy Fitzgerald should have got the All-Star that year because of his performances. I had stood behind him watching the Clare–Tipp game that year and he was brilliant – truly brilliant.

When people ask me about Davy I always tell them that first. Then I tell them about the Railway Cup trip to Boston in 2005.

There was a lot of bad feeling on that trip. At one point there was abuse being hurled between Kilkenny and Cork players across the lobby of the team's hotel. They got into a lift and we actually thought for a minute to chase in after them and have the fight there and then. We could have been killed, in fairness. Anyone who knows about lifts knows that they stop handy enough if there is much movement. I remember thinking afterwards that that would have been some space to have been fighting in.

Anyway the Munster manager, Joe O'Leary, was looking after the

Munster selection. He called myself and Davy Fitz together and said that the selectors couldn't decide which of us to play in the game so he was going to give us a half each. Davy in the first half, me in the second.

I was grand with that. Davy stood up and he was literally shaking with rage.

There was a team meeting that night. On the whiteboard when we walked in there was the confirmation where the teamlist was written. Beside the number 1 was written Davy/Dónal Óg. The meeting was no sooner started when the conversation turned to the issue of puck-outs. Davy stood up and made a speech about how he could drive the ball longer and more accurately than any man on this trip or any goal-keeper in Ireland. Clearly all directed at me. He was furious. John Gardiner was beside me, and he was furious too. John asked me if I wanted him to get up and fuck Davy out of it in front of everybody. I told him to let it go.

Next day, Davy was still in a sulk. We were going out to puck around and he wouldn't speak but kept deliberately stopping to osten-tatiously sign autographs, letting it be seen that he was the big star.

So I said to myself, Well, Davy boy, you won't treat me like this. I'll show you that whatever level you go to I'm capable of going there too.

So we were stewing in this surly silence when I caught a ball and moved straight towards him and drove it as furiously as I could straight past him and into a forest behind him.

We stood and stared at each other for about a minute. This made him think! Finally we broke off the stare. I think he got the message that he needed to stop fucking acting the bollox with me now, and we continued pucking. Someone told the media about it and a version of the story was in the *Irish Independent* the following week.

That day in the game, just coming up to half-time, a ball fell into the Munster square. Davy went down and didn't get up for a few minutes. At half-time he went off, limping like a fucking war veteran. Every report that went back to Ireland made it clear that Davy Fitz got injured and was replaced by the substitute, Dónal Óg Cusack. He might be mad but there's method there too!

7

When we were young lads and coming up through the grades we knew for sure that we were bulletproof. We'd get name-checked in the local papers and talked about in clubs and photographed as we won minor and under-21 titles. Bulletproof and scratchproof. Good-fellas. Success shields you when you are young. Rules and Leaving Certs are for other people. We knew we were good. We were the future, the next big thing.

Probably we hadn't enough respect for anybody. That's a good thing when you are starting off. And probably it's a very Cork thing too – the old joke about a Cork fella with an inferiority complex believing he's only as good as everybody else.

Back then, Frank Murphy, the County Secretary, was a grand and commanding figure on the stage. He would make big heroic speeches to us. It never seemed odd, even if the speeches sometimes struck us as funny. He has a way with words, Frank, and the bigger the words the more special the way he has with them.

Even then, Frank had been the Cork County Secretary for ever. Theoretically he served the Board. In reality, as the only full-time officer, he controlled everything. Frank Murphy held GAA life in Cork in the palm of his hand. And when the lads up above in Croke Park needed to be shown the error of their ways, Frank was our man for that.

The stories about the man went ahead of him. He was God, except he moved in more mysterious ways. Dropping a word here and a word there so that his will would be done. Providing jobs for good players or tickets for that fella or connections for this fella. Nothing for the other fella. Getting people off suspensions because of his legendary familiarity with the nooks and crannies of the rule book. His epic speeches to GAA congress. He was and is such a figure in Cork life that no surname is really necessary. He was and is Frank. The don of

Cork GAA. I remember in the days of our under-21 team, Frank would come into the hubbub of the dressing-room and stand there in the small space not taken up by our egos, amid the clouds of anti-perspirant spray, and he would wax eloquent as only he could. The other officials would stand respectfully to the side like curates listening to a hymn being sung by the Pope. We boys used to find it amusing – we'd sit there wondering, What is the story here? This figure in the suit and comb-over with the grand phrases and all these guys nearly bowing to him?

We had a couple of fellas back then, strong-minded bucks who weren't really the ideal audience for Frank. Seánie Farrell, for instance, was a fella who never bowed to anybody and who was making up his own legend as he went along. When Seánie encountered Frank, this strange grey man who the whole county was afraid of, this man who would come among us to orate and declaim occasionally, Seánie just found it all very amusing.

I can remember Frank making a speech before we played Clare back in 1997 as under-21s. Ideally there would have been tension in the room but . . . Seánie had his back to Frank as Frank spoke, so we could all see Frank's face as the speech came at us and at the same time we could see Seánie. Frank was speechifying and Seánie was laughifying. Just laughing like crazy.

Afterwards lots of us had to see the physio, having strained muscles with the effort that went into not laughing along with Seánie. Even at that, one of us would occasionally crack, the shoulders would begin shaking and we'd have to look at the floor and start rooting in a kitbag while thinking of tragic things to make ourselves stop laughing.

I still reckon Frank caught me having a little laugh. But the words he was using were fantastic. I remember he used often say, 'Boys! Hurl with abandon!' – and that used to kill us altogether. Abandon! Boys!

He was the boss, though. Even at under-21 level, when we had more than a few notions about ourselves, we could see he ruled the world outside. If he thought it was due to us he would call us into a room and give us a dressing-down. I remember one night in the mid-nineties he brought us in and the abuse he gave us was unbelievable. Harsh and funny at the same time. Frank actually accused poor Alan Cummins of being a tennis player! (Myself and Cummins used to play a bit of tennis when we were young. I used to say to Cummins that Frank had his spies out. Cummins reckoned it was bad enough that the great Frank Cummins of Kilkenny would have come to Cork in the first place to hurl, but then to have his young fella going about the place with a tennis racquet!)

I remember at minor level, fellows would be coming into the room and almost bowing. Literally. I don't know what they were doing, but anyway I remember wondering what the story here was. Frank worked for the County Board. He didn't own it or invent it.

One thing that seriously pissed me off about Frank from early on was the abuse he would roar at players and selectors. I remember being a sub on the minor team in 1994, and afterwards with the seniors, and I would hear it at close hand, there on the bench. I'd sit there thinking, Who the fuck does this guy think he is?

Now we all generally got a great kick out of Frank's carry-on and he was never truly frightening to us because I suppose there was always a bit of rebellion in that group, a generational thing. And winning indemnified us. Cork had been in the doldrums and now we were riding along, or so we thought, to be the next great team from the county.

Anyway, there was one icon and one alone for us. Jimmy Barry-Murphy. I remember being in the dressing-room before games and just saying to myself, 'Jesus Christ, I am in the same room as Jimmy Barry-Murphy.' But Frank, the fella who was meant to fill us with shock and awe, had no real effect. And the power he had over the rest of the county, the fear he struck into committee men, the labyrinths he controlled as full-time Secretary and guardian of the tradition and secrets of Cork GAA, it meant nothing to us.

So our attitude was to sort of say, Well fuck this fella then, why is the whole county afraid of him? He was one of us but not part of us. He had access to the dressing-room but wasn't part of the dressing-room. We kept him at arm's length but we knew what he could do.

We didn't even dislike him. I didn't, anyway. He was Frank. He was the face of the Board. He was the law. He was eccentric. He was part of the bigger scene and he could be generous and he could be fun, and to have him on your side was a good thing. Once we went on a team trip to Scotland playing shinty and the boys were teasing Frank, trying to get him to drink, giving him bottles of Heineken and egging him on. The lads didn't care, and eventually Frank humoured everybody by putting a bottle up to his lips. He didn't mind too much either. There was a picture around for a long time of Frank putting a bottle of Heineken into my mouth for the crack too while I was asleep. He was a good character in many ways, this almost mythical administrator and operator who tagged along with us.

We went to Thailand after we won the All-Ireland in 1999. It was a great trip, even if the Board were in control of the whole thing. (Or thought they were. We were asked to help finance the trip by selling team pictures about the place and passing the money back to the Board. There was a fair-to-bristling trade in unofficial team pictures in Cork that winter. Maybe that was a sign of things to come.) First of all, a few days in Bangkok. You have to admire the optimism of the Cork County Board to dump thirty young fellas from Cork in Bangkok and to hope they'd go to the museums and perhaps to the opera.

I nearly get the shakes when I think about it. Myself (twenty-two) and Neil Ronan (nineteen) were rooming together and hitting the town so hard that we hardly saw the room at all. We drank and messed around a lot – it was some adventure for two young fellas. One night, seriously ill, I just collapsed. And Ronan (here's how mature and responsible we were!) just put me into a tuk-tuk and sent it off back to the hotel.

I got sick and I was dizzy and weak. I threw myself into the bed and waited to die. I passed out and came to in the middle of the night.

I went looking for Sully. I knew that if I said, 'Sully, there is something seriously wrong with me here,' he would take care of me. So I went looking for him.

I couldn't even find a way out of the room, I was vomiting and I was shaking and collapsing. I lay down again. And the next morning I went looking for him again and couldn't find him. He was still out somewhere. I met some of the lads and said it to them.

'Lads, I'm fucking sick. Seriously – fucking – sick.'

The boys thought this was hilarious. Little patronizing lectures about the effects of alcohol followed.

Next thing, in my delirium I went and stood underneath the hotel's ornamental fountain, treating it like a cold shower. The comrades who had been lecturing me about what a poor friend the drink is realized then that there was something wrong beyond the usual. They brought me back up to bed and sent for help.

A nurse came and put me on a drip straight away. I remember the drip hanging from the lampshade. I was shattered. I'd done nothing but train on the roof of the hotel and drink.

Next thing, of course, Frank was informed of my plight. This is the side of the man people don't know: he stayed with me for the best part of the next two days. He made sure I was looked after. A couple of the boys would be calling in and out at any given time between partying. Frank would always be there.

I remember Sully called in and found myself and Frank eating tea and toast! Sully brings it up still when we are at war and cursing Frank. 'Still and all, Ógie, it was grand and cosy when he looked after you with the bit of tea and toast and the drip.'

I recovered after a couple of days and myself and Neil sensibly resumed our schedule of non-stop partying and hell-raising. It was by chance then that a knock came when we were both in the room. We looked out the peephole. Frank! For fuck's sake what does Frank want?

He stepped into the room and announced with pleasure that our team sponsors, Esat Digifone as they were back then, were buying suits for every member of the party. All you had to do was go down to this place in town and claim your free threads.

We weren't as impressed or grateful as we should have been. I said to Frank that we were in Bangkok, we hadn't a clue where we were and we had as much chance of finding that street as we had of staying in for a night.

'Well so, I'll take you down myself!'

That was Frank. It was a genuinely good-natured offer. So Ronan and myself got ready and followed him downstairs, assuming we'd get one of these little tuk-tuks downtown, they were great old yokes and we were laughing to ourselves saying, 'Oh Jesus the boys are going to see us heading off with Frank here.'

But Frank had a car! So we sat in with Frank and off through the chaos of the little streets till we arrived at the shop of a man called John the Tailor.

John the Tailor was good fun. He knew Frank and he addressed him as he hurried about the place as Mr Frank! 'Oh Mr Frank this and Mr Frank thanks you. Suits you, Mr Frank. Suits you!' If Frank had been secretary of the Bangkok county board John the Tailor's devotion to him couldn't have been more impressive.

By now the kick myself and Ronan were getting out of Mr Frank was immense. We got measured up but, with all due respect to Mr Frank, the colours he was telling John the Tailor to bring out were shocking. He was either amusing himself or John the Tailor needed to look at his stock. In the end we entered into the spirit of it and Ronan and myself ordered a couple of vile green suits. They were fucking desperate outfits but Mr Frank was pleased to have helped and we had a great old time with him in John the Tailor's.

When we were done Mr Frank was up for more.

'Have you had anything to eat, boys? We'll go for something to eat.'

Myself and Ronan were having the crack now but, Jesus, Frank took us to a beautiful place out by the river. He was king of this town already! It was genuinely lovely and we had a great conversation. He was telling us about Cork down the years and about old matches. I was delighted with him, he's an intelligent man and he can really tell a story. You could listen to him for hours and, as well as being entertained, get a good idea of the environment he has come from and the things that shaped him. It appears as if his life has been the GAA and almost nothing else. I often think of that conversation when we are at war with him. He is a product of the environment he grew up in. So are we all. I'd probably be no different if I'd had his life experiences. It's a pity all of us haven't been on the same page working for Cork GAA and sharing the same vision, because he is a powerful friend to have and a tough enemy to fight. I liked the man and a lot of me still does. But if we need to go back to the trenches again in the morning, I'll go.

After dinner we were walking around the streets and next minute Frank turns and says to us, 'Have you had any massages here, boys?'

'Eh! No!'

Whatever about the car, the suits, the dinner, this was the capper! Myself and Ronan were looking at each other. If the boys see or hear about this we are screwed! But what could you say to him? Myself and

Ronan would be adventurous fellas anyway, so we said, 'Ah sure right we'll go with you so, Frank.' He was delighted to be showing us around.

'Do you know what we'll go for? We'll go for a foot massage!'

So off we went anyway, myself, Neil Ronan and the legendary Mr Frank, in for a foot massage. If anyone had a photograph of that they could blackmail any of the three of us for life: the musketeers fed and watered and the three of us laid out on three little beds all in a row beside each other. Little Thai women fussing about, rubbing our sweaty Irish feet! The pride of Cork manhood!

Afterwards I took Ronan aside. Just in case.

'I'm fucking telling you now, Neil. Nobody has to ever hear about what happened today because we'll get such a doing over from the boys that it will last the rest of our lives.'

We agreed solemnly. Then we got a few pints into us that night and he told all the boys about it anyway.

After Bangkok we all went up north to a resort place called Chang Mai and we were brought one afternoon to this show that I didn't like the look of it at all. It was basically elephants being demeaned playing basketball and the like. It was horrible to see animals doing something which didn't come naturally to them at all. The whole thing was taking the animals' dignity away.

Afterwards there was the chance of an elephant ride through the jungle. Forget about dignity now, everyone wanted the chance to go for a spin on an elephant and to have their photo taken on board giving a big thumbs-up. We queued up in two loose lines as they loaded the elephants up and sent them off. I was well to the back by myself and daydreaming as usual and, Oh Jesus Christ, last minute I realize that Frank is in the same place in the other line as I am in my line. And they are taking one from each line and loading them up side by side on these seats on top of the elephant and letting them off like newlyweds.

I know my fate. I'm a young fella here and after the tea and the toast, after the foot massage and the dinner by the river, if I'm seen up on an elephant now with Frank the boys are going to destroy me! I wouldn't give a shit now, but back then as a young fella . . . Oh Jesus.

So sure as God the queue is getting a bit shorter, a bit shorter and, as predicted, it is myself and Frank! So he says: 'Mr Cusack! We're going on that elephant there.'

'No problem, Frank, great job.'

So up we went on top of the elephant: Dónal Óg Cusack, trouble-maker from Cloyne, and Phrionsias Ó Murchú, Secretary and defender of the Cork County Board.

I realized to my relief that most of the boys who had wanted to experience a go on the elephants had gone ahead. The rest had wandered off. In the clear! Presuming that our elephant didn't fancy himself as a sprinter and start overtaking other comrades, I might get away with this one.

Now I wasn't comfortable up on the elephant for two reasons. First, I was with Frank and I knew what an absolutely comical pair we made, sitting up there, side by side. And second, I didn't really like the idea of what was happening anyway. There was a little fella up on the front of the elephant. He was sticking a hook into the elephant's ear to basic-ally steer the animal. I remembered the old stories from childhood about the elephants being intelligent and having long memories and I said to myself, if this poor fella has half a brain left he's going to kill someone one of these days.

Now the little fella with the hook was steering the elephant, but the other half of the gimmick was that when the jungle got dense you were supposed to make the elephant go by feeding him bananas. Local people were literally hanging down from the trees selling the bunches of bananas that you would feed your elephant with. Frank being Frank, it was himself who took control and bought the bananas on our behalf. Grand! Now it's me and Frank in the jungle on top of an elephant, and Frank clutching a huge bunch of bananas. You couldn't make up a picture this comical on Photoshop.

Next minute the elephant trudges into this swamp and stops still. He knows the game. He stands in the swamp till he gets some bananas. No bananas, no movement. That's the deal. You keep giving him bananas, he keeps moving.

The water was well up on the elephant and rising slowly. He stood and he stood. Definitely in the deepest part of the swamp, I noticed. And his trunk was waving back at us, as much to say, 'Lads, if you don't feed me here now, I'm going nowhere and we can all drown. I haven't much of a life as an elephant with a fucking hook in my ear and you clowns up on top of me, and I know you're afraid of your lives like, so if this is the way ye want to die, the way ye want to be remembered, that's grand! Otherwise give me bananas!'

I remember saying to myself, 'Right, Frank, give the fucking elephant some bananas, we need to get out of here.' But Frank is sitting there, clutching his bunch of bananas as if he is bringing them home as presents from the trip. I'm not kidding, you couldn't make up a better metaphor for all that followed over the next few years. We're all drowning! Frank wants to hold on to all the bananas!

Eventually I nudged Frank.

'Feed him for fuck's sake, Frank.'

So Frank examines the bunch and picks off one banana and gingerly hands it over next time the elephant lifts up his trunk. And the little fella with the hook is getting all excited and saying, 'No, no, no,' trying to explain that one poxy banana isn't going to get us through the swamp here.

The elephant goes on another couple of yards and stops again, and Frank sighs and hands him over another single banana! And I'm looking at the fella with the hook and he is getting agitated, so now I freak because I'm starting to panic.

'For fuck's sake, Frank, give him the fucking bananas! Give him the whole lot of them!'

And onwards we went through the fucking jungle like Darby and Joan.

Finally the elephant let us off as we were to continue our journey on a raft. It had turned into me and Frank doing a sort of jungle triathlon. So on we step on to this floating square of planks and the raft is pushed out into the river and I'm still a bit jumpy. Myself and Frank are out in the current now, and next thing an elephant on the bank lets this godawful screech out of him that frightens the life out of me, a huge roar. Not a bother on Frank, though.

'That's our fella saying goodbye, Mr Cusack. Give him a salute.'

And I swear to God, I'm a worse eejit. There I am in the middle of a river with Mr Frank Murphy and the two of us waving goodbye to an elephant who has supposedly just roared a hearty farewell to us, the last shreds of my credibility drifting down the Swanee ahead of me!

And the next thought that strikes me is that, just like a roller-coaster ride in Disney World, the organizers have taken an 'official' snapshot of myself and Frank on our elephant as we trudged through the jungle. A copy is available for each of us to purchase when we get to the end of the expedition. Which would be grand except . . .

I need to get to those pictures before one of the boys wanders past the stall and spots them. Now this raft expedition is a race against time. I'm on the water, praying for whitewater rapids, a typhoon, anything to get us to the end quickly now. But the damn thing just moseys along. No point in feeding bananas to a raft. Frank is reminiscing about our elephant as if the animal had won All-Irelands for Cork.

Finally we get off the raft alive and my number-one priority is to get to this stall, to find this place where the pictures are being sold. I gallop ahead of Frank. There are two pictures of everybody available, but when myself and Frank get there, there is only one picture left of the two of us. Not funny. I look about the place, my eyes scanning the horizon for a group of Cork players gathered around a photograph which they will hastily put away when they see me. But nothing. I had to let Frank buy the remaining copy for himself and head back to the real world, knowing that some smart bastard had my picture and that I was snookered. Someday, somewhere, that photo was going to resurface. I couldn't ask around about it without drawing attention to the whole thing. Just had to wait and wait till my man played his hand!

So I said to myself, 'Right, I'll keep the ear to the ground now and I'll find out in time who bought that picture.' But nothing happened. And yet I knew it was out there. Somewhere.

We played Kilkenny away in the first round of the 2000 National Hurling league and JBM had been travelling with Frank up front in the bus.

We arrived. JBM crooked his finger at me. 'Come here, I want a word with you. For fuck's sake tell me this, were you up on an elephant having the crack with Frank in Thailand?'

'Ehm.'

'And did the elephant wave ye goodbye?'

'Frank thought so.'

'Tell me this, though: were you down on the raft and did your old elephant not fucking recognize you, so you and Frank, ye had to wave at him?'

'Sort of, Jimmy.'

'Well, he hasn't spoken about anything else all the way to Kilkenny.'

I'm hearing this from JBM. A legend in the game. I'm thinking some fucker is going to show Jimmy the picture of me and Frank on the elephant. Me, Frank and a bunch of bananas going down together in the swamp of history.

This ain't over, whoever you are!

8

Waterford today. We lost, but we went down fighting. At least there was some guts and spirit there, that was the most important thing. We were thirteen points down with fifteen minutes left, but we got back to within three points at one stage. We proved to ourselves there is something there inside us still.

At half-time we were nine points down and I actually got a bad feeling that this game was going to unravel again, just like Kilkenny had. It was going to lurch to disaster. There was a danger of it. At half-time Denis spoke, but no player said a word. Tom Kenny asked me to speak because he's captain at the moment, while John Gardiner is injured.

I was tense. I said it to Tom: 'Listen, if I talk here I'm going to freak, or else I'm going to say nothing.'

Tom looked at me, obviously sensing where we were. 'I think you should freak.'

And I freaked. Nuclear freaking. I unloaded everything that had been in my head since Kilkenny dismembered us. I unloaded my fears that losing would somehow become acceptable, that we'd accept smaller margins and make excuses for ourselves.

Halfway through . . . shit. I got this idea in my head that my forehead was bleeding! I swear to God! Bleeding! I actually said to myself, 'Oh Jesus Christ, this will be embarrassing because there is blood coming out of my forehead now.'

There's about half the dressing-room who know me and the other half who think I'm a cross between a madman and the antichrist, and now that I'm ranting and bleeding from the forehead they are glancing down to see if I am sticking cloven feet into my boots!

I think my head is going to fucking explode.

'Don't fucking go back out on the field if you haven't got it inside of you. Any man who doesn't have it, don't go back out.' I said it with all the passion I could find in myself. 'We can't accept. We just fucking can't. We can't wake up on Monday morning like we woke up after the Kilkenny game. Never fucking again. Ever!'

And in fairness Denis came in afterwards and just backed up in about five seconds what I said without any veins popping from his head.

The second half we fought harder anyway, the fucking umpire did me for going outside the square again but I know by now that's a trophy for those guys. You look at Kilkenny's goalies, count how often they do it. See if they get pulled!

We nearly got there, though. We lost, but there was good fighting spirit in the second half and Denis spoke brilliantly afterwards; he spoke about how we fought well but there was a difference between a victory and a three-point defeat by Waterford at home. We had to remember that.

It came home to us today how our little world has been changed by the strike. Like any player who has been around a team for a while, I could tell you where any player sits. You walk into this dressing-room or that and you have your seat and you know who your neighbours are and who you will be staring at across the room.

In Páirc Uí Chaoimh, I'd always sit in the same place and Tom Kenny would sit next to me. For years. And today I came in and Kenny was up in my hatch, leaving a tiny bit of room for me. Barry Johnston, one of the young fellas who played instead of us when we were on strike, was sitting in Kenny's seat. And I knew by the sly grin on Kenny's face that he was half delighted with this and waiting to see what would happen. So afterwards I said it to him, I said, 'Look, Barry, I know this is awkward and you might go out of here saying that fucking Cusack threw me out of my place, but the fact is that's my seat there. Now Tom Kenny is sitting in my seat because you are sitting in his seat. You've to sort it out amongst yourselves but that's my seat.' That wiped the smirk from Tom's face.

It's not just the seats, of course. There is a genuine awkwardness among us as we try to become a team. We played a couple of league games together under an interim manager, John Considine, before Denis Walsh was appointed. Nothing was said about the strike. I would have made it my business to shout at the new players during those games, the same as I would shout at other players from the goal line. Tried to be normal. You just do your best. I don't know whether things are ever going to be perfect. I don't know if we are ever going to talk about the strike and why we all did what we did.

We tiptoe around certain things. I don't know if they know, really know, how we felt about things or why we did what we did. I'm looking at these young fellas and I'm thinking that they just didn't understand it. They don't give me the feeling that they did, they're not those type of characters. Sometimes I look at them and I think they were just young fellas who saw the bright lights and they went for it. Then on bad days there is a bit of me, all right, which would be saying, 'Fuck it, I don't know if I should be so charitable.'

Everyone is back now and these few new guys have survived, just a handful of them despite the promises from Gerald McCarthy and the Board that they were the future of Cork hurling. Whatever they were promised when they were breaking the strike, it obviously wasn't this. So we all just get on with it. It's sport, and in sport and life you have to drive on.

It could be that we'd all be better off having it all out in the open. A truth meeting. I think once the championship panel is named, we will have to do it. We have to put the past behind us and walk out of this mess. There would be an irony if the strike succeeded in giving us a good manager whom we could work with, but we failed because we couldn't work with a few fellas who replaced us when we were on strike.

We've our own stuff that we do every year among ourselves. The players' fund, for instance, we look after that ourselves, hand out the expenses or whatever. Soon one of the boys will need looking after somehow. Or the helmets, we all wear Mycro helmets. Ronan Curran works for Mycro and it's just a thing we do. We have an agreement that if sixteen fellas vote one way and fourteen vote the other way then everyone goes with the majority. It's just the culture of our team.

Who is even going to sit down and explain these things to the lads who are thrown in with us now? We shouldn't resent them or treat them differently, but unconsciously perhaps we do see them as different.

There was a huge number of fellas in Cork who turned down the chance to play in those circumstances, a lot of good men who said thanks but no thanks when Gerald and the County Board came calling. A lot of fellas that were close to the panel over the past couple of years and some of them even had a bit of a raw deal. You could understand fellas like that if they said, 'Fuck it, this may be the last chance I get.'

Jason Barrett in Carrigtwohill comes to mind. He was on the panel and you'd think that he'd go for it, but he didn't because he was principled about the thing. Meanwhile other fellas reached out for the chance, they bought the promises of the County Board and they enjoyed being high-profile around Cork for a while.

If that had happened back in 2002, I imagine I would have been very bitter, but seven years on I'm not sure. We are all older now and we've been around the block a few times. You just have to take some things on the chin in this life. It wasn't nice for us, knowing that players would step in like that and grab our jerseys while they were still warm from our backs. It wasn't nice for them after a while either, I imagine. It's not nice for them now.

Towards the end of the strike, after Gerald had gone and an interim management team of John Considine and Tony O'Sullivan had been appointed for two games, John Gardiner was asked in for a meeting with the new regime. He asked me to go with him.

With my reputation being the way it was at that stage, I really didn't want to go. I thought it would prejudice the meeting, that the two boys would be thinking, Here's Cusack coming in to stir the shit again. But Gardiner wanted me to go with him and I wouldn't let him down.

Considine and O'Sullivan were excellent. They just said, 'Look, we're not going to disrupt anything, we're gone in two weeks' time and we just want to keep things together, keep ticking over and see what can we do.' John Considine said it to us straight that there were going to be changes on the panel. We said that was fine, which it was, we were just going to drive on anyway. Strike or no strike, we always knew fellas would be moving on and new players would be coming in. We were never under the illusion that we would be the one and only group of players for years to come.

So on the first night we had a training session above in Páirc Uí Rinn and it brought the first hint of the dressing-room problem. In Páirc Uí Rinn, Benjy sits on my right, Sully sits there, Hartnett, Shane O'Neill, Patrick Cronin – I could keep going right around the room, telling you where every fella would sit. It's an unwritten rule that nobody will take your seat, but I walked into the dressing-room and in my peripheral vision I could see at least two fellas I didn't know sitting over where I sit.

Fuck that. But I sat over the other side anyway and the boys who knew me were aware of this and were probably half amused. What could I do? If I went over and sat in between the boys, word would be around Cork that night that Cusack came over looking for a fight or something. So I sat on the other side at the door and I remember I was going into the toilet and who was coming out against me but Ray Ryan, captain of the team that Gerald had built during the strike.

He said hello. I said hello. John Considine came in and said, 'Right lads, there is a meeting upstairs, come up for it.'

I was nearest the door and I was first out. The boys who had taken my seat, they were near the door as well though, so they would have been next out or very close to it. We went through one set of double doors and then through another set of double doors. I sensed that these fellas were behind me so I held the doors open but I didn't look back and we went into the room and there were too many chairs there anyway and they were laid out in a huge semi-circle.

I went in, sat down. Three or four of the new fellas sat down exactly across from me. All the new fellas sat over there and then for the next minute or thirty seconds all of 'our' fellas were streaming in and every fella would look left and look right and suss out the lie of the land.

For a couple of seconds it was desperate because the four or five new boys seemed to be huddled beside each other for comfort and protection. There was a couple of seconds' worth of us all staring over at the boys. I remember looking at the lads huddled up over there and I was still raw and I said to myself, 'Lads, you're not fucking making speeches about us now, are ye?'

John Considine spoke very well that night and left us under no illusions that we would pull together for Cork. Fuck it, he was right. Anyway, most of us had enough to be worried about, getting ourselves right physically and mentally for hurling again. I told myself that I didn't have time to be hating those fellas. And I parked it there.

We went to Clare to play them in the league in the first match after the strike, and things weren't any better really. The young lads sat together, well up the bus. Myself and Seán Óg sat in the back seat. Either they were afraid of us or we have a reputation for being boring.

In Clare we ate at a number of little tables, not one big table like usual. The new boys were at their own little table, and again it was obvious and it was awkward. I remember saying to Eoin Cadogan and Shane O'Neill, who were two-thirds of the full-back line in front of me that day, 'Listen, lads, we're playing for Cork, we need to talk to your man from Sars.' Conor O'Sullivan was playing in the corner, filling out the full-back line. Shane had played with him at UCC anyway, so he brought him up and we went through the exact same things. I introduced myself to him, said Best of luck today and Look, this is the way we do it. He couldn't go back to anyone and be able to say Cusack acted the bollox to him!

Today's comeback will have helped us all along the road a bit, I reckon. As a group we faced getting annihilated just like two weeks ago against Kilkenny. But we stood up and stopped it. We got the crowd behind us. We got a little sense of ourselves as a team again.

Step by step. Maybe some day we'll all laugh about that first night's training in Páirc Uí Rinn. For now, though, we are playing together. It's a start.

9

After 1999 we deflated slowly. In 2000 we were complacent and we got beaten by Offaly. Jimmy Barry-Murphy, who had half reared us as players, felt he had done his stint, won an All-Ireland with us, brought us to the summit. He said goodbye to us.

Things got frayed. We wanted to step on from 1999, to evolve and to leave a mark on hurling history, some legacy bigger than a single All-Ireland won when we were young. We had grown up not just with success but with the knowledge that Cork expected success. By winning in 1999 we had ended a brief but painful famine for the county. Tradition demanded that we drive on. So did our own sense of ourselves.

Every team sees a version of itself and its place in the world. We were young and we had graduated to a senior All-Ireland, most of us, within a year of completing back-to-back under-21 titles. We wanted more.

We were pushing against an invisible force field, though. A lot of us wanted to train and prepare and immerse ourselves in excellence, to be as close to full-time hurling as we could be. We had at least a decade ahead to claim as our own. We wanted to look to the best methods of preparation that professional sports teams used and to bring them to our own sporting life and our own game. We wanted to create a culture of excellence for ourselves.

And we had a County Board which felt that there was no need to do things differently from the way they always had been done. The years of famine and underachievement in Cork were quickly forgotten. The Board had a winning team again. Cork would always have winning teams, sure. And the world would stand still for us.

I had a plan once upon a time, when things were going well with the club in Cloyne, that we would put our players' names on the backs of their jerseys. And in my daydreams I hoped that Cork might do the same thing soon after. It wasn't an idea that came out of my ego; I just liked the idea that Frank Murphy and the Board might look at a Cork player ahead of them in the tunnel in Páirc Uí Chaoimh one day and see more than a number. They might see a name and they might subconsciously register that the name belongs to a man who has worries and concerns and responsibilities that he lays aside to play hurling for Cork. The player knows the privilege of playing for Cork and he honours that privilege and tradition by giving it everything he has. The Board man might see the name and feel that part of the tradition of Cork and part of the privilege of being a Board member would be to honour the men who wear the jersey by giving them the means to pursue the excellence that the county demands.

Instead they look at Seán Óg Ó hAilpín in his number-7 jersey and they just see number 7. And if Seán Óg isn't wearing number 7, sure there'll be a queue of fellas who want to wear it, so Seán Óg had best keep his mouth shut and his head down and remember that fact. It would be years before the Board would openly put that theory to the test, but that is the way they ran things.

Of course, Seán Óg might go on to become something of a legend in his Cork shirt, and when he was done, if he had played the game in the right way with the Board, he would be one of the good ol' boys of Cork GAA, part of the Masonic system, looked after with tickets and bailed out of the odd harmless scrape and sent up to Dublin on the eve of big matches with a few tickets and an invite to stay in the Burlington and to go on RTE the night before the game and flog anecdotes about the good old days. Meanwhile, all he would have to do is keep his mouth shut and be a good number 7.

You only have to look at Páirc Uí Chaoimh to see what many of those on the Cork County Board really think of players and fans. Numbers is all we are. The place is dilapidated, a badly run death-trap with facilities that are inadequate for anybody who uses it. It's home for us and I actually like to train there, with our voices echoing around the empty stands and terraces. When training moves to Páirc Uí Chaoimh the championship isn't far away. But even those of us who love it there know it is ramshackle and a disgrace to Cork GAA.

In 2001 we played Limerick in Páirc Uí Chaoimh. We met for a pre-match meal in Páirc Uí Rinn and waited for the team bus which would take us down to the stadium. We waited. It was a hot sunny day and we waited some more. We got tense and anxious, but we waited a bit longer. Eventually we had to accept that there was no team bus going. So we squeezed into our cars and we drove down from Temple Hill towards Páirc Uí Chaoimh through the matchday crowds.

The overflow from pubs mixed with those shuffling slowly towards the ground, and through it all our little procession of cars inched, with fans cheering us and people abusing us and banging the roofs of our cars and generally laughing at us crawling towards the ground in this state.

And at Páirc Uí Chaoimh? Hassle at the gates. Fellas who had been playing for Cork for several years having to state who they were and what they were doing there before eventually being allowed in. Dr Con had a man called Dr Tadhg O'Sullivan come in to work with us as backup that day. After 2000, when the 'blood rule' had been introduced, Con had a worry about getting players back on to the field. Anyway, they stopped Tadhg coming into Páirc Uí Chaoimh that day and caused a scene. More distraction and unhelpfulness.

The dressing-rooms in Páirc Uí Chaoimh are minute and dingy and badly positioned. They are in the main tunnel which runs around the ground and takes up the full length of the space under the main stand. To get in and out of the dressing-rooms on a big day you have to force your way through the press of the crowd in that dark, confined space. When there is a senior double-header, we're forced to share our tiny dressing-room with one of the teams playing the earlier match.

By the time we arrived late for the Limerick match in 2001, the other team, understandably failing to grasp that they had to share this tiny space with us, had colonized the entire dressing-room, so we had to make our way out the tunnel to a makeshift gym.

This is a major championship match. We are a team who are very serious about our mental preparation. The gym is not a dressing-room and it has no toilets or benches. So, before we play Limerick, any player who needs to go to the toilet has to make his way out into the main tunnel and force his way down along through the match crowd, taking back-slaps and abuse before he gets to use the public toilets.

A few lads tried it. Impossible. So we were reduced to urinating on towels in the corner of our own gym before a major championship game.

Those players who like to go into a toilet stall and just sit with their eyes closed, gathering their thoughts and preparing mentally, were lost altogether. We were all a little stressed and a bit *trí na chéile* when we hit the pitch.

We went out that day and we lost by a point: Cork's first defeat in Páirc Uí Chaoimh ever. I wouldn't take anything away from Limerick's achievement; Barry Foley scored with an amazing sideline cut to win the game. They beat what was in front of them, but we weren't prepared the way we felt we needed to be prepared that day.

Things happen that way sometimes. Misunderstandings. Bad days. Seán Óg had been in a bad car accident earlier in the summer, and we were missing him. Brian Corcoran had broken his finger and he was out. Pat Mulcahy played centre-back that afternoon.

Yet all that happened that day just seemed to be a symptom of something bigger. We were happy with Tom Cashman as manager and after the previous year we had been well motivated; but our belief was ebbing away, a thousand little things with the County Board were niggling at us and distracting us. The spirit of the team was being lost. Fellas were glad to go back to their clubs that summer, I thought.

Tom Cashman left that winter without telling us. One day he was manager. The next day we heard he was gone.

In 2002, on the day we wore the socks around the ankles, we lost the league final by a point to Kilkenny despite a decent comeback which nearly caught them. Then in the championship we lost to Galway in Thurles in one of the most dispiriting and gutless performances that a Cork team has ever put in. Our morale was a damp patch somewhere in the soles of our boots. The sparkle and optimism of 1999 had been crushed out of us totally.

On the day we lost to Galway, Sully played football for Cork in the curtain-raiser. That was a signal that a lot of the things you'd have dreamed of about being a Cork hurler weren't going to happen. If we were serious about this sport, how could they put Diarmuid O'Sullivan, who was one of our main players, on a team to play a different sport before a big match? There was something missing there. I knew that

day that this had to be sorted, something was wrong. I realized that
there were things that I thought playing for Cork was all about, and
there were things that people like Frank Murphy thought that playing
for Cork was all about. And these were very different things. Either
we needed to go or they needed to go.

We could either walk away or we could do something.

That August I did something that I felt that one of us had to do. I
lit the blue touchpaper. I did an interview on the radio in Cork and I
poured all our grievances out on to the table. A lot of people paid
attention. None of them had anything to do with the County Board.

That autumn we spoke to Frank Murphy and to the Board about
the shabby treatment of players, about issues like proper medical care,
playing gear, decent transport, payment of expenses, the possibility
of reliable hot showers after winter training sessions and a raft of other
basic requirements. They were unimpressed. We went public again.

The Board were still unimpressed. In fact they were hostile and
uncompromising and fairly bolshy about stonewalling us.

Kilkenny were pushing on as a team, looking to claim the decade we
had earmarked as our own. We were faced with a long slide into medi-
ocrity, years of being asked to put the maximum of ourselves into a
system which would never allow us to get the maximum out of ourselves.
That could be our career. Lads with a great future behind them.

Or we could do something.

We did something. We went on strike. The public backed us. The
Board and Frank Murphy capitulated on just about everything. We
proved our point and got to the next four All-Ireland finals, but the
Board never forgot and they never forgave. Not the Board, and especially not Frank.

The good ol' boy system had been faced down and Frank, I think,
was especially aggrieved. For decades he had been the good policeman
on the block, the copper who did things his way. And then, just like
in the movies, when he has a day to retirement or a week to retirement
or five years to retirement, trouble breaks out. His entire way of doing
things is questioned. And he knows he can't walk away into the sunset
until this is settled.

The sad irony is that if we had all worked together for Cork hurling, all pushed on to act like the best teams act and prepare like the best and honour the red jersey by continually being the best and expecting the best, Cork GAA would have no greater friend or advocate than Frank Murphy.

Frank withdrew for a while, but I worried that he would come back and that the next time it could be personal.

Meanwhile we delivered.

In 2006 we lost the All-Ireland final to Kilkenny by the width of a goal. Under Dónal O'Grady, who managed us in the 2003 and 2004 championships, and John Allen, who took the reins for the next two years, we had reached four successive All-Ireland finals, winning two. Before losing to Kilkenny we'd had a run of thirteen championship wins on the trot and been to the four previous Munster finals, winning three. Against opposition in hurling's top nine counties our win record stood at 87 per cent.

I don't know what way they were preparing in other counties, but under Dónal and John we brought attention to detail to new levels, we explored entire new areas of preparation of playing together as a team. We motivated each other and inspired each other and drove each other on.

We were a happy and achieving team when John Allen stepped down in the wake of the 2006 defeat. None of this was a consideration for Frank and the Board.

The Board didn't much like Dónal O'Grady. John Allen, I don't think they could take or understand at all. This quiet and philosophical man who attended training in his sandals or bare feet was a mystery to them and an affront to them. John had the wisdom to let us grow as a team and to carry the weight of responsibility within the group. He knew the value of the journey and the importance of the destination. John's own words, from his *Irish Times* column, best describe what happened after his departure:

It was time to dismantle this efficient, well-structured, successful management team and bring in a new backroom team who would bring a return to the traditional Cork style and even more success would follow.

The most important cog in the wheel was allowed to leave without any acknowledgement of the hugely significant role he played in the success of the previous four years and very little effort was made to keep him involved. The team trainer, Seánie McGrath, played the key role in the preparation of the team in those glory days. He was a fitness expert, dietitian, nutritionist, psychologist, funny man, and friend to each and every one of the players. He made the team tick. But he was let go by a board who refused to recognise his importance.

So the thread which had brought us almost continual success was snipped by the Board. We were given Gerald McCarthy instead. Strangely, for a group who allegedly have a predisposition for conflict, we accepted his appointment and got on with working with him. He came out publicly and he demeaned our style of play – 'I'm not a fan of their overpassing style' – before we had even met him. We made all the right noises, though, and again and again we went to him with ideas which generally he took on board.

A manager needs to inspire and he needs to convey to players that he is in control and has a passionate conviction about the way he is leading the team. Gerald took our ideas on board readily enough. But it didn't say much about his own convictions, and the way in which he would go about things just drained our confidence in him. It was an arranged marriage between two different faiths and it was just never going to work.

10

Here's how it works these days in my life. Timmy O'Sullivan has the team in Cloyne and on the day of a training session, or the day before, I will ask Timmy if he wants me to take the session or if he wants me to participate in it.

It would be normal down the years for me to take the sessions, but after some of the troubles we've had in the club lately, the sensitive thing to do is to ask Timmy so that at the end of the year nobody is going to turn around and say that Timmy had the title of manager but that fucking Cusack took over as usual.

We are on the verge of a championship game against Bishopstown and they will be decent. Us? We don't know where we stand really this year.

Anyway, between the Cork training and doing my own stuff, I go out and I train Cloyne. And I do it because I want to do it. Nobody forces me to do it. Nobody pays me to do it. I do it because I love the club and I love the place.

We maybe aren't quite as engaged and as hungry as we were before we got to our three county finals, but it still matters. It matters deeply. Some nights I might finish work, go get something to eat, train the Cloyne team, go to the gym and do my own stuff, and then lock up the pub. I'm not complaining. The opposite. That's the way it has been for a fair number of years now.

What I have a problem with is the fellas who would be on about me trying to take down the GAA, the accusation of being elitist, the idea that my life is devoted to fattening the bank accounts of the very top strand of players at everyone else's expense. All that kind of lazy, reactive, bullshit thinking.

Where am I going to end up when I finish playing? In a gated community in Florida? With a vineyard in Tuscany? I'll be working, and if I'm not training or playing for Cloyne I'll be doing something for the club till they hit me over the head with a shovel and tip me into a newly dug grave and vow to keep their mouths shut about my demise.

Last week, say, we were doing a lot of hooking and blocking in training, and we have been having bad trouble with the hurleys breaking like matchsticks, so there was good crack and the texts were going to lads to bring any hurleys they had around the house and my father was bringing old hurleys down from the attic. He's the water man for the team these days and he has a museum worth of sticks up in the attic.

Even the father's supply of ash couldn't solve the problem, though. The sticks are breaking if somebody looks crossly at them, so the club got ten of these new plastic hurleys that they are making up in Offaly. There are men who would turn in their graves if they saw these things being used, and when I came down on the night for training the father mentioned he'd got out whatever sticks he'd blown the dust off in the attic, so I said, 'Grand.' The plastic sticks were held back.

Anyway I took half a glance at himself and his great friend, Dinny O'Shea. They were leaning over something in the corner; when I take the glasses off, my eyesight isn't great, but I imagined they were sanding a stick and I wondered why the two boys were sanding the old hurleys we were going to be doing the blocking drills with.

So I investigated, and what were they doing? The toilets were blocked and they're both handy men and they're down, clearing the toilets before the boys go training.

And I'm taking the training session.

So to a lot of people I'm the elitist.

But this is what the GAA is about. It goes back to a very serious thing. I train the team and my father runs around with the water bottles, and himself and Dinny clean the toilets if needs be but don't come to me and tell me that because of that when I go up training and playing with Cork that I have no right to feel that the Cork players should be looked after well and that those high-profile fellas shouldn't benefit from exploitation of their own image. I'll argue that point to the death with anybody.

My father and Dinny and men like them all over the country are down in their clubs clearing the toilets and doing whatever else has to be done because they want to be doing it, because they are putting something back or paying something forward, or because they just love their club. And if the day ever came when big and successful companies wanted to make money by placing advertisements and logos on my father's back and Dinny's back as they went about their business in the club, and Cloyne sold the TV rights to my father's day and Dinny's day, I wouldn't begrudge them the chance to get something back from all that.

It doesn't sit with me at all, this pious argument that wanting county players to be well looked after is tantamount to killing off the GAA by poisoning it with toxic semi-professionalism. And I don't believe that if top inter-county players are well looked after it will demoralize the men who work in the fields and put up the nets and line the flags.

A few years ago I did a radio documentary with Gareth Southgate, the Middlesbrough manager, and David Walsh of the *Sunday Times*, and the point I made about players who go on to the top was that even if I had been part of Roy Keane's underage career in Cork and had done anything for him, surely if I saw him playing for Manchester United and being captain of United, I would be delighted for him. I wouldn't be sitting at home surely kicking the dog and saying, 'Fuck it he gets paid for that and I get nothing for coaching kids, I'm not going out any more.' I'd be delighted and proud to have done something for him. With the next bunch of kids I trained I would be able to hold Roy Keane up to them and say he was once just like you are now and if you work like Roy did, etc., etc.

My remarks on the documentary were taken out of context in some way, because when we were in South Africa very soon after it was broadcast, every headline at home said Cusack had called for semi-professionalism. I remember one day I was sitting with Frank Murphy, eating a bit of grub, and I got a voice-mail from Today FM saying that they would be calling me to interview me about the views I had expressed. All I could think of was, Wouldn't this be perfect, to take the call sitting with Frank and to say, 'Frank Murphy is actually here beside me, we're on holidays out here in South Africa, perhaps Frank would like to comment on the points you are making there?' It would have raised a few eyebrows!

It's an empty argument that drives me insane, this notion of resentments seeping up the line. If fellas are up there and they're doing what they're doing at the county level, Seán Óg and that calibre of guys, let them earn as much as possible from their fame and from their image.

I don't think I will ever change on that. Lads go full circle, I know. And people say that maybe in a few years' time I'll be grumbling that them fucking GAA players are getting too much. But I doubt it.

I know there is a line. When I was younger I would have loved to have been a professional hurler. It was almost an objective of mine. But I think now that the GAA could not sustain that.

Two years ago I would have said that to Nickey Brennan when he was President of the GAA. I was working in New York for a week and I flew overnight back into Dublin and Dessie Farrell and myself were going to a meeting with Nickey Brennan and Paraic Duffy.

(It's not well known and will probably never be fully appreciated that the GPA has been a journey undertaken essentially by a group of people who have worked beyond the call of duty and enjoyed a great friendship along the way: Dessie, Siobhan Earley, Kieran McGeeney, Seán Potts, Pat Coffey, Dónal O'Neill, Dara McGarrity among others.)

Dessie and myself had been doing a lot of talking and thinking about the whole thing, where we thought the GPA should go and where we hoped the GAA would go, and we did the figures and considered the facts, and we would have come to the conclusion that professionalism is not the way forward.

What has the average inter-county player got now, anyway – five or six years? If you pay him, you're not going to be able to pay him nearly enough that he's going to be set up for the rest of his life.

And I don't think it would be a very good character-building exercise or that you would be equipping him with the tools that are needed to go on with the rest of his life. So you would actually be doing a disservice to him, even if the GAA could sustain such a system.

Now a young fella like I was could say, 'Fuck it, this is what I want to do,' but in terms of getting as much as possible out of the thing, compensating him for loss of earnings, proper expenses and proper insurance are going to be the best that can be done. I've no problem with an inter-county fella being on a separate insurance scheme from a club player. Why do we drug-test only the inter-county players? Because there is already a distinction.

So. The objective. Why not create an amateur association that looks after its players better than any other sports association, and then invest your money in offering guys extra education and other benefits that are tailored to them? I think that there is an acknowledgement at certain levels of the GAA that that is the way it has to go. If we take it to that point, then I'm happy, I'm out of there then. To a certain degree that's what we did ourselves with Cork over the last couple of years. We recognized that the Association isn't going to look after us, so we started looking after ourselves. We built up our own funds to look after ourselves. A few lads started driving sponsored cars. If one of our fellas got injured over the last couple of years, he'd get his money straight away through our players' fund. No other group would be doing that. If you got injured with Cork, you'd straight away get your week's wages. If you had any other costs, you got money out of that fund.

The guys benefited and felt reassured from being looked after properly, and the irony is that they all committed to bringing money into that fund. It's gas, though: I put that model to people and they see it as entirely reasonable. Players should be well looked after; but then something like what went on this last winter, and the old accusations get thrown up again. This is a slippery slope to professionalism! The professionalism agenda is somehow behind this!

All winter Nickey Brennan knew the truth, because we've told Nickey Brennan and Paraic Duffy that we'll work with them to bring the GAA to that stage. We've said that what is needed is for the GPA and the GAA to join hands and make the great leap into the future together.

Things evolve. I first got involved in the GPA back in 1999 when Brian Corcoran would have been the only GPA voice in our dressing-room. Things went on in the early days of the GPA, provocative stunts, which people don't forget or forgive easily, but those fellas had to travel that road: there was no other way to make people take notice. For example, the furore over the 'free-dinner merchants' – I used that phrase in a speech once, referring to a certain element in GAA administration, and the skies went dark and there were bolts of lightning hitting the ground around my feet.

I'm amazed. Fellas would still say that to me and they'd remember it bitterly. I know though where the GPA was at that time and I remember reading that phrase out and knowing the impact it would have. Do I really think they are 'free-dinner merchants'? No, I do not. Mainly, they are not.

We needed a response, though. Some fellas needed to take the hard yards and do the things to raise the GPA's profile to get fellas talking, to get an argument going. We needed to bring the GAA out and draw them into the fight; otherwise it would have kept on going the same way until we were irrelevant.

All that early GPA stuff, the inflammatory remarks or the stunts like trying to get into the GAA's Annual Congress – all that had to be done by certain fellas. Things were done by design. I would even have had a good smirk to myself, 'Oh Jesus the guys are going to go apeshit over this – well, fingers crossed they will anyway!'

If I make a long boring speech at the GPA AGM (and believe me I am capable of it!), that won't make the front pages of the sports supplements on Monday morning. Throw in a few sidewinders, though, and it guarantees a debate, it gets fellas in clubs and dressing-rooms talking. I know it draws fire on me but it's something which has to be done. For the GPA to survive the early years, there had to be things happening, big events and necessary confrontations.

As a group of hurlers in Cork, we knew that we would be able to sort out our own problems (we would have to), but we believed that in the long run players as a whole were better served by having an organization looking after them and that anything we won as a result of our strike in 2002 should become the standard for all county players. No other group would have to go out in the cold like we did.

In years to come, what the Cork hurlers have put together for themselves shouldn't be necessary at all. There shouldn't be a need for a quasi-secret fund, where the boys are like a secret society raising money to look after themselves and welfare needs. It shouldn't be the case that when we are having our corporate dinner at the end of the year the County Board pays us €1,500 for a table, unembarrassed by the fact that their own players are having to run this dinner in order to be able to look after themselves.

I grew up and I live and play under the shadow of the great Christy Ring. I have huge passion and respect for the history of the GAA, and I see no conflict at all between that history and the GPA. I hope that some day, sooner rather than later, the GPA will be accepted as part of the GAA. That we will have offices in Croke Park and be funded by Croke Park and that we will be seen as a positive connection to the players as another means of moving the GAA forward.

I won't be still playing when the benefits of what the GPA has done come through. It's a joke in the dressing-room that lads will be driving past me on their way to games saying to themselves, 'Your man there, the skinny fella we almost hit, used he to play?' They won't know what we went through to put in place proper welfare for them, and we won't care once it's there.

This whole thing embraces the entire GAA, whatever happens, because the GPA should be owned equally by the Sligo or Leitrim hurler and the Cork or Kilkenny hurler. Equality and respect can never be bad things. An elite group will never take over the GPA. That is the GPA I want: equality and respect. Part of the broader GAA. The positives in having the GPA as part of the GAA church will always outweigh the negatives.

In a way, progress towards official recognition by the GAA is slowed down by the way the GAA is and by the way we have to be. GAA life passes in cycles. There is a time for playing and a time for talking generally. And the presidency changes every three years. The GAA likes to leave dealing with the GPA to its President – which is a pity, but that is how things are. On the other hand, we have to be seen to be active and vibrant, and we engage on courses of action which are necessary but which don't represent the long-term future of the GPA.

Some day, I think, we will make the great leap forward together. I think Paraic Duffy may be the man who will take the GPA's hand and make that leap.

I like Duffy. On the last night of his involvement in the attempted resolution of our strike, I said to him that I hoped some day he would be able to come to Cork and meet with fellas like myself and John and Seán Óg, and it won't be in circumstances of stress and strife, but just us talking as GAA men together. We really had to respect the fact that he came in and got involved in Cork at all. It was a minefield for a senior figure within the GAA, but Duffy had the balls to come down and get his hands dirty.

He rang me one day and he said, 'Look, Dónal Óg, can I meet up with you? Myself and Fergal McGill will come down, and if you want to bring someone else, do, but this meeting has to be kept completely confidential.'

I said to him, 'If you say that to me, Paraic, no one will ever hear about it.'

So that was the way it would be. I said to John Gardiner that we had to go to a meeting but nobody was to hear about it because that was the deal I had made.

John wanted clarification.

'So I can't even tell Diarmaid Falvey or Seán Óg or any of the lads?'

'John, you know if the man wants to do it this way, we ought to do it this way.'

So Paraic came down and met with us and we had a very honest discussion and learned from each other. He was involved again, not too long afterwards, when all parties convened at the Airport Hotel for a long night of negotiations. Paraic asked at one stage, could he come in and talk to all of our lads along with Christy Cooney, the President-elect.

That night myself and John had arrived at the hotel first to meet with the Croke Park people. They had produced a document that laid out what was going to happen over the next couple of years. The document basically outlined a position where the County Board would be put into suspended animation and Cork's affairs would be run from Croke Park.

We read all this and said, 'Oh Jesus, we need to get the boys in here because there is some stuff in this document that is big.' It looked bad for the County Board and yet apparently they were accepting it.

So we rang up a few of the lads. About seven or eight arrived at short notice, and Cooney and Duffy asked, could they come in and talk to the lads.

We said, 'No problem, no problem at all,' and in they came.

Almost straight away Paraic inadvertently let slip that myself and John had met with him previously.

Now I am the guy who insists that there be no secrets within the group. Everything is put on the table, everything gets brought back to the centre. And now the boys hear that myself and John had this secret meeting with Duffy.

Diarmaid Falvey! I thought his eyes were literally going to pop out of his head when Duffy left. He was stunned. I had to explain that I've utter respect for Paraic Duffy and if he said it had to be kept confidential, well then.

Diarmaid snapped at me that night, he gave out to me big-time in front of the boys. After all our years and all my talk of how we were doing things and how we were keeping it so good, I wasn't living by the code.

I did some cursing of Paraic Duffy that night, but I believe he sees quite clearly on issues of player welfare (which was the issue he really cut his teeth on as a GAA politician) and that if and when we make progress, it will be Paraic who has the guts and the leadership to make that leap towards recognizing the role of the GPA and the possibilities of the GAA and the GPA working together.

Anyway, what the GAA had put on the table that night was interesting in that it damned the County Board. They published the document afterwards, but the one part they held back was that they offered me a role in coaching the team!

Some of our players liked what was on offer but I wasn't comfortable with the idea. Joe Deane was very strong on the notion that it would be a way of killing me.

At the end I had to face Cooney and Duffy again and tell them that there was no deal. I hated doing that to Paraic Duffy, as I have had to do it too many times at this stage. They said we were leaving a great deal behind us. Maybe we were and maybe we would lose by gambling for more, but that was the decision we made that night.

At 9 a.m. the next morning I was on my way to work after being in the Airport Hotel till the early hours.

Graham Canty, captain of the Cork footballers, rang me and asked me straight.

'Have you got a problem with me?'

'No, Graham.'

'Have you got a problem with the Cork footballers?'

'No, Graham. Why?'

'Well, why the fuck . . .'

He blew me out of the water. We had never informed the footballers about what had been going on the night before. We had sat and considered a document that would change the entire face of Cork GAA and never thought to consult the footballers. Stop! Graham kept machine-gunning me. He was right – we were inside, negotiating a deal, and hadn't involved them.

To be honest, it was just the way things had worked out. We never expected the format that Cooney and Duffy went with in terms of the proposal and the meeting, and it was tough going all night . . . Now, within another couple of hours, I was having another tough conversation with a guy I like, trust and admire . . . We worked closely together during the strikes, Graham and I, more closely than any of our panels really knew. We had needed to – otherwise the football–hurling relationship could have weakened us rather than strengthened us. Now I had made a fuck-up. Nothing to do but put the hands up and apologize.

Thinking about our battle with Gerald and the County Board, and about the things some GAA people have said about the Cork hurlers and the GPA, I always remember a quote that Dónal O'Grady used to use from a fellow Corkman, Terence McSwiney. Victory will go not to those who have inflicted the most but to those who have endured the most.

Myself, my father, Dinny O'Shea, we are all in the club these nights as the club gets ready for the championship. There is no elite. We want the same thing. In our club we will fight each other and argue, and we will come together again. We are club people. In the beginning and in the end.

And GPA members will always be club people. That's where players come from and that's where they will return to. If the county player's journey is a little different along the way, let him be looked after not just because of what the county games give to the GAA, not just because of what the full houses and TV coverage generate. Just do it because it's the right thing to do.

Meanwhile Bishopstown are waiting. Till they are out of the way I am not a Cork hurler. Or a GPA man. I am a Cloyne man.

II

Text to the boys:

> **LADS GOING 2ALLEY AT 11. 30 IN THE MORN IF ANYONE INTERESTED
> IN JOINING PROB CASE CUD B MADE 4KEVIN AND CADS NOT WANTIN
> 2SHOW UP AFTER LAST WEEKS DRUBBING BUT THE FACT THAT IT
> ACTUALLY CAN'T GET ANY WORSE 4YE THAN 7ZERO PROB SHUD B
> CONSIDERED WHEN MAKING YERE DECISION**

Sunday morning at the alley in Rochestown. Nice drive. This is my hardcore workout and my hardcore company. Eoin Cadogan and his younger brother Alan, Kevin Hartnett, usually Seán Óg, increasingly now Aisake too. Tom Kenny might drop down. John Gardiner.

I love the alley sessions. I take them fierce serious and they bring out the competitor in me. We'll do drills with the ball against the wall and then play games against each other.

The competitiveness is crazy. The game we play is like squash and the boys have never ever beaten me. Now, I know that this will sound terrible and you'll cringe at what a small petty man I am, but they've never beaten me and I drive them insane about it! I never shut up. I rub it in, every chance I get, and when I do I make Muhammad Ali look shy and retiring.

Tempers run high sometimes. I aggravate the lads and they try to aggravate me and there would be a viciousness sometimes among the boys as they plot to beat me. There have been incidents where men have been stretched out on the alley floor.

We're close friends, though, and the work we do together in the alley brings all of us on.

I'm worried about Kevin Hartnett. He's one of my closest pals on the team and he has been around the panel a few years now without making the breakthrough he deserves.

Kevin is another Seán Óg, in terms of the way he prepares for hurling. I always think that you should try to surround yourself with fellas like that when you train. If the effort you put in is in any way close to what they put in, they will drag you with them.

Denis Walsh said a couple of things to me there recently. He said there are a couple of fellas on this panel that are here a couple of years now and they haven't made the breakthrough.

Fuck it, the first fella I thought of was Kevin. I think there's a possibility he's in trouble. And he does too. He hasn't got a look-in since the Kilkenny game. There is a cut going to be made in the panel soon and my worry would be that Denis and the lads haven't been in charge long enough to have gauged properly what a fella like Kevin Hartnett offers.

Then again, maybe I'm reading too much into things. Every fella on a panel thinks he's the only one really worried, every fella, at every level. Once there is a pecking order, every fella is worried about slipping in it. I know Kevin, though. He'll be going through torture, thinking about that every day. Am I going to be dropped? You know when fellas look at teams, they don't see things the same as people outside the panel do. There are all these little things going on, a million factors that they are summing up. Kevin may be as safe as houses for all we know. But he's anxious.

It's one of the things people seldom consider when they think of the GAA and one of the things which I bring to the table when I work for the GPA. Take a guy like Hartnett. There he is with his junior club, Russell Rovers, and he has made the jump to the Cork senior panel. That's a huge jump, and while the club will be proud they need him all the time, he's their county man. But being a Cork hurler is almost a full-time commitment so Russell Rovers won't see too much of him. So I imagine there are small resentments and jealousies, as in every club. Fellas always think that you shouldn't do anything outside your box.

Then if a guy like Kevin is to get dropped, they'll say, 'For fuck's sake, who did he think he was anyway?' That mentality is brutal, but clubs are like that. Smaller ones especially.

He said to me there a while ago that he would go mad if he got dropped off the panel. We were doing a session and I was thinking to myself about what I was going to say to him about that. I think he will stay and I think, come the summer, he will be involved; but when a fella gets worried, you need something more concrete to say to him than that.

So before he went away I said three things to him. Number one, to stop thinking negatively and to just go to the death with it. Number two, that he is a great player and the odds favour him. Number three, hurling could all end with an injury tomorrow. He has a great girlfriend, Keara, and a great life ahead of him. So if one door closes for him, another door will open up for him. He'll go away and he'll do other things.

And one more thing. You know where I am; any time you need to talk about it, I'm there.

What makes it hard and what could be killing Kevin is that he is from a junior club, Russell Rovers. All the boys are playing senior games all over the place and it's championship time and they are getting talked about a lot. The word goes round and fellas would go out and see senior league games in Cork in the springtime. One good game and the word would be around the street, your man was very good the other night.

When you play for a senior club you get talked about. Fact of life. And if there is one thing worse than being talked about, it's not being talked about.

Russell Rovers? Grand club and neighbours of ours, but 90 per cent of Cork don't even know where Russell Rovers is, and half of those who do know who Russell Rovers are only know because Hartnett has been on the Cork panel for the last few years. You play well for Russell Rovers and the word (if there is any word) is that you marked Johnny What's-his-face out of it, but that Johnny is forty-seven now and was stuck for the bit of pace twenty years ago.

And of course you can't leave. His father is in the club, just like mine is in Cloyne and, well, it shouldn't work that way but it does. (Strangely, when there was a split in Cloyne back in 1939, Paddy Joe Ring ended up moving to Russell Rovers for a while, but *sín scéil eile*.)

Denis Walsh and the selectors appear to me to be dead straight and fair, but it still raises your profile if you're playing the bigger games.

It's a pity because Kevin has invested a lot in it. He identifies himself as a hurler and as a Cork hurler. I don't think he'd have the motivation going back down to a junior because of his nature, the way he has committed to the thing.

And that is what people don't see when they moan about inter-county players and this perceived elite. If you watched Hartnett play for UCC earlier this year, you would pick him as a county player. If you watched his lifestyle and his training and his commitment, you would be astonished. He's getting worried, though. The pressure. And there are hundreds of guys all over the country in the same situation.

Or Eoin Cadogan. He's such a proud young fella he wouldn't even reply to the sort of text at the top of this chapter. But he'd turn up in the alley, rearing to go. Mad for action and revenge. The other day Hartnett was away for the weekend with Keara, and Cadogan was there and he was unusually quiet. His form in the alley was poor and even his performance was poor.

Afterwards I said to him, 'Look, is all OK, Cads?' And he came out with it then that the work thing is on his brain. Things have been getting tight at work and there is talk of layoffs in the air.

So it is spring. The championship is coming. And here are two fellas among the greatly despised Cork hurlers, just two lads out of the small group of us who go to the ball alley to work on our game, and their brows are knitted with worry.

We have newish management which will be making its presence felt in the next few weeks. Neither Hartnett nor Cads is sure of his place on the panel, let alone the team, and the game which takes so much of their time and energy brings worries for them instead of being an escape.

Somebody will see them playing somewhere over the next few weeks, and maybe one or other of them will be down and it will be announced grandly that your man couldn't hurl snow off a rope. There'll always be somebody glad to see a lad fail. In Australia they call it 'tall poppy syndrome', the tallest poppy gets its head cut off first.

In Ireland we have a plainer word for it: begrudgery.

12

This is an awkward enough one for a hurling story and it's been an awkward enough one for this hurler – but it's my story. Once long ago I denied myself, literally I denied my own name. I swore I would never do it again.

So. Since I was young, in my head anyway at first, I've known that I'll sleep with whoever I want to sleep with, I'll fall in love with whoever I want to fall in love with, I'll be with whoever I want to be with. My business. That isn't me putting a fight up or making a stand. That's just a given in my brain.

That's how it has been since I was young. That's how it is.

Have I slept with men? Yes. Have I slept with women? Yes, I've slept with women too.

I hate labels, though. That's the way I am. How does that sound to you? Does it matter? That's the way it is. I live with it and I am fine with it. So be it.

The people I would be close to will tell you, there were never tears. There was never agony. I just know this thing. I've had to say this to people I'm close to again and again. When I was young I said it to Diarmaid Falvey, I said it to Sully, I said it to my good friend Thomas O'Brien. This is who I am. This is what I do.

I spend a lot of time trying to work things out, but once I know something about myself, I know it. I don't agonize. I get great ease out of that. It's logical to me. Since I was thirteen or fourteen I knew this about myself. And that was it. I just knew it was a bit different.

I thought about it but never had any problems dealing with it. Anything I have done in life, I need to be able to say afterwards that I did it for the right reasons. It's the same with this thing.

I tried to go out with women to make sure, to see what kind of feeling it gave me. I went out with nice women and good women, but sure I still knew. I wanted something else. I get more out of men. I just do. Always have.

Why? Well, Dr Con and myself have had fierce philosophical conversations about that. Con has had his troubles with it, mainly as the man he is and the friend he is, trying to protect me, and with his questions he would actually have troubled me for all my confidence, but still nothing changes.

Listen. I'm in Cloyne, growing up in Cloyne, and I'm not stupid. Even at thirteen or fourteen I'm not stupid. I know what matters in Cloyne because the same thing matters to me, it matters in my house with my brothers, my father, my cousins. Hurling comes first.

And I know from early on I am different, just in this way. But whatever you may feel about me or who I am, you should know I've always been at peace with it. However, I can well see that if things were another way, life would be easier.

I still see it. I often say to Billy that I'd envy him when I see him with his kids. If I were like him, if I wasn't the way I am, I'd be married with a couple of kids by now. I'd probably have a family to come home to. I see him and his young fella, Danny, playing hurling, and of course you'd like that for yourself. What Cloyne man wouldn't? My dad once told me how proud he is when he sees the three of us, his sons, playing senior for Cloyne together, and that makes me think. It would be easier. No question.

Then again, other times the lads are on to me – this woman is driving me mad. That woman. Grief at home. I go away, laughing and thinking, Am I a lucky man or what?

I'm from Cloyne. I'm playing the only sport that matters in a village and a city and a county that is mad about that sport. Demented mad. I'm playing hurling in a town more steeped in hurling than anywhere else could ever be. Christy Ring himself looks over everything we do. I'm a Harty Cup player. A county player. And that's a challenge in itself. To the world I live in I'm a man's man.

And in the early years I was that and I was also going into gay nightclubs in Cork all on my own.

There was no choice but to go in alone. No choice but to find out where one of these places was and get in from Cloyne and just walk in there. The first time I was inside a gay nightclub was a joint in Cork which was called The Other Place. It was a bit of a dump. A pub upstairs, a bar downstairs with a dance floor. A weird layout to the place, especially if you didn't know that layout beforehand.

I got to the door. Nervous. I said, 'Right, Ógie boy, this is going to be a bit of a challenge,' took a deep breath and went in. To add to the tension I recognized the bouncer, but by that time there was no turning back. I felt I had to do it.

I went in and I hadn't a clue what was going on or what the structure of the place was. I would be the sort of person who goes into a place normally and wants to know the layout of everywhere, and who sits where, and how to get out in a hurry, but I'm here and I haven't a clue.

That's part of the life, though. Part of living that life. New things, strange things happen. At first you recognize it in yourself, this small difference. Then you begin to recognize it in others. If a hundred fellas are in a bar and ten of them are gay, I'd pick out nine of them. A sixth sense. I'd known it with fellas I served my time with, worked with. Serving your time at a trade on a building site in Cork City you wouldn't imagine there was any place for free love, but you see it. And you know it. Those were the first fleeting encounters I ever had. I was nineteen. I would know. He would know. You just know.

And now I am in this nightclub and everything is strange and new and my confidence isn't what it should be. A fella comes up to me and says, 'You're Dónal Óg, yeah?'

Sheer panic. I shake my head. Deny it. I just say, 'Sorry, no.'

And that's the worst feeling. People say it would be easier, wouldn't it, to just fit in with everyone else? But you can't live that denial, you can't be somebody else. I woke up the next day and made a vow to myself: that will never again fucking happen to me now, because I'm not going through this thing all my life, living like this. Never ever again.

Any fella that ever asked me about it afterwards or any fella that said it to me, I told them. I never denied it again. Whatever came my way, I would always be me.

The first person I told was Diarmaid Falvey. We've been close since I was young. I would have recognized in Diarmaid that he has a broad mind and would be able to handle that kind of stuff. Funny thing is, Diarmaid's wife Mary is a smart, intuitive woman. I don't know how she reckoned she knew but she says she knew. Just by certain things I had said, etc.

Ger Cunningham's wife Deirdre wasn't surprised either, according to Ger. Ger had a slight heart attack, but that's another story.

I told other people, but only when they needed to be told. The gay life and the life of Cork hurlers don't really overlap and I could step from one world to the other with more and more ease as I got older.

There is lots of crazy stuff there. The gay world, for a lot of young men, is not a lot different from the straight world. It's full of drugs and clubs and one-night stands and searching for a buzz. It's often about waking up in the morning and not knowing who is beside you, where you are. Because I went into those places on my own, I lived a load of that shit. Loads of it, and nobody back in the other world I lived in would have known.

I'd be a healthy-living person well into my sport, but I could tell stories that would embarrass myself. The easiest ones are when you wake up and escape. I woke up one morning not knowing where I was. I looked out the window of this place and I saw the temporary courthouse in Cork. Most people in Cork wouldn't know where the temporary courthouse is, but I worked in there as an electrician. I looked out. I saw the courthouse. Rang one of the lads.

'Drive in along the quays. Collect me.'

I had to be getting out of the place before anybody in the house woke up.

Even when we went away on holidays as a team, I would head off by myself. From doing it in Cork you would develop skills and instincts. One night in Ho Chi Minh City I remember myself and Ronan Curran heading out on those motorbikes that the locals drive you around on.

And I suppose Ronan copped later, but I gave him the slip. Ronan thought we were going out for a few late-night drinks. I remember saying to the fella that was driving my bike to drift away in the traffic.

I hated that in a way. It's a lonely enough business. I love going out with the lads and having the crack and the slagging. Slipping away alone in a foreign city to do your own thing isn't easy. But that is the way and it's its own form of adventure.

Next morning I woke up with a fella. Hungover. Demented. Lost. It's all right waking up and not knowing where you are in Cork, but in Ho Chi Minh City it's another story. Who is beside me? Where am I? Shit.

I needed to get out of there. I'm thinking, This is my life and at times like this, well, it's not ideal, is it? I headed for the door and opened it. Good Morning Vietnam! A dog came at me. There was a wall of cages with dogs in them, each of them going mad. Now, I have to stay here or wake this fella up. I gave him a shake.

He drove me back to the city. I couldn't believe it. We were miles out of the way. Miles and miles.

I came back to the lads. Before I got to my room I heard a noise in another room. Ben O'Connor and Pat Mulcahy were in there. It was eleven or twelve o'clock. The boys were delighted. Noon and Ógie is only coming back from the night out. The slagging started over it. Team stuff. The lads.

My night had its own history that they aren't imagining and that doesn't really matter. I'm back with the boys. One of the team.

13

If you were to give Gerald McCarthy the benefit of the doubt, you would say that we were never a traditional sort of team. And we would have given him that benefit if he had given it to us.

In the years between the strike of 2002 and the All-Ireland final defeat of 2006, we grew as people and we grew as a team. Dónal O'Grady developed us as players and John Allen had the wisdom to let us evolve as people. We were a self-motivating group and we looked after ourselves in many of the ways in which other county teams get looked after by their County Boards.

We had a big benefit dinner at the end of each year, an event organized by the players for the players and for benefactors of the team. People in Cork are generous and, even at the end of 2006, having failed to win the three-in-a-row, we had our dinner and it was a great success.

The lads asked me if I would make the speech this time and, on the principle that it is far better for the lads to let me down than it is for me to let the lads down, I said I would. John Allen had just left at that time and we were in a state of limbo. We had little forebodings. One of the things I said that day in the speech was that we hadn't come to a time for the settling of old scores. This was before anyone was appointed to replace John, and the words were directed at the County Board and at Frank.

We were going away on holiday as a team fairly soon afterwards, but it was as if the skies had darkened and a cold breeze had blown through the town. We knew what was afoot, that there was a chance of retaliation coming our way.

We headed off to America with the three-in-a-row gone and heavy worries about the future hanging over us, but we were determined to have the best holiday we could. It had been a long, long grind for us all and we were determined to put the defeat to Kilkenny behind us.

Looking back, it was a great holiday. We had a brilliant system in

place. We went to San Francisco first; and then anyone who wanted
to, the people with kids or whatever, went down to Disney World
and the other fellas went to Las Vegas. And then we all met again in
Mexico, in Cancun. A serious break and run by the players on a fair
basis for partners and kids.

Historically, the Board brought you along on holidays; now we
made it clear to the Board that they were guests of ours. Also, if you
had four kids, then the four kids got paid for. Nobody complained.
The sacrifice put in by a man leaving a wife at home with four kids
for so many nights and weekends in a season is greater than that put
in by a fella on his own. That used not to be the way.

Funny, but I'd actually be the first to accept that sometimes the manager
whom players think they deserve is the last manager they should get.
That can be too cosy, and a panel has to have an edge to it. A new
manager often sees things in a fresh light and shakes a team out of old
habits. But amateur players who want to give everything to their sport
need a manager who at least reflects and respects that team's drive and
dedication.

We were lucky enough for a long time in that regard. We grew up,
most of us, under the wing of our idol, Jimmy Barry-Murphy. Jimmy
was replaced for a year by Tom Cashman, and then we had Bertie Óg
Murphy. All of them were fighting a County Board that was living in
the dark ages and working with a team which had outgrown that era.
They were good men, though, and we had no problems with their
management.

Dónal O'Grady brought us to a different level. He was a manager
who considered everything and tended to have everything written
down on the back of a cornflakes pack when he arrived at training.
We feared him and respected him.

And when Dónal went, John Allen took over. There could have been
no John without Dónal O'Grady, but John's personality was such that
he took things on and developed them in a way that Dónal never would
have. He was less methodical and more intuitive and he allowed us to
grow together more as a group of people. John is a schoolteacher, like
Dónal, though he brought less of the *múinteoir* into the dressing-room

with him. He was always the Boss and, as much as people would like to spin the story that John was soft, nobody ever crossed the line.

All that time, through five different managers – none of whom the Cork team complained about and three of whom won All-Ireland titles with us – we grew and evolved and closed in on the prime of our hurling lives. Losing the three-in-a-row hurt us but it wasn't a final chapter. We didn't think so anyway.

While we were away in California and Vegas and Mexico, Gerald McCarthy was appointed for the 2007 season. The general reaction was a shrug. The first real discussion of Gerald was beside a pool under a blue sky one day. Somebody at home rang one of the lads, who went to the computer and printed off a piece from a national newspaper back home. He showed it around. The new Cork manager, Gerald McCarthy, was telling the world he wasn't a fan of our short hand-passing style of play. By the pool the reaction was pretty much the same from every deckchair: 'Who is this fucker? He's coming in now and picking a fight with us?'

To most of us the only contact we would have had with him was when he managed Waterford against us. The jury was out as to whether Gerald was a County Board stooge, put in merely to help the Board in reclaiming those things they lost control of, back after the 2002 strike.

Our first meeting with Gerald was held out in the Rochestown Park Hotel. He spoke to us and you could have scraped the sense of disappointment up off the floor. A guy gets to manage his county fairly late in his life, you imagine he will be inspired by it and have something to say to you about it that might inspire you too. Gerald didn't have any memorable words to throw on the table. He finished by asking, had we anything to say. Silence. I knew then we were in trouble. I will never forget the silence inside that room. Lads just staring in disbelief.

The silence limped on. I was wondering to myself if the boys were thinking that I should perhaps say something under the circumstances or if I had something prepared. Nope. None of us had anything to say, so we all sat looking at Gerald. It was like one of those intensely embarrassing scenes from *The Office*.

In the end one of the lads asked a fairly obvious question.

'When are we training?'

'Oh yeah! The training bit! Right! Mick, have you got the training stuff? Have you got that there now, Mick?'

The fellas' jaws were dropping. Mick Dolan, Chairman of the County Board, started patting his pockets. What have these County Board hacks got to do with our training sessions?

Whether these fellas should actually be at a team meeting is highly debatable but now the boys are fiddling around, looking for bits of paper, and we knew we had just been frogmarched back to the dark ages before the strike of 2002. The boys in the blazers were back.

During the 2007–8 strike I said to Gerald that that first meeting, and the Mick Dolan incident, marked the beginning of his own end.

'Gerald, what exactly did *you* think the players were thinking that night?'

I honestly don't know if he really knew what was going on, if he'd taken much notice of the movement to get rid of the Board's interference in team affairs because they were getting in the way. I don't think he had paid any heed to all the attempts to create something that was special.

There was a machine being created in Kilkenny. The game was changing year on year. Kilkenny and Cork were in a race to build the perfect hurling machine, a process we had started. A great sports team needs to be like a cult. The great teams are built around faith and commitment. We were in a race with Kilkenny, two teams built on those principles. The old players, previous generations, might love to romanticize the way things once were, but the game changed in those few years. Kilkenny and Cork pushed each other on to new levels.

Gerald certainly didn't see that, with his arrival, the whole system collapsed. They'd gotten rid of everybody except an assistant trainer after we had been on one of the longest unbeaten runs of any Cork side in history. Now everything was collapsed, folded up and taken away. No logic or sense, but Gerald seemed oblivious to it all.

Training was dire. He had an obsession with overhead pulling, which was his trademark as a player apparently. Pretty as it is to watch, there is a reason nobody pulls overhead much any more. Instead of gaining possession you are just creating another fifty–fifty situation down the field. At times goalies and corner-backs were required to practise overhead pulling with the same obsessiveness as midfielders.

The relationship wasn't good from the start. We went down to Waterford for a Waterford Crystal Tournament match and we ate inside in a nightclub beforehand. The smell of the place and these lousy sandwiches – we knew we were in deep trouble.

Every drill I had done for the previous couple of years was geared towards a certain style of play. When I'd grab the ball, I'd look for my wing-backs or my corner-backs or my midfielders, and we'd try to move the ball out. It wasn't short play for the sake of short play; we were trying to transfer the ball from A to B with the least amount of risk rather than lamping the ball down the field where it would be contested fifty–fifty. When it goes wrong, the short strategy can cost us a goal and it leaves me looking bad. Enough of them have come back past me over the years to know that. But firing the ball down the other end of the field as far away from myself as possible might in a less obvious way cost us five or six points in a game. So we play the percentages. I don't insist on short puck-outs and force the team to comply; it's something we are all on the same page about, something we worked out. And when it goes wrong occasionally, as we know it will, it's something I'll take the rap for.

It went wrong that night against Waterford. I caught a ball, moved and struck it out quickly, and I fucked up. I think it was John Mullane of Waterford who caught it and put it back over my head and the bar. It was bad but, as I say, we had established a long time ago that occasionally this was going to happen and we believed in the system.

We got into the dressing-room at half-time and Gerald said: 'Puck out in front of the boys, just fucking clear the ball.'

I wasn't happy. It was high-handed, but it was stupid too. You don't mind being the fall guy for the fellas behind on the terrace or the guys in the press box but you expect the manager to understand what is going on. So when I was going out to the field – I think I was the last out the door – I said to Gerald: 'If that happens again, I'll do the exact same thing.'

Now, I was a bit out of line, I knew that, but the way he was handling it was going to the heart of what my game and Cork's game was about. I felt that it was a cheap shot for the benefit of showing the dressing-room that he would be boss. He'd made no attempt to understand that it wasn't me who had decided on the short puck-out policy but the team. We'd been in four All-Ireland finals in succession, playing that way.

I understood that we needed to evolve and I understood that the team needs to change – any team does. But this business of just coming in and throwing everything out for the sake of it, and not replacing it with anything, that didn't sit in my head at all. There needs to be a reason for you to ask a team to stop doing something that has been successful. As far as I could tell, he never understood what had actually been happening over the four years before he arrived, he never had a feel for it or an understanding of it or a curiosity about it.

He had a view that he was what Cork hurling had been standing still and waiting for, over the previous thirty years. The team felt there was nothing new there, though. We felt we could see through him like a glass of water.

After that match, we were dumped back into the same nightclub in Dungarvan for a big feed of greasy chips. With the Waterford team.

Nothing against Waterford, but it was a long time since we'd eaten chips after games. Let alone be dumped into a nightclub with a team we had just played, to shovel this grease into ourselves. And Gerald was back with his old pals from Waterford, in his element, greeting everybody, and some of the lads were grumbling as to why the hell he just didn't go and sit at the Waterford table altogether.

The chips thing was such a psychological blow. Jerry Wallis, our physical coach, almost resigned over it. For years Cork teams ran around in the concrete tunnels underneath Páirc Uí Chaoimh and got fried chicken and chips and a fizzy drink thrown at them afterwards, just to make sure no good could come of the work. It had stopped in 2002 and we had started eating as athletes should.

Anyway, I got a phone call the next day from Martin Bohan.

'Gerald wants to meet with you tomorrow before training for a disciplinary meeting.'

'What's that all about?'

'What happened yesterday.'

Something struck me when I'd agreed and hung up the phone. I called Martin back.

'Ye know now there will be someone going with me in there tomorrow night.'

'I'll check that out and get back to you.'

'No. I'm not asking. I am telling you that this isn't a special request, this is the way we've always done it. I'm not going to be going in there alone. There will be another player with me. There is going to be a couple of you there. No big deal or anything, but there will be another one of the players coming with me.'

'I'll check that out.'

So he came back and said that no, Gerald didn't want that at all. No way. So I said fine, maybe ye don't know me but when I say it I mean it: I will be going straight down to training and there will be no meeting. Then it got better.

A few minutes later he called back. 'Gerald has said that Mick Dolan from the Board can be there.'

'Am I listening to this, Martin? You're saying that Mick Dolan, the Chairman of the Cork County Board, is coming to a disciplinary meeting to ensure that Dónal Óg Cusack gets fair treatment! For fuck's sake, boys, I won't be there tomorrow, end of story!'

'Well, who would you bring?'

'Seán Óg.'

The next morning he rang me yet again and said that Gerald had agreed to it, Seán Óg could come. I met Seán Óg down in Fermoy before the meeting and I said to him that I had a feeling that the meeting wouldn't be about Sunday at all. It might start out that way but there was a bigger agenda.

True enough, pretty soon the meeting was all about how we had our own ways in the team and how we were too set in those ways. Supposedly Gerald wasn't being made welcome in the set-up.

I pointed out that after his appointment the team had been away on holidays and the first view of his that we knew of was his comment in the national papers that he wasn't a fan of our hand-passing style.

He said a few times that he wouldn't have his authority questioned. And we got into a big and stupid debate about how I had been the last out of the room and nobody else could have heard me question his authority. It was a private exchange that he had decided to make an issue of.

The meeting went on and on and on. It was proposed that I be suspended. Seán Óg wasn't having it. 'After the debate we're after having here and all the issues we have covered,' he said, 'there is no logic to suspending the man, this isn't right what you're doing here.'

In the end they grandly announced a solution. I wouldn't be suspended for the forthcoming game with Tipperary, but I wouldn't be playing either. Marty Coleman would be playing in goal. I don't know if I was supposed to throw a tantrum and turn against Marty. I had no problem with them dropping me and playing Marty if it was done in a straightforward way. But this was just a gutless thing to do.

Meanwhile, at the ground in Fermoy the team were waiting to be trained. Neither myself nor Seán Óg had turned up and the word was going around that something bad had happened. So the lads decided not to come out on to the field at all. When we got there finally, a couple of them were trickling out for a puck-around and we all went back in and explained what had just happened.

That weekend was the beginning of a slow decay in the panel. My friend Billy was just a fringe player at the time, but he announced that he couldn't hack it any more. He went to Gerald when he was leaving and told it to him straight. 'Gerald, the team is a disaster. Can you not see that? Can you not see the boys don't respect you?'

'I can't see that.'

'I'm sitting down with them, though, and they're totally demoralized by you and the set-up, Gerald.'

Then Wayne Sherlock left. Just like that. He met me out in the middle of the field and he said, 'Look, I want to talk to you, I'm packing up here tonight.' He was like a prisoner announcing his intention to escape. 'I can't take it any more,' he said, 'and I'm going to fucking tell him that on the way out as well.'

Wayne Sherlock was a very quiet and earnest fella and a great corner-back; but he did, he actually waited till the game started and walked across to Gerald and said he'd had enough.

I remember looking out in the Munster semi-final against Waterford in Semple Stadium that year. It was almost the end of the game and we were losing and I just wondered, where had we gone? Nine of the team which finished the previous September's All-Ireland were missing by the time we got to the end of the Waterford game.

It was pretty much the same when we got beaten by them again a few weeks later, in the All-Ireland quarter-final. Stupid decisions. Key fellas like Joe Deane taken off when a game was still winnable. The culmination of a hundred little things which had been done wrong along the way.

We made a mistake at the end of 2007. We were asked by the footballers to support them in their own troubles with the County Board. While we were at it, a number of the lads wanted us to get rid of Gerald too.

We had set up a meeting to discuss whether or not to support the footballers. It took ten minutes to decide that we would. Most of the meeting was taken up with the question of Gerald. I argued fiercely against moving on him. I said it was the wrong time. The Board could just stick in somebody who would be no better, so I argued that we were better off to try and work with Gerald. He had come around to certain things already and maybe he would improve.

That debate turned out to be the most bitter internal disagreement we experienced since I joined the senior squad. We had a vote. It was close enough, but we stuck with our system whereby everybody would stick together once a vote was over. Everybody settled for a policy of co-operation.

I was wrong. We should have gone for it. The last year was such a waste of men's lives and hurling abilities that it drives me insane with regret. We should have gone for it. It might sound harsh but this is a harsh business and the man driving the bus was not going in the direction we hoped for when we climbed on board. Instead we set ourselves back another year of our prime.

A short story about looking after players.

I've played in five All-Ireland finals and conceded three goals in those games. The worst was the first. In 2003, Martin Comerford went to hit his shot one way, across my body, but Seán Óg got his hurley to it slightly. It bounced and beat me at the near post. Probably won them the game. That year Croke Park were all over their place with their policy on sliotars, and the ball being used had a freakish bounce at the best of times. The bounce was off and my weight had gone one way and I couldn't get back in time. It looked like a bad goal.

The goal burned a hole in my heart and gnawed at my brain all that winter. I put myself through hell over it.

The following spring we were inside in Páirc Uí Rinn and out of nowhere Dónal O'Grady took me aside and said to me that he'd watched the video of that goal twenty times at least, and as far as he was concerned he could see no fault in my positioning or anticipation. It was one of those things.

He released me in the space of a few seconds with those words. He gave me my own confidence back and showed me that he had confidence in me. I'll never forget him for that. He switched the light back on in my head.

And I continued to work harder. I wanted to repay the man's faith in me. I realized that people had been nurturing me along the way, but that I could be better. I could make the move beyond D, I could press on to E this year, and further next year. I could do this thing to the best of my ability while I had the chance and while I had it in me. Or I could be a passenger and that would kill me.

I lost out narrowly for an All-Star award the next year. Ger Cunningham texted me that night that I was still a work in progress. I drove on. The following year I was an All-Star. I felt I had reached a new level in my game.

Guys like Dónal O'Grady and Ger Cunningham and John Allen had the wisdom to bring that out of me. To make me want it. To me, that's management.

14

Semple Stadium, Thurles, 3 May

If we have a modern history with Tipperary it's that we have never really feared them. When we started out we would have had an awe when it came to Clare. But Tipp? Not really. I'd imagine they worry about us much more than we worry about them. Up until 2007 I had never been on a team defeated by Tipp in the championship at any level.

I suppose we became men that day we got past Clare in 1999. Anthony Daly and the boys held no more fears for us.

Tipp flared to an All-Ireland in 2001 when we were in the doldrums, and then they went away again. Mostly, when we play them we beat them, and when we don't beat them we know why. They beat us last year, for instance, but Gerald had us set up all wrong. The game was a depressing experience and gave great encouragement to their new manager, Liam Sheedy. If they were to beat us this year it will be three years in a row they have done us. Not great against a team we don't truly rate.

To be honest, we miss Babs Keating. We always believed that as long as the Babs show was running in Tipperary we had nothing too much to worry about.

Babs made some of the mischief we got up to all the more worthwhile. For instance, there is a long history in the GAA of playing close to the wind when it comes to sliotars. One manager used to soak a consignment of new sliotars in a bath for a day and then dry them out in the week of a Cork match. The idea was to get them to Ger Cunningham to puck out. The balls would look new, but that bit of zing would be gone from them and they would shorten Ger's legendary puck-outs accordingly.

Babs had a short and selective memory about this sort of thing, having himself been involved in one or two great sliotar stories in his playing days. When we played Tipperary in the Munster final in 2006, Babs came down behind the goal for the first puck-out of the game and got the umpire to throw me another type of ball. I just threw the ball away and pucked out the ball we were using anyway. It made what happened later all the sweeter.

There was already a bit of history between Cork and Tipp with regard to sliotars. The previous year, they won a penalty against us. Eoin Kelly stepped up.

We had a plan. Once we had been awarded a penalty or we had given away a penalty, we were to create a bit of commotion, a diversion through which to get the right ball in play. If we won a penalty we'd be getting rid of the O'Neill's ball and getting one of our favoured Cummins All-Star balls in to use. If we conceded a penalty I'd get rid of the match ball in use at the time and the dud ball would be rolled in. Never handed over. Rolled in, so that it would just appear to be lying on the grass waiting to be picked up. There was nothing obvious. It would just appear there. On the day, Kelly picked up the dud ball. It had been a job of work for one of our men to soften it up and still have it look like a newish O'Neill's ball.

It gave me great confidence to see him pick it up.

To reassure opposing players, what we used to do was write the opposing county name in marker on the ball. Tipp! Eoin Kelly picked up the ball, looked at it and placed it for the penalty. I said to the boys, 'We've a chance here now with this.'

He took the penalty with it and we saved it.

(Kieran Murphy got a point with the same ball seconds later when it broke downfield, so if anybody ever argued with us, we could say that for fuck's sake Kieran Murphy put the same ball over from fifty yards!)

You'd get a great kick out of something like that afterwards. Before a game it would be a little something up your sleeve, you'd have the thing organized and be waiting. Pulling it off in the heat of battle gave great satisfaction.

And we'd have a bit of crack with it. Sully nearly got raped by Limerick fellas in 2006, running the length of the field with an All-Star sliotar in his shorts for us to take a penalty with.

It was mischief, but there was a gap there for it and we got some fun out of it. Paul Codd of Wexford copped one day. He picked up a ball with Wexford written on it and knew straight off it wasn't one of theirs. He drove it out over the stand.

There was room for all this carry-on with sliotars because the GAA left room for it. We'd always be for pushing the edge with stuff like that where the GAA leaves the door open. Any advantage.

At the time they hadn't standardized the sliotars used in games. Nothing about their wishes concerning sliotars appeared in the actual rule book and there was no penalty for replacing the match ball with one of our own. There is no other sport in the world that you could play where you wouldn't know beforehand exactly what type of ball you would be using. So in the gap where there was uncertainty we decided to try to influence things.

For instance, once we decided on the tactic of going for distance with our puck-outs in the All-Ireland final in 2005. The next thing to make sure of was that we were pucking out the right sliotar. We wanted to use All-Star balls, made here in Cork, because for distance they are hard to beat. So everything possible had to be done that day to allow us to use the All-Star ball. We decided that, whatever had to happen, we'd do it. If we'd to throw away every other ball that was in the stadium, we'd throw them away.

It was after that season that the whole sliotar issue would become really controversial again; but it occupied a lot of our thoughts in the lead-up to the final as we tried to come up with different ways to get the All-Star ball on the field. People were telling us that when we got to Croke Park there was a good chance we wouldn't be able to use the All-Star at all, that Croke Park were going to insist on the use of O'Neill's sliotars.

Nobody knew exactly what the story would be. I had an idea though. My brother used to work as a printer. Surely . . .

When I get the bit between my teeth on things like this, there are parts of my brain that won't switch off. We got stamps made up to see if we could fake things. We basically wanted to get an O'Neill's logo on to an All-Star ball!

It didn't work, though. You couldn't get blank All-Star balls to put the O'Neill's logo on to.

A lot of the outfield players didn't like the O'Neill's ball either. Joe Deane talked about it a lot, saying that if he was taking frees and he bent down and saw an O'Neill's ball he'd have a negative thought straight away, whereas if he saw an All-Star logo, it was, Yes, I've a better chance of putting this over.

Down in training one night a light bulb popped in my head. I went over to Ger Cunningham and I gave him the master plan. We needed somebody who made sliotars. We needed to talk with them and get them to make an All-Star sliotar but put an O'Neill's cover on it. Do the job properly. So wherever in the world these things were actually made they'd cut them out and, instead of putting the All-Star stamp on the All-Star sliotar, they'd put an O'Neill's stamp on it. Nobody would know the difference, except we'd be happier with it.

Ger looked at me and he said, 'Hmmmm, for fuck's sake go back into goals will you.'

I asked for a meeting with two of the members of the management team. Jesus, they didn't want to hear it.

I figured management had no need to know. The All-Star balls were legal and so were the O'Neill's balls. We just had a preference and wanted the edge we believed we would get.

So I rang up a fella I knew who had contacts in the sports equipment game, swore him to secrecy and asked him, would he meet with a few of us in the Rochestown Hotel. I gave a big spiel about how we needed a favour from him for the good of the county, etc., and all this kind of stuff, and then asked straight, would it be possible to get an All-Star ball made and then to cover and stamp them as O'Neill's sliotars?

The scheme sounded worse every time I repeated it but I stressed nobody would know. There would be no controversy. And in the end he agreed to look into it. Obviously he made a big speech about how this would be a massive scandal, but between the jigs and the reels he said he could possibly do it.

When I spoke to him next he said, 'Yeah, it can be done.' He just needed to check out one or two things. He rang me soon after and said the gear is on its way, he was going to get it done out in India because, he said, if someone found out about it, we could all try and distance ourselves from it! He said he couldn't trust an Irish guy to do it.

So we were happy. We spoke about how we'd exchange with the fellas behind the goals, take ones off them if we had to, every ball I'd puck out would be a nice ball, it would be one of ours.

The GAA stole my pleasure, though. Within a couple of days of our deal being done they came out and said that they would now allow the All-Star ball to be used, but each ball would be stamped with a unique match-day stamp. It was all sorted.

I suppose it was a triumph but deep down I preferred my own plan!

Tipp beat us last year, a historic win for them in Páirc Uí Chaoimh. The game was a depressing experience. A match we gave away rather than one that was taken from us.

If last year was a landmark for Tipperary, beating us down by the Lee for the first time since Tipp people began walking upright or whatever, this year we know they have their sights on games way beyond us. Rightly so. We don't know if we can get ourselves healed and hurling in time to play them. But there is a chance. Part of our best opportunity lies in Tipperary's belief that they will beat us and go on to better things.

Today they played Kilkenny in the National League final in Semple Stadium. They lost, but tomorrow the headlines will be about the way in which Tipp thundered into Kilkenny and how for a few minutes in the first half especially, Kilkenny looked distracted and annoyed by the booming challenges and thunderous mood.

In the first few minutes a Kilkenny defender got mugged in his own square. James Ryall, who is big enough to expect to be safe in these circumstances, got turned over. James Woodlock hustled the ball over the line into the net for Tipperary. Seconds later, Shane McGrath came up with an overhead point while effectively being pinned in by Kilkenny defenders. Whatever else they have been doing, Tipp have been working on their physical strength.

And, next thing, John O'Brien went haring through. Bang. Goal. Eight minutes gone. Tipp had been through for two goals. The second one, O'Brien's, interests me as a goalie. He came through and shot for goals from a spot where at that stage of the game most players would be taking a point. Obviously a policy decision.

Brian Hogan, the Kilkenny defender, was stretchered off. His replacement was Martin Comerford. Comerford came on, got a red card for fighting with Tipp's Declan Fanning, and went straight back off.

Tipp took Kilkenny into extra time before going under to the champions. Not bad, not bad, considering that, just before Kilkenny beat us by twenty-seven points in the league, they had beaten Tipperary by seventeen.

They were impressive today but in a way which doesn't leave us fearing them. I'm not sure why.

They beat us last year on a day when we had young lads playing all over the place and experienced men on the bench. And when it was over, Gerald never went to the boys and told them what had gone wrong or why they had been taken off. I remember Páidí O'Sullivan had been played at wing-back in training all the way to the game. He'd been put in as a corner-forward. Then taken off. And not a word said to him.

Things like that kill players. There was a steady drip of things like that.

15

We're on a balcony in South Africa, having dinner. Seán Óg, his girl-friend Siobhan, Jimmy McEvoy and myself. My phone rings. It's my sister Treasa. She sounds panicky, so I move away from the table.

'Dónal Óg? Are you gay?'

'Oh, for fuck's sake, Treasa.'

'I've no problem if you are, but listen it's going around everywhere here. Daddy is going mad with worry.'

'Oh fuck.'

In early 2006 we had begun to let our heads turn to the three-in-a-row. It's a special thing in hurling to win three All-Ireland titles back to back; it puts you up there with the greats and the immortals. We wanted that for ourselves and for Cork.

The team had a holiday, to South Africa, early that year. Myself and Seán Óg, being perhaps the maddest, were training twice a day over there. We were so much into the training that when the boys would go playing soccer we wouldn't play with them in case we got injured. Even when we were in Sun City we used to take a taxi ride out of the resort to this field we'd found. We'd train out there.

I remember some of it as pure torture. Seán Óg is one tough man to train with. He has no mercy on you. Not a drop. Running with Seán Óg is different from running with anybody else. He is hardcore. And even on the good days I'd be feeling sorry for myself. I've scoliosis! He's a fucking Olympic-level athlete!

But I wouldn't give in to the mad bastard, so this was the big thing for me, just to keep up. Seán Óg would be talking to me about this and that and I'd be trying to breathe, just trying to stay alive.

Anyway, this one morning I was sick, actually genuinely sick, and I kept saying, 'I don't feel well at all, Seán Óg.'

And he's striding on. Oblivious. 'Ah yeah! Blah, blah, blah.'

'No, I'm telling you! I've something wrong with me!'

So I actually stopped. Dying a death in the sun. Sweat coming in buckets. Wanting to puke.

'You carry on, I'm all right, I'm actually going to get sick all right. I'm actually sick, it's not sick sick, its not sick from running with you. There's something wrong.'

'OK, I'll see you back at the hotel.'

'Huh?'

And off he galloped. I just remember thinking, That bastard! He's so interested, he left me here! Not just had he kept running away fast when I was telling him I was sick, so that he was making me worse by having to chase him, but he's after heading off and leaving me on this stretch, miles away from the hotel! The langer!

That's how it was. We were training so much at the time that Hartnett, who used to come with us, gave up on it. He was only a young fella and he had guts and desire, but one morning he put a note in my door: 'Can't go this morning because I'm too sore!'

Now that was some rookie mistake to make. He still gets reminded of that message! By then, myself and Seán Óg were used to the regime, we were training solid; and poor Hartnett, even though he was a fierce fit fella, he couldn't take the shock to his body out there at all. He was just shattered.

Anyway, the trip was coming to an end, and we were in this place called Knysna on the Garden Route, and a lot of nights I'd eat with Seán Óg and Siobhan. On this night we'd been sitting with Jimmy McEvoy on the balcony above the sea when Treasa had called. Suddenly I was a long way from home and poor Treasa was talking to me as if I was dead.

I remember I went back to the table and I was eating away, saying nothing, and I remember thinking, There is something gone badly wrong here, there is something gone wrong, I could feel it.

In late 2005 I'd been going out a lot and I didn't care really, to be honest. I know that sounds like bravado but at the time I didn't. I had a very good friend that I used to talk to, and he would be very much on the scene in Cork, he would have been totally immersed in the whole thing, and even he would be saying, 'Dónal Óg, there's common talk about you, it's just taken for granted on the scene.'

It had to transfer over from that scene, but I never seriously thought about it till it happened.

When Treasa called, I carried on as if nothing was happening. I tried to ring her again later but I didn't get through to her. So the next day, first thing, I made my way to Joe Deane. If there is something going on, Joe most of the time would know about it.

So I found Joe. On the team, at this stage, I'd spoken to only a handful of guys about the issue. I've always gone along, assuming that the others would just put two and two together, but we are hurlers. They aren't even thinking that way, it turns out.

'How's the form, Joe? Anything happening that I should know about?'

I often say that to fellas because it puts them on the back foot a bit. You can see it cross their face. Oh Jesus Christ, is there anything I need to tell this fella about? Do I really want to tell him about that other thing? I better tell the fucker because he's after asking me, he's after making that statement, isn't he? He knows that I know!

Joe is smarter than me, though. He looks at me for a second. This is at the breakfast, the morning after Treasa's call. He's wide awake to me and my tactics.

'Did you hear anything?'

'About what, Joe?'

'Aw for fuck's sake. Come on.'

He rolled his eyes and took me away from the group. He said there'd been a couple of boys on to him from home and there were some emails going around. 'They're saying that you came out to the team as gay during this holiday.'

'But that didn't happen, Joe.'

'I know that, but this isn't one fella now. It's going around. I spoke to Dr Con last night and we decided to leave you alone and leave you enjoy your holiday.'

'Joe, you know the drill that, whatever gets said about any of us, we tell each other. If there is something going on it needs to come back.'

'I know, I know, I know, I probably would have said it to you anyway, but we said last night that we'll leave the man alone.'

And that was the conversation. I asked Joe not to say anything to anybody, to just keep his ear to the ground.

I rang Thomas O'Brien, who was living in the house in Ballinacurra with me. We bought a house together a few years ago. Thomas isn't gay or anything and is now married to a lovely woman, Joan, but we're best friends since we were young fellas and he would have known about that side of me since we were young fellas. Thomas runs his own business and he's sharp, very sharp.

So I rang him. 'Is anything going on at home?'

'No.'

'I'm after hearing stuff is going around about me.'

'I would have heard about that. Or maybe fellas wouldn't say it to me because they know how close I am with you.'

'Right. Thomas, you know the drill, you need to check that out for me.'

I wasn't worried about myself. I was worried about my parents and what was going on. Was there something up or had something happened?

Dependable as ever, Thomas called back a couple of hours later. There was something up all right. He'd rung Mark Landers. Good call. There is a gossipy old woman in Mark trying to get out; at times he can be the twenty-four-hour version of the *Evening Echo*! Mark was all talk about it. This had happened. That had happened.

Now Thomas was worried. 'It's not normal, the stuff that's spreading.'

In South Africa I was rooming with Timmy McCarthy. And I knew Timmy. He'd know any gossip that was going. The boys that I'd have around me, the lads I'm close to know the drill, we have an unwritten rule between us: if there is anything going on like this we tell each other. Now the rule was becoming unstuck a bit. Gatchy would be one of those fellas loyal to that way. So would Timmy. Poor old Timmy called Gatchy back in Cork and said he'd been getting these texts from home about Dónal Óg. Timmy was worried and he was asking Gatchy, what was the story. And Gatchy, playing by the rule, was ringing me now, telling me that Timmy Mac had been on about this, and what was going on?

I was in the room with Timmy and he'd begun acting all bloody awkward with me so I said to myself, I've known Timmy a long time and he's the same age as me and he's a tough enough lad, so how long is it going to take him to get around to this one with me? I'm not going to save him! He can bring it up.

Timmy was being all kind of nice to me, tiptoeing about the place, and I was half amused by watching him, so I left it and didn't tell him that I knew until we were well back at home. We were back training on a bad night and he sat into the car and he said to me, 'Is everything all right with you, because there is stuff going on.'

'Mac, how long did it take you! You know when you were ringing home? I knew who you were ringing and why. They were ringing me!'

And poor Timmy actually snapped over it because he got all embarrassed, but we had a great laugh over it before he left the car.

'You fucking knew that I was on about that and you wouldn't say it to me! Some bollox you are.'

That was the funny side. When we were in South Africa, though, things were tough enough at home.

My father rang me one night. 'Dónal Óg, is this true, what's going on?'

'Ah, Dad, I'm a long ways away from home.'

'There was a fella on to me today and I'll kill him, I'll kill him.'

Now my father is a man who would physically fight with you, he would fight for his family, but he's sixty-three years of age. He was driving a crane on a building site. Building sites can be cruel, hard places. He didn't need this. Plus maybe the bigmouth that was on to him would come back at him with a hammer to the head or something.

Still, I can't have this conversation 6,000 miles away from him. I said, 'Look, don't do anything – hang tough and I'll be at home asap, I'll be home early, I'm going to get on the next flight out of here.'

I had been meant to go on from South Africa to do more training at Club La Santa in Lanzarote with Jimmy McEvoy, a fella called Paul Tierney and Juliet Murphy. Tierney was a sub with Cork in 2004 and is a serious athlete. Juliet was the captain of the Cork ladies' football side and was seriously into the training too, so by going to

Lanzarote I'd have a base of really good training by the time I got home.

But I said to Dad that I wouldn't go to Spain. I'd come home. I half expected him to insist I go on to Lanzarote, but he didn't.

'Grand job, you better come home, Dónal Óg, because the stuff going on here is crazy.'

He was genuinely bothered. He rang me again the next night and he'd obviously thought more about it. He said not to worry about coming home, to keep training because it was important. We'd sort it out whenever I did come home.

But by then I was worried for him and Mam. They were at home, listening to all this stuff. It was a lot to ask from them.

It was hard for the team as well. I went to Sully because you go to your trusted fellas when you are in trouble. I was asking him to find out what he could about where all this was coming from. We had a good chat.

Seán Óg was in the pool at the same time, and Seán Óg, typical Seán Óg, in at the front door, no back door with the man, he was way over at the other end of the pool but he obviously sensed from the way I was talking to Sully that there was something wrong. So he rang me in my hotel room.

'I don't know now and it might be none of my business but there is something up. Will you come down and meet me?'

Typical. So I went down and met with him. We went away for a walk and I told him the whole story, stuff that I thought he would have guessed.

He was unbelievable. Content that I'd told him, happy to open up to me about his own life and about things even I had never known about him. We were always close friends from the time we met as under-14s for Cork, but our relationship has never been the same since that day. We had a long conversation, about two hours long because it was a deep and complex conversation from both sides, and we came out of it like brothers.

Other times it was a bit awkward around the hotel. Everywhere I went, I was asking myself how many of the boys were talking about this. I knew Ben O'Connor was talking about it because Joe came back and said that Ben was talking about it, concerned. Pat Mulcahy had asked Ben about it, had he heard what people were saying, and Ben was saying he didn't give a fuck.

Joe told me what Ben said, and it sticks in my head: 'If there are thirty of us out here, there is surely one fella among us who is gay and if Ógie is gay I don't give a fuck, it won't change one bit what I think about him.'

Things like that you always remember.

I remember coming home on the plane as well. Brian Corcoran came to me with his baby daughter in his arms. Whoever it was that was sitting beside me at the time, Corcoran told him go away off down the plane. He sat in beside me and talked. That's the way the Corcoran would be. He was the boss when he was there. He'd done everything. In two sports. He paved the way. He was a god. And he sat down beside me and stared at me.

'Are you in trouble?'

'I don't know, would you call it trouble, but this is the story anyway.'

So I went through the whole story with him. I'll never forget it. Corcoran has a fierce habit of staring at you when you're talking to him. He's taking in your every reaction. I remember I was looking at him, wondering, Is there a chance this man could take this badly? I'm very close to him but there is always a chance that somebody you know and like will turn out to be homophobic or something, and I remember thinking this would be a very strange place now for me to fall out with Brian Corcoran. On a plane with his baby daughter on his lap.

I shouldn't have doubted the man. We couldn't have had a better conversation and he said to me the same thing that every fella said, 'You know the drill, Ógie, I'm there if you want me.'

So, except for things with my father and mother and with the likes of my friend Dr Con, who was worrying a bit for me, I was getting through it.

Again and again in the next few weeks I sat down with friends and comrades from the team and told them the story. They were draining conversations, hard talks. My relationship with fellas got closer, but I always said to them, 'Look, if you have a problem with this I don't mind.'

And I wouldn't have minded if lads were troubled because I know fellas and I know how we all grew up. Cork and a GAA upbringing in Cork isn't the same as growing up in California or Sydney.

I worried too because I'm not a person who wants people being protective of me. I just wouldn't want that. I can stand on my own two feet. I'm comfortable being the leader in certain situations if required. I did say to fellas, 'If you don't want me having certain roles come and tell me,' but there was not a chance with that group and the men they are.

All those earnest talks. I'd say to them straight, eye to eye, 'If you've a problem because I didn't tell you about it, well I didn't think it was your fucking business! The reason I'm telling you now is I didn't want you to be hearing about it or reading about it in a tabloid and then worrying about it. If you have a problem now you'd better come to me first. If you've an issue with this, come back to me.'

But no, that was it. They stood up and said they were there for me. The way things were done in the group and the way we do our business never changed, far from it.

When it all ends, those are the things that live on beyond matches and dressing-rooms and medals. The journey is what matters, and ours has been richer, longer and at times more beautiful than most teams'.

To hell with the begrudgers. And I'll be there to welcome them.

16

As it happened, that Tipp game would start an entire spiral of events which Tipperary would have been unaware of at the time. We spent more time putting ourselves together again than we ever did about wondering how Tipp had beaten us.

We went to Gerald after the game. There was a review meeting arranged but a couple of players got together beforehand – again there was a push to get rid of Gerald and the selectors, but again we decided to go along. Morale was lower than a snake's belly.

One of the areas where we were lacking was mental training. We wanted a mind coach, somebody who could perhaps tap into the spirit that had once been in us. We had a guy in mind, John Carey was his name, but another team had snapped up his services. We went to Gerald and, as usual, he took it on board and tried to do it in his own way.

The next week he came up to me one night in Páirc Uí Chaoimh. He said he'd been having a think about the entire mind coach thing.

'Ógie, you could do that. They listen to you. You could do that.'

'Aw Jesus. Mind coach?'

I remember looking at him and wondering whether I would fuck him out of it or not, but I realized he genuinely felt it would be a good idea.

'Yeah, sure, well I'll think about it.'

Gardiner came up to me after training. He wanted a word.

'Wait till you hear this, he's going to get Seán Óg to do the fucking psychologist thing!'

We both knew that Seán Óg is so earnest and committed that he would go away and speed-read through a degree course in sports psychology if he thought that him taking on the role could be of any help.

'For fuck's sake, Ga, he said it to me earlier as well. For me to do it!'

'Hold on a second, he came up to me and said Ógie can do that job for us. I just assumed it was Seán Óg.'

'We need to put a plan in place.'

So we came up with three things and spoke to Gerald.

1. We should look to see who is the best at what they are doing right now – Munster Rugby. And we should go to them and ask about their systems. We should benchmark against the very best.

2. We'll get another guy apart from John Carey, Seán Óg or myself to do the psychology thing right.

3. One of the biggest problems was that management and players were not getting on. We needed a facilitator.

I knew a guy, Cathal O'Reilly, who had captained the Galway team, St Raphael's, that beat us in the All-Ireland Colleges final in 1995. He'd played Cork minor and Cork under-21 and a bit of senior as well, but he lost two of his fingers and that ended it. He's a business transformation manager now, and I figured that they wouldn't put him in charge of transforming businesses if he wasn't a capable fella. I had first-hand experience of working with him in the area of getting groups to work together, and he knows his business.

We met Gerald in Páirc Uí Rinn and we said it to him: 'Here's the options that we think that we should look at, Gerald.'

And again Gerald is, 'Yeah, yeah, yeah.'

I said to him, 'What do you think about Cathal O'Reilly?'

Gerald said he'd like to meet him. So we arranged to meet with Cathal the following Sunday night in Rochestown: myself, John, Gerald and Cathal.

At the meeting I remember Gerald himself saying that things were bad. Cathal drew up a triangle and listed, from a famous book by a guy called Patrick Lencioni, the five dysfunctions of a team. And for every one of them Gerald was nodding and saying, 'Yeah, that exists with us!'

Absence of Trust?

Yeah.

Fear of Conflict?

Yes.

Lack of Commitment?

Afraid so.

Avoidance of Accountability?

Bang on again.

Inattention to Results?

You're reading our minds.

Cathal was very impressive as he is basically just one of those very impressive fellas, and Gerald said, 'Yeah we'll go with that.'

The first thing Cathal did was try to do a bit of analysis on the Tipp game with us all. We had gone far into the lead that day and then lost. He analysed it all like a business, and one of the things he noted was that ten minutes before half-time in that game and in others we were effectively stopping playing.

We'd done the same against Galway in the league a few weeks earlier. I remember that day because Gerald came into the dressing-room and said, 'That's it, lads, ye're beaten.' I remember saying to Ben that I'd played on a lot of really bad Cloyne teams in my time and taken a fair few beatings but no fucker had ever walked into the dressing-room at half-time and said, 'That's it, boys, ye're beaten!'

Cathal put us to work on some documents which would become infamous. Now, this is my kind of thing. I enjoy it at work and in training situations and team-building environments. It fascinates me. In Cloyne a couple of years earlier we had actually done the exact same exercise as Cathal was proposing. I thought it was a good idea and was enthusiastically behind it.

How it works is this. Suppose there are three of us, you, me and Jack. Jack will write down all the positive things he can think to say about you and me. I will write down all the positives about Jack and you. You will write down all the positives about Jack and me.

The facilitator takes the papers away and comes back and gives me what you and Jack said about me. He gives you what Jack and I wrote about you, etc. So in a team situation you might get back 30–40 sheets full of positives.

Now, some of the lads were in the horrors about what to write about Gerald and some of the selectors, and there were a lot of phone calls between ourselves. Some lads wanted to put down things like, 'He is always on time.' Or, 'He is very neat.' (Well done, Timmy Mac!)

When Gerald received his own feedback he made a speech to us; he said he'd won all these things in his life but this document meant more to him, etc., etc.

My blood turned a little chillier. I remember saying to Gatchy and Sully, 'See that document, that document has serious chance of coming back to haunt us!'

So it came to pass.

During the strike I was working in the University of Limerick and I got a phone call from the *Echo*. The journalist said to me, in the sort of way you'd break very bad news to a person, 'We're after getting possession of a document . . .'

I knew what it was immediately. I said, 'That document was supposed to be confidential, if you print that . . .'

I trailed off – sure, what could I say to him? In the *Echo* offices they had struck gold. I was probably on speakerphone!

So, meekly, I asked him to read out what I had said. Oh god. Like people telling you what you did when you were very drunk at your grandmother's month's mind Mass. Like your best mate showing everybody a picture of, say, you and Frank Murphy aboard an elephant.

I was one of the people who was sceptical at the start about Gerald, probably paranoia. Now I have grown to realise that this man wants this team to be as successful as anyone and is prepared to do or try anything to get us there. We will climb the steps of Croke Park together, and we will say it was some journey to get here. I respect you for everything you are and your total commitment to this team —Dónal Óg Cusack

Sweet mother of divine fucking Jesus! Word for word, worse than I even remembered!

We called a meeting that night. My phone was hopping all the way home. If I would take one call, I'd miss half a dozen. Every one of the boys rang me. Furious, every one of them. Cathal called, livid at the breach of confidentiality.

At the meeting that night, there was a copy of the *Echo* lying there on a chair and I grabbed it. I knew what I had said, but I was looking for what the other fellas had said; was there any fella, just one, who had made a bigger fool of himself than I had?

No! I was fucked. All the fucking enemies laughing, and most of the comrades seething.

Seán Óg described it as being like a little child in the school yard who gets his trousers pulled down in front of everyone and he has no underpants on him. And of course the *Echo* described it as an assessment – in my mortification I forgot to mention to them that the idea of the exercise had been to write as positively as possible.

My instinct was to turn the flame thrower back on to Gerald. I had a text, we all had a copy of it, that had been sent out the day after the Galway game later in the summer:

It's 6 a.m., couldn't sleep, how could I? All I could think of is what an honour it was to be with men, not just men, legends, yet another glorious chapter in Cork's great history, what an honour, stand with them, observe them, embrace them in victory, how can hurling still do this to us, our job now is to make sure they realise last night is only one step on the road to greater glory, maybe I can sleep now Gerald Mc

If those words were coming from a fella like John Allen or Dónal Grady, who we knew had been along on the journey with us, we would have appreciated it. But coming from Gerald?

No.

We considered making Gerald's text public, but there are some things during a war that have to be kept inside of you. There just have to be. If we'd thrown that text out there after what had been said about us by Gerald, we would have got a brief satisfaction, as I am sure he did from the O'Reilly leak, but the whole country would have been recoiling at the spectacle we were making of ourselves.

Probably they were anyway, but in this one instance at least we held back.

Now it is early May and Tipperary await us again at the end of the month in Semple Stadium. There is a danger that they could bury us deep in a hole. We've spent a year getting out of last year's narrow grave. We haven't the energy left to go clawing the earth again this year.

17

Since my brain nearly bled out through my skin at half-time in the Waterford game I've been feeling a bit off. I trained with Cork again the week afterwards on Tuesday and on Thursday.

On the Tuesday night we were in Mallow and by chance I'd a fierce conversation with Denis Walsh afterwards for about an hour. I was delighted. I have a good idea how he came to have this job, and the more I see of him the more I like and believe in him.

There was a slight problem tonight as we were talking, though.

I am definitely sick. I played a game out in the field at home during the week and I got dizzy and had to ask Luke Cahill to go into my home to get some chocolate for me. I thought I was going to pass out.

So I was talking to Denis Walsh, still at the stage of getting to know each other, and I was slightly dizzy and the sweat was pouring out of me. I could feel it coming in rivers and I know he must have been saying to himself, 'Shit, it's true what they told me about Cusack, there's balls of sweat pouring down his face just talking to me. He's mad! His mouth will be foaming next.'

So I had to say it him, 'Look, Denis, I'm not feeling great and I know about these balls of sweat.'

And he laughed. 'Fucking hell, I was looking at your head there and wondering about that.'

So the next morning I went in to Dr Con. Now the usual trouble with going in to see Dr Con when you're sick (and I think this is a big part of his great medical capabilities) is that you forget what you went in to him about as soon as you get there. The man is the upside to feeling sick. I can go in to Con and be so entertained that I would forget to tell him what was wrong with me. Fact.

So I said to him, 'Con, before we start chatting about anything now, I'm telling you there is something wrong with me. We can talk about this first, maybe spend about ten per cent of our time talking about what's wrong with me!'

So he took all the tests and we chatted on.

Cork played Tipperary in the league this year, of course. Under lights in Semple. One of the GAA's set-piece events, reduced to the level of farce as Cork were fielding a replacement team.

I remember nothing about the game. It took place on the night of Smurf's removal.

In the middle of all our dramas and crises our old friend just removed himself from the stage. Left us all wondering if there hadn't been so much going on with ourselves that we had never fully noticed his pain.

Aw fuck. Smurf. Smurf. Smurf.

Once I met him on the street and he wasn't supposed to be there. He was supposed to be at an Old Firm match in Glasgow. He'd got turned back on the way because when he was asked for photo ID he took out and unfolded an old picture of himself from the *Imokilly People*. Smurf hurling for Cloyne!

And fuck, you know what? If you wanted Smurf's identity? That was it. A hurler who was always on the way to see Celtic play.

He'd told me a couple of times he would do it and that he would do it on a Thursday. You never believe the fellas who talk about it, do you?

We were up there in the bar on a Thursday night and I was after locking the bar. Thomas O'Brien, who used to manage the senior hurling team, had left about fifteen minutes earlier.

The mobile rang soon after. It was Thomas. If that happens, ninety-nine times out of a hundred it is the Gardaí on the road. The boys see the cops, they ring the lads.

But Thomas said that there was something wrong over in Smurf's house. He said he thought it was serious. I just said straight out, 'He's dead, I think.' Straight away it was in my head. All the times Smurf would have said it.

I left the bar and I went down the road. Thomas was across the road at his own house. He was very bothered. I said I would go over. When I did, I saw there was panic in the house. A brother came out.

'Mick, what's the story?'

'He's after killing himself, Ógie. Come upstairs.'

We went up to the room. There was our friend dead.

He was one of the fellas you were always glad to see. A feature of all our lives. From the days when I was small and I'd be out pucking a ball against a wall every evening and he'd come up the street. 'Put it away, boy, you'll never be any good!'

He was omnipresent in Cloyne. One of the characters. Everyone in Cloyne knows everyone and everyone loved Smurf.

I came up home after 2 a.m. and broke the news to my parents.

The next morning, Friday the 13th, I was due to do a live radio programme in Cork about the strike, Neil Prendiville's show. I didn't really want to do it after what happened to Smurf, but during the strike you had to do a lot of stuff you didn't enjoy doing, and I knew the lads were depending on me. So I did it and I came back later to the Alley Bar, still dazed and distracted.

And of course drama is unfolding.

Smurf was a great customer and a friend to us all since we were young lads. There's a few candles lighting to him in the bar. The place is quiet and sombre.

Gatchy was in behind the bar when I arrived. Nobody else there, and he was doing the favour of looking after the place for a few minutes. He needed to go. So I took over. Then Cathal came in. Cathal Cronin, one of my partners in the bar and the big lad who had turned me in as a child for joining a Cloyne training session, having hidden in a bush while the team slogged around the parish.

And then an old hurler came in. A bit of a legend and a man about whom we would tell a lot of stories. A bright man.

'Dónal Óg how are you.'

He has a lovely speaking voice, the same fella. I'd be wary of him, though. I don't think he likes me.

'All right, thanks.'

'Will you have a drink?'

'No. I'm grand, thanks. I'm not drinking at all.'

'Will you have a Coke?'

'No, I'm grand, thanks. Look after yourself there and get your own drink.'

'Would you have a Diet Coke?'

This is a bit loaded. A little cut there.

'No, thanks anyway. Go on away by yourself there.'

He turns to Cathal, who has just come in. Cathal is a man who would be well capable of looking after himself. Everyone in the bar knows this.

'Cathal, I will have a pint of Heineken. Dónal Óg won't drink with me.'

'Grand job.'

Cathal starts pulling the pint. Cathal is wary, too. Our man has an observation to make.

'Cathal, you are after getting very heavy.'

Now since those days as kids when I jumped out the back of training and found Cathal lagging along behind, Cathal has been conscious of the weight thing. So this is dangerous ground. There are a couple of regulars sitting there with ears pricked now.

Cathal puts the pint up on the counter.

'Do you think so?'

And there is silence now. All ears cocked. It's like a tense scene in a Wild West saloon.

'I do! Do you know you are actually getting fatter every time I see you.'

Now in the Western this is when the saloon-keeper starts clearing the more expensive bottles from behind the bar. Cathal turns to me and says: 'Dónal Óg, you go in behind the bar there.'

I do as I am told. Cathal goes over to our pal and speaks to him urgently. 'I want to talk to you out the back.'

Every pair of eyes in the place is on the two of them now. Nobody wants to step in front of Cathal. Everyone wondering, would our man have the guts to go out the back with Cathal. Because nobody else would. But he just says, 'I won't go out the back with you, Cathal. I'll sit down beside the fire with you.'

Cathal storms over to the fireside. Our friend takes a newspaper, slowly folds it, puts it under his arm and goes over to the fire and sits down.

Now there is tension you can cut. Cathal is seething. I stand behind a pillar in the bar trying to listen – trying to get a head start if things are going to explode We're all trying to tune in.

Billy comes in. Cathal's brother. Our man with the newspaper and the bit of borrowed time likes Billy.

I say to Billy, 'Go over and tell Cathal you need to talk to him upstairs urgently.'

So Billy says to Cathal, 'We need to go upstairs for a meeting.'

The bar is quiet and only half lit with the memorial candles for our friend Smurf. We are all in pain. Nobody needs this.

Between the grief and the insult Cathal can hardly take a breath. I go upstairs with Billy and Cathal and we talk. 'Leave it be. Leave it be. Leave it be.'

I came back down to tend the bar.

A while later a guy called Dónal Kelleher, a good friend of Smurf's, comes in and says to us that there is a horse running in Wolverhampton at ten past five. The horse is called Smirfys Systems. 'On the sad day that was in it we should back him,' thinks Dónal.

I tell Donie that I'm not up for it, but most of the lads place a bet.

The horse wins. Our man by the fireplace survives Cathal.

Cathal's grief is uninterrupted.

Another night and another day in the life in Cloyne.

We gather soon after at the church for Smurf's removal. We are in the guard of honour, waiting for the coffin to come along, all bothered and grieving over that. The village is hurting deeply over the loss of Smurf, but religion keeps its hold.

A whisper from behind the guard of honour. Ten minutes gone in Semple Stadium. Tipp not pulling away yet.

There is annoyance. 'Fuck, lads, put the phones away. Jesus.'

The cortège is late. Time passes. Somebody goes over and whispers in Diarmaid Falvey's ear. 'Tipp just a couple of points up.' What is going wrong? Diarmaid's face is troubled enough.

We file into church soon after and when we walk up the road to the bar after the short ceremony the end of the Cork–Tipp match is being played out on the TV, and I'll never forget but the loudest noise in the Alley Bar is coming from a fella shouting for Tipperary. In our bar with the candles lighting for Smurf.

*

Con calls and leaves a message. 'Dónal, can you ring me back?'

Alarm bells. I call him straight back.

'Con. What's wrong? My whole life you are calling me Ógie, now you've done a few tests and it's Dónal. What's the story?'

To my relief he laughs. 'Reading too much into everything as usual,' he says. 'The tests I have done have shown something unusual in your blood.' He wants his brother-in-law Dr O'Halloran, who has helped me greatly to control my thyroid issue, to have a look at me at twenty to one on Thursday.

'Hold on there till I check the diary, Con.'

'Ógie, it's twenty to one on Thursday. That's final. Put away your diary.'

So I do. And on the Thursday I'm checked by Dr O'Halloran and dismissed with a virus, but I take away this sense that the time is well past thirty years of age and everything now is a bit more serious and a bit too grown up.

A picture of you playing hurling isn't enough any more.

18

Midleton, Co. Cork, 9 May
Bishopstown 1-13 Cloyne 0-12

I don't even want to begin unravelling what happened in Midleton last night. Let me add the ending to an old story before starting into all that.

When Sully settled down – or went dormant, as they say about volcanoes – he settled in Glanmire. Often after big games, himself and myself would have a drink or two for unwinding and when we were done there would always be a bed for me in his and his partner Gráinne's house.

A few years ago I was above in Sully's house and I was feeling a bit shook as it was a Monday morning and we'd had a fair bit of unwinding to do the night before. Sully was clattering about the place, doing stuff, and I was in the sitting-room, looking at the pictures he keeps on the mantelpiece. For a hard man he is fierce sentimental. I lifted one photo to have a closer look at it, and as I was looking I noticed that I had uncovered another photograph behind.

Two men on an elephant somewhere in Thailand. *Dónal Óg agus Phrionsias ar muin n' eilifint.*

Sully!

The bastard!

The cute hoor!

Every time I'd come to his house for years he'd covered over this entertainment showpiece! Everyone who came into the Sully house, except me, except his childhood friend, his comrade, his teammate, his fucking brother in arms, everybody was being shown this famous picture for years afterwards!

So I put that picture into my gear bag and disappeared it.

*

Last night we lost to Bishopstown in the first round of the Cork championship and we are in trouble.

It's not so long ago that we were wiping teams out at this stage. In the good days we beat Sars by about twenty points one night above in Páirc Uí Chaoimh. Now they are county champions and we are cracking. We beat the Rockies up in Carrigtwohill by fifteen points or so one night. We were hammering good teams because not long ago we were very good and we had a system that we believed in. We had a woman, Valerie O'Sullivan, as a physical trainer and she was excellent. We spent a lot of time talking about the game. We talked about how we wanted to play. What we would do in every contingency.

And we talked about each other. We used to have meetings which we called 'truth' meetings. The truth meetings were scary and bruising at first but the boys wanted more of them when they got the idea.

We'd sit and we'd talk and we'd criticize each other within the room, within the circle of the team. We didn't go to the Alley Bar and snipe behind each other's backs. We didn't sell each other out in our homes so parents and brothers and sisters would do the dirty work, spreading the word around the place.

We sat and called each other on things. It was a bracing experience, but we took it all on board for the sake of the team and each other, and it worked. In the early days of the truth meetings lads had their doubts and one of the team was sore about them till the end. (That player later left the club. It was when he was in the process of leaving that he described the truth meetings as abuse. The Chairman at the time asked for a meeting with the player, hoping to persuade him to stay. The Chairman asked me, would I attend and help plead with him. I said to the Chairman that if I was there at all, it would be to tell him to go from Cloyne as quickly as he could! So maybe I wasn't the best person to go with the Chairman. He agreed and went alone.)

You could take those meetings as abuse if that was what you wanted, but for the rest of us they were frank and manly conversations between people who wanted to achieve something. We learned from them and grew from them.

I was the captain, so first I'd comment on each fella as honestly as I could without bringing my own personal likes or dislikes into it. A fella couldn't come back straight away, because that would turn into bitching. If he calls Dónal Óg a bollox, Dónal Óg can't be coming straight back with a genius retort like 'Oh no, you're the bollox.'

So you'd go through the whole room – everyone, selectors as well – and there would be desperate raw stuff said, but everybody would have to wait till it went right around. Then they could say whatever they needed to say back to you or whatever they had come to say in the first place. And that was it. Done. It took a lot of confidence to hear yourself dismantled by teammates and it took a lot to criticize to their faces fellas you had grown up with. We used to have a big thing about not talking about each other even around the town. What needed to be said about each other got said in the room, between us and the four walls, and it stayed there.

Those meetings used to happen most often after things went wrong, and some nights we'd be there until half twelve, one o'clock in the morning, unravelling the mess we were in. And as a group we'd always make sure that we ended standing in a circle or a huddle and we'd have one squeeze and say that all this was going to be left here in the room.

And then we'd drive on. Next session. Next mission. Next challenge. Next match.

Last year, having lost three county finals in a row, we got Dónal O'Grady in to train us. And we lost in the championship to Sars. I made a major mistake with five minutes to go. I passed the ball straight to one of their players whom I had mistaken for Sully. I'd made a couple of point-blank saves in the first half and was playing well, had even scored a few from frees. But my mistake killed us.

Along with another Cloyne man I had put a lot personally into getting O'Grady down to work with us in Cloyne and had done my best to convince him that, even though most people thought we were finished, we could still do it.

To make a long story short, Dónal didn't want to be named straight out as manager of Cloyne. So I had to be the Trojan Horse. Without revealing the master plan, I had to work things through till I was given sole responsibility for hurling matters – otherwise another coach would have been appointed. Once my appointment was secure I would bring Dónal in and the whole plan would be revealed and everybody would be happy. In the meantime I was to say nothing about Dónal and carry on as if I just had an insatiable lust for power!

Needless to say I had been on the wrong side of some of our officials at this stage, so getting full responsibility for hurling matters required some manoeuvring. It was like going to the church and asking for full responsibility for religious affairs.

Anyway, it was done and Dónal arrived. We needed to back up and repay his commitment and I, of all people, didn't want to let him down. That night when we lost in the championship I felt it was me who had let him down.

I couldn't face anyone after that loss to Sars, but neither did I want to stay at home by myself as I knew my brain would start to test me. So I went to our gym, turned off all the lights and skipped for an hour. I worked in the dark because I knew that the lads would be looking for me, and if they saw the lights on through the big windows of the gym on the main road they would guess it was me and try to convince me to go drinking with them . . .

Maybe that's how the end begins. More and more games come down to the last minutes and you lose that cold talent for putting the others away. You stand up for yourself when somebody asks why this or that happens, but by little degrees it slips.

Last night against Bishopstown we had five minutes to go and we were losing. We won a free, a scoreable free, and needed to cash it in calmly. Next thing, Sully clocked your man that had fouled him. All hell broke loose. We lost the free. Lost a man. Lost the momentum. Fucking snapped.

I don't know. In my head I am just thinking at that stage that if it was the other way round and a fight needed to be started to preserve our lead and distract Bishopstown coming down to the wire, I'd be happy to get involved in that fight. My brain just goes like that. In fact I love that feeling, being in there, knowing that you don't care about anything else, only that you're in this thing here together and that you're going to do everything you can to get out and that's all that matters.

For it to happen this way, though, for us to hand away the momentum and the free, my mind started to fry. So I was up to Sully while the big fight flared. Just as I arrived on the scene, Sully's brother Dónal got a red card. I said, 'Wrong time, boys, we should be taking frees, focused, why are we fighting and in front of everyone?'

And next thing, the bold Sully fucks me out of it in front of the whole of Midleton. He roars at me to fuck off back into goals and mind my own business.

A couple of Cloyne fellas have said it to me today, but that's Sully. He's my friend and I know him better than most. He hasn't any badness in him. He carries a lot of pressure when he is playing for Cloyne.

We should be cuter than that, but our frees were desperate anyway. I came out to take our last 65, to drop it in front of the goal for the lads to fight over it. What did I do with it? Put it fucking wide.

So I can imagine now what the old enemies in the crowd were thinking. It finished beautifully for them! What a finale: Sully turns on me; I come out to take the 65 and I drive it wide. Some of them would have paid twice to see that.

It's not like we don't know how to finish out a game. Just a few weeks ago we played Blarney in the league. It was not long after Kilkenny had gutted Cork above in Nowlan Park. There was a big crowd out as Blarney had won the Intermediate Championship last year and this was their first senior game.

A serious fight broke out midway through the second half – Billy (Killian Cronin) was in the thick of it. I stood watching and wondering to myself how he was remaining standing with all the belts he got. We had been losing for most of the game, but after the fight we picked it up and they lost their way. The last puck of the game was a 65 – a very dodgy ball that just came in over the backs and forwards. As it was near the full-time whistle there were a lot of bodies around and everybody was pulling as if their lives depended on it.

I called the ball as mine and Billy protected me, but still it was dodgy. I grabbed and cleared it. I know a top keeper should catch balls like that, but I also know that most people wouldn't be comfortable in that situation.

As they say, everybody likes the idea of being a goalkeeper except on the day of a championship game when the pressure is on. Nobody really relishes the idea of a ball dropping into a square full of bodies with hurleys swinging all over the place in the last minute of a game either. So taking that responsibility and performing well made me feel good. And the way we closed out the game made me think we had a chance this year.

Now this. A dumb fight. A loss of focus. And bickering among ourselves.

Of course, I'm trotting back to goals having put the 65 wide, and Billy smiles at me. He was ripping a minute earlier over Sully and now I've hit this bad wide and he grins at me, this grin that says: Cloyne!

Conclusions? We're slipping. Sully is doing his thing because Sully is slipping. If Sully's slipping we're all slipping.

There was a song, I think the Dubliners recorded it: 'Don't Give Up Till It's Over'. We used to sing that together during that time when we were a great team. We'd all be inside in a circle and we'd put it on the tape and we'd all sing it and it was special. Not too many teams would sing a song together before a game, but for all the championship games we did the same.

We knew fellas would be talking about us, the lunatics inside singing away, but that was part of getting ourselves ready. Men who grew up together in Cloyne would be crying in that circle because there was such a fierce bond. We were training hard, we were a big strong team, we won great games against good teams and we were getting to county finals.

Now we are cracking. If we'd played well against Bishopstown last night we would have beaten them. They are young and eager, but we should have known too much for them. Get into a two-horse race for the last ten minutes and then back yourself, Dónal O'Grady used to tell his teams. For the last ten minutes last night the odds on us just got longer and longer.

We were in the Alley Bar afterwards and there was music and the whole town seemed to be sardined in there. When we lose, the feeling is more acute than when we win. Winning means you don't have to stick together, there is the next day, the next chapter. No post-mortem requires your presence.

The Alley Bar. Backstory. Back in the boom, in November 2006 to be precise, four of us took over the place. There was nothing going to stop us. The other three boys were in the building trade, they were building estates and so on. Take on a pub? For fuck's sake sure, we could rule the world!

So there was Billy, he's playing with Cork; Cathal Cronin, who was a selector with Cloyne; and Maurice or Mossy Cahill, who was centre-back for Cloyne. I would have grown up with Mossy.

It's been a good but sometimes tough experience, the Alley Bar. We have had some mighty nights there, and I have come to know and like a lot of people I would never have met in Cloyne only for the beer. But there is also a nasty side to bar life. Drink does desperate things to men, you see an awful downside to it. You see fellas in trouble. Sad sort of trouble usually.

It's another world at times. There is a separate economy inside in that pub. They all borrow off each other. At the start we got caught some by that, the four of us. The boys were borrowing from us and our own money was circulating the bar. Somebody would borrow from Mossy to pay Cathal back.

It's a village pub and you realize there are some fellas that own that pub and they aren't us. If a taoiseach or a millionaire came in the door or whatever, he'd know he's in their territory. And that's where we live. In their territory!

In the Alley the atmosphere was loud but morose and bad-tempered. The older crowd didn't like the music and wanted to pick the bones of the match. The younger fellas wanted the music to drown out all thoughts of the match. There was some bitter drinking being done.

There was no point in trying to think. The music was too loud. On a night like that we turn up the music real loud and turn down the lights in the bar. It's safer if we can't hear or see each other. Everyone was already too hard and set in their opinions and a bit too generous, giving them to everyone else.

I was half going to mention to Sully about fucking me out of it but I said to myself that this was the wrong place to be going at it. Strangely, we found ourselves, he and I, on the street outside the bar just talking, and we fell into each other's company easily like often before.

Sully had a notion.

'Will we head off out of here into town, Ógie?'

'Ah, fuck it we will, Sull.'

And the two of us went into Cork for the night and forgot about hurling.

That's part of what we are. We have our rows and push on. One day a few months ago when we were still on strike with Cork, my father spotted some of the Sully uncles over by the dressing-rooms in the field with a few other fellas. He went into the garage and pulled out one of the supporters' placards from the strike: 'We Support The Hurlers'.

And madman that he is, he stood over in front of the boys with his placard. This at the height of the troubles, with feelings running at boiling point and that generation of Sullys all firm, staunch County Board men.

At the end of the day, though, we are all Cloyne men first, and we come together again as a law of nature. We were training there a couple of Sundays ago and I was taking the session and the training was torturous and vicious. I was inside at home having the breakfast afterwards and Dad and myself were talking about what the GAA is, what fellas will put themselves through for the love of the game, and he said something there was no arguing with. The Sullys are the men of Cloyne; when they're gone this team is gone. There was five of them there that day, training and tearing into each other. And you'd want them on your side in any fight or any war.

Funny thing was, last night there were a couple of people back in the Alley Bar saying to me that we needed to go back to the truth meetings; they were a forum and a valve as well. If you had a problem with a fella, you'd say, 'Look there is a truth meeting, we'll have it out there.' You could sort it out with Sully, they said.

They have a point, but for Sully and myself, we know where we stand without having to say it. Same as it ever was. And maybe too late in the day for truth meetings for either of us anyhow. When the Sullys are gone we are all gone, and Diarmuid is starting to take his leave.

19

Last Sunday, like every club in the country, we held a Lá na gClub or Club Day to mark the GAA's 125th birthday. We'd lost the Bishopstown game the night before, and as the sun came up I was in no mood for a day at the club. I rang my sister and she came and collected me as my head cleared from the night out with Sully.

I'm amazed, but we had a great day. The club had rung me during the week. They were looking for a piper to lead off the festivities. I told them that the only piper I knew in Cork was a fella widely known as Pa the Piper. He is a good buddy of the Bomber Roche, and the pair of them must have been the most enthusiastic fans of the strike that there had been. Pa mightn't be politically acceptable!

The club said, 'Oh for fuck's sake we'll get him down.' So the President, Bunty Cahill, put up the flag and then forty young fellas, under-8s and under-10s, marched up behind Pa on the pipes and the Bomber, who was on drums. Then they lined them up, like two Champions League teams, and Bunty and myself went along then to shake hands with each of them.

And then great excitement! We played a game – the Married Men against the Single Men. My father was in goals for the married and I was in goals for us and, ah fuck, it was great, everyone was in fine form and everything went well. There was a fierce crowd around. We had such a laugh just being a community out there in our field, playing hurling for the crack.

The field is the venue for childhood in Cloyne and it is the venue for so much that comes afterwards. It was a gorgeous day, and to have generations of Cloyne people together in the field was right and perfect.

It was here in the field that we learned hurling, where we came to understand the game and let our imaginations become infected by it.

As a young fella there was nothing I would love more than to finish work below in Cahill's, trimming the windows for them, and then wander up through the fields and the lads would have started gathering on the pitch. I'd be in the house for thirty seconds, nothing to eat, just grab the stick and back out and over the wall.

You'd remember the sunny nights, those long ones when it never grew dark, the endless games of backs and forwards which came to matter more than anything else. I remember Paddy Joe Ring, Christy's brother, would play in goals for backs and forwards, out here in the same field where his brother chased my father around. And the games would still be filthy. Desperate. Desperate.

I remember one day my brother Conor hit me on the head. Somebody had been winding the pair of us up in the match, and all of a sudden I was reefed open. I came in and presented myself to my poor mother. My father was gone away, working, and there were no cars about the place. My mother went up to a soldier living up the road, Harry Farmer. 'The young fella is bleeding like mad,' she said.

Harry, fair play to him, brought me to the doctor. The doctor couldn't stitch me, so Harry had to drive us on to the hospital. Every house in Cloyne has stories like that, memories of childhood, memories of first games, great games, last games. The field is where we gather and where we celebrate and where we take our beatings. Sacred ground, I think.

Last year somebody got the bright idea to sell it.

In this country right now we're looking back on a lot of the crazy things that went on when we had more money than sense, and we'll wonder what the hell we were thinking at the time. In Cloyne we'll talk about the time when the field was going to be sold. And all the murder and madness that followed.

It happened so fast. The thing went from being a rumour to being put to a vote to being passed by a margin of about seven or eight votes. The field would be sold as a chunk of real estate in the middle of the town. We'd get some land on the outskirts of the town and we'd start again.

My argument about the field was that, number one, it's in the middle of our town and it's more than a field. Old women go down the field for a walk while men are hurling. There is only one way into the field and it's overlooked by houses; parents leave the kids off down there, and there is no fear of anybody harming them when they're pucking around.

The second thing was that if we were getting more green fields nearby, it would have been easier to take; but the plan was to build a massive complex and we were getting no more green space than we already had.

And last. Our history. Every club in the country tries to create a history for themselves and they all try and create *laochs*, warriors, the great men that fellas will look up to and talk about and compare themselves to. A lot of it is only bullshit that they make up because that's what drives young people, but every day when I was a young fella I'd be in that field and I could look and there was a statue of a fella out there who was the greatest warrior of them all.

I mightn't have known who he was at first but, once I worked it out and I could see that all he had was a hurley, a ball and this exact field here, it was something. We all could work that out, and when we did we could map the road from the field to playing in front of 50,000 people because the fella that lived in that house there, the fella we have the statue to, he did it. We have the turf that was trod by the greatest *laoch* of them all and what were we going to do, cover it in patios and walkways.

During all this Willie John Ring on his bed of death made me promise to him not to let the field be sold.

All that put me in one corner of the ring when the row started.

And at first, to be honest I couldn't understand the people in the other corner. And the people who wanted the sale to go through, they couldn't understand the rest of us. So there was a bitterness there that divided us badly for a while.

The faultlines broke like this. All the fellas who grew up in the town, in the four streets, people like the Cahills and ourselves, were the people who didn't want it sold. The people who were living around the periphery were happy to make the sale. So my argument, which didn't go down well, was to say, 'You don't love that field as much as we do.' Not a great argument in terms of winning hearts and minds.

On the one side they were saying, 'We do, we love Cloyne, we are Cloyne, we love the field.'

On the other, I was saying, 'Sure you don't, because if you love that field as much as we do, you wouldn't fucking sell it!'

After a while the town was in danger of collapsing under the weight of the tension. There was a massive move to get us all in under the one roof to hammer it out before we went at each other with scythes and pitchforks!

My friend Diarmaid Falvey pushed and pushed for this meeting because the town was coming apart at the seams over the issue of the club and its pitch. He was right, but he was taking a risk. Getting us all together could cause an explosion too.

We talked of nothing else meanwhile. If a fella came into the pub and he didn't want the field sold, the talk would turn to how we would all blow up the developers' machinery and sabotage the entire thing. Seriously! Some talked about how we would start the club again with just the four streets and we'd begin at junior and work our way up. Four streets and a field, and fuck them all.

If he was against you and wanted the field sold, he wouldn't be talking to you at all; he'd be in a pub with like-minded men and women muttering about progress and how it was wrong to stop progress.

Meanwhile the economy had come to the edge of a cliff and was about to throw itself over the edge. The developer asked if he might have a further year's grace on the deal. So we had the meeting in that light, and on the night I felt that rage you get sometimes when you feel passionately in your heart about something and you know you are right and you think you have an argument that will end all arguments and send everyone away nodding their heads and saying, 'Fair play to Cusack, the scales fell from my eyes when he said that.'

Anyway, in the end I said something which in the heat of that night was easily misunderstood and fellas chose to misunderstand it for their own reasons. And later they misquoted me out of context!

I said that I couldn't believe what was happening to us and that we needed to do something one way or another. We needed to get rid of the field and get the development started and have it as a closed deal. Or we needed to forget about selling it. But we couldn't have it all hanging over us for another year, with more and more trouble being caused, trouble that was even reflecting on the senior hurling team. I said, 'You're all Cloyne men but we'll get to the point that when I look at you I won't look at Cloyne men, I'll see this fella over here as a Midleton man because he came from there originally.' And I said to the Sullys, 'Sure we'll see you as West Cork men.' (Their father came to Cloyne from West Cork.) There was a fella who used to be the club Chairman and I said to him that we'd go back far enough to see him as a Scotsman. The point was that the argument was regressing to the stage where we were defining the love of Cloyne on the basis of whether you were for or against selling the hurling field; and those of us with long roots in the four streets and close to the field who couldn't understand how anybody could sell it would start judging the others differently. We'd all go back to our caveman instincts – which, in a town whose name means the meadow of the caves, would be a fairly short journey!

I thought it was a reasonable point, but things had gone too far by then. The priest had said to the developers, 'Yep, drive on, lads, do this, do that, knock down walls.' Knocking down the walls adjacent to the church gave the development side all sorts of access in anticipation of the deal being done and work commencing quickly. That is how mad it got among us all. At a meeting one of the pro-development side said that they'd slipped one over on the bishop.

So word has it that next thing the bishop himself received a phone call: 'This is what they are saying about you in Cloyne!'

And of course the bishop came down and witnessed the pure madness of Cloyne. He saw that hurling is our number-one faith, that we are worshipping false gods and so on. The parish hall had been taken over for use as a gym by the hurlers. So His Grace freaked.

Everything stopped until walls that had been there for more than a hundred years got put back up stone by stone. Around the same time a new priest came in who was not for playing ball with the developers at all.

So now the project was in all this trouble and when I stood up and made my little speech about ancestry and roots – and I believe this 100 per cent – they saw their perfect opportunity, they had the bogeyman! Dónal Óg Cusack!

The bogeyman had said these terrible things to them, calling them West Cork men and Scots and, tough men as they were who had seen many a thing on the hurling field, this was too much! So the Chairman, the Secretary of twenty years, the Chairman of the Finance Committee and two members of the Finance Committee – all long-serving members of the club – packed up and resigned!

So on my side of the fence there was disbelief. People were asking over and over, 'You mean after all everyone has been through over this, these men resigned over what Dónal Óg said!' And on the other side of the fence they were too mortally offended to even come out of their post-traumatic-stress counselling and explain it all.

My argument to them was, I didn't say that they were West Cork men or Scotsmen! I said we would degenerate into defining each other in those terms. I apologized if they had taken offence, but by then it all had a life of its own.

Walls had been rebuilt, but in the wrong places. The town was split, the club was in chaos. So Diarmaid Falvey, the Vice-Chairman, took the rudder.

Now this is how bad it was in Cloyne: Diarmaid wouldn't talk to me when he took over. He'd only speak to me if it was documented for the record. He couldn't be seen to be plotting with Cusack. He's a solicitor in town and he wanted to play this thing straight down the middle. Normally he'd be a fella that would give you a heads up on this or that, but now he was under so much pressure we could only talk on the record. So Diarmaid at meetings would read out minutes and there'd be things like, 'At this point Dónal Óg called me and I told him that I could not speak to him.'

During the row our strike problem with the Board rumbled on too. One weekend there was some brutal stuff in one of the national papers about my role in the club. Someone in Cloyne, hiding behind a wall of anonymity, told the paper that I would never even put my hand down a toilet in the club if that needed doing. There's nothing lower in the GAA than fingering somebody as a bad club man.

A couple of people in Cloyne rang me and said that they were confident they knew who the person was. They'd heard that person use that phrase before in different contexts. My parents were mad, but to be honest I was in a conflict and knew I needed to keep the main goal in mind. The same people in the club and in that particular paper had tried to label me in this way before but never succeeded. For a while there were stories going around the town that some time before Christmas some people in the club were going to take their chance and make a move to get rid of me . . .

For some of them I had been a thorn in their side for many a year, a troublemaker and an embarrassment. I remember them calling me into a committee meeting, straight from the middle of a training session, back in 2002, and putting me in the middle of the room facing all of the officers. They asked me not to go ahead with the strike. One guy said I was doing myself a disservice. I told them my views and told them that what they had said to me didn't do anything to change those views. In fact they had only reinforced my attitude, if anything. And I went back out to the session.

When I was involved in running the senior team for a few years I had to keep the executive out of the team business – not that I got any kick out of it, but it needed to be done if we were to be successful. I remember one meeting at the end of a year when we had reached a county final. Bunty Cahill brought up that he was hurt and annoyed that he couldn't travel in the bus with the team to big games.

Bunty is a great man and I wouldn't have had any problem with his travelling, but it was in my head that I just wanted the team travelling alone with no distraction from others on the bus. So Bunty got left out.

Worse, I had an outburst that even those on my side nearly killed me for afterwards. I said, 'Bunty, don't be worrying because as long as I'm taking the team you won't be going on the bus, so make the same arrangements to get to the games next year as you did this year.' And left the meeting. I've regretted it ever since.

That's one of the things that made Lá na gClub special last weekend. Bunty and myself walking along, shaking hands with the line of young fellas and just having a laugh and a chat in the sunshine.

In the end, the economy tanked and the field was saved. In Cloyne we had to introduce a Cloyne solution to a Cloyne problem: we made a rule in the club that there could be no more talk about it. After it had all ended, fellas would be winding each other up about it. They'd know I was touchy, for instance, because I'd been burned, so the lads would be marking out little patches in training.

'I like it over here, Dónal Óg, I'm actually going to buy this patch, this time next year I'll be sitting out here in a deck chair!'

So we had to stop. There was no more talk about it.

It was a hard time and we still feel it, but we're starting to laugh about the madness now. The madness and all the stuff that cut to the bone. The Secretary is gone, the Chairman resigned but is back on the committee. That's a fair upheaval in a small rural club.

One of those fellas who left and is back now though is Sully's uncle Timmy. He is the main man looking after the senior hurling team this season and I'm working with Timmy. We'll be grand, we'll drive on. The friendship survived and I'm glad.

I couldn't hack us not getting on, so I rang him and asked could I call to him at home. I went to him and said, 'Look, Timmy, I don't dislike you, you know me long enough that if I didn't like you I'd fucking say it to your face. I don't mind fighting about the land but that doesn't mean I dislike you.'

And Timmy said, 'Ógie, sure look, I'm the same. Look up on that wall – there wouldn't be a picture of you still up there if I didn't like you.'

So we're looking after the senior hurling team now and we're all part of the process of trying to get the whole club going again. That's how it should be. And the day last Sunday put a lot of things back in perspective.

Most of us think that the life of the senior hurling team is everything in the club, but there were people in the field that (gasp!) didn't really care about the senior hurling team. People there with kids, and they're new to the town perhaps and just getting to know the club and the area. Brilliant.

It was a great day. The club sold loads of stuff in the club shop and a couple of new people signed up to the club. There was even one person who said she hadn't even known the field existed there!

The lads had done a load of work tidying up the place and then taking down all the wire that was around the field, just to make it look like a nice friendly place. There was a great feeling around Cloyne last night, even though we lost the match the night before; we just felt like a good happy club again. There was one fella there in the Alley Bar, I was talking to him and I hadn't talked to him in years. It was great. It couldn't have been fecking better and it was Lá na gClub did that.

I'll remember the match in the field for a long time and smile every time. Paddy O'Sullivan is Diarmuid's uncle. Paddy was playing full-forward in the match and I swear that man thought it was the All-Ireland final. He even looked the part, kitted out in his 1970s gear.

He was playing with us Singles (even though his status in that regard was debatable) and he was delighted to get a goal. My father let in a bad old goal and you should have heard the two of them. Paddy was telling the father how artfully he had caught him off his line but the father was genuinely savage over the goal. When I went home the next day he was still shaking his head and saying, 'Fuck it, I should have stopped that goal.' And I was saying to myself, Is he messing with me here, showing me how bad I am, or is he really serious about this? And he was serious!

The night of Lá na gClub ended in the Alley Bar and there was a small thing happened which I will never forget. Paddy O'Sullivan, still pleased with his goal, was there, Dermie O'Shea was there, Deccie Motherway, a selector with the seniors, was sitting there too, and Timmy O'Sullivan was beside him.

Timmy had a heart attack about eighteen months ago, but Paddy and Timmy are gas men, tough men who work laying blocks together all day every day, but they have a love for each other as brothers that is unbelievable.

At one stage in the night Timmy was mad for a cigarette and cadged one off Dermie and they disappeared out the back for a smoke. One of the lads squealed! 'Timmy is gone out the back for a cigarette.'

And poor Paddy nearly collapsed. The lads started quizzing him as to why he was so worried that Timmy was smoking.

Eventually he turned to me and he said: 'I don't want Timmy to die before me because I love him and I don't want to have to suffer that.'

And when Timmy came back in, a row started about the cigarettes, and soon Dermie, the youngest of the fifteen O'Sheas, is asking if he is being accused of trying to kill Timmy and half of us are laughing and half are upset and fuck it, there and then, that moment at the end of that day, we should have nailed it down because that's what the club is about.

It brought it all home to me yesterday. There is such great pride in the club and friendship and love and we have our rows, but we pull together again. We drive on.

One last memory. The Bomber Roche and Pa stayed around drinking with us of course, and every now and then they would start up with the pipes and the boys would all be up marching around the pub behind them like it was a match, and next thing we noticed there was two English fellas had come in, one fella asked for a Coke and the other fella had a pint and they sat in a corner. And that made our day. The thought of them wondering what the fuck was going on in this place, with the pipes and the band and the big crowd in there, drinking and hopping up every now and again to march behind a fella they called the Bomber.

Tourists. But they saw the real Cloyne! A place where it doesn't matter what you are in your private world or what side you took in a strike or a row or an argument. There we were, all of us who had been in the pits of dejection twenty-four hours before and at each other's throats over the strike and the field and my words, and now together in each other's company with the pride coming back into us as Cloyne men. As Timmy would say, we were happy out.

20

We flew home to Dublin from South Africa. My original plan had been to attend a GPA meeting in Dublin, stay overnight at the Airport Hotel and then head on to Lanzarote for more training. Now things had changed. I decided to attend the meeting, sleep the night and head home to Cork.

Usual drama, of course. While I headed to the GPA meeting Jimmy McEvoy got me a room at the Airport Hotel and texted me the room number. He told reception I would be collecting a key. In due course I arrived, shattered. I went to reception in the hotel, said to the girl that I was in room number whatever, that there had been another man here earlier, etc.

So she gave me my key and I wandered off. I found the room, opened the door and could hear the shower going full blast. There was a computer on the table. Jimmy is always on the computer. I remember saying to myself, 'Fuck it, Jimmy is just home from South Africa and he has the computer out again. You'd think he'd have people to call or whatever.'

Next minute I notice a suitcase that's not my own. And not Jimmy's. Sudden panic. Jesus Christ, that's women's gear there, all over the bed. Not mine. Not Jimmy's.

Clear visions now of the papers kicking off a week's coverage of my private life with Cusack Arrested Inside Woman's Hotel Room.

I ran out of the door.

After a night's sleep in my own room I caught the plane to Cork. My father was collecting me and, men being men and families being families, he collected me and we drove to Cloyne as if nothing was going on in our lives. We talked about the holiday and we talked hurling and all that chit-chat kind of stuff. Down home, typically, my mother had dinner just about ready for me.

So we sat down in the kitchen, Dad and I avoiding any silences and filling the gaps with small talk. My mother was doing what she does with the dinner, rattling about and staying busy. No silence. A lot of tension.

Eventually I said, 'Look, Dad, we need to have a little chat. We need to talk. Can we go to the sitting-room?' It was getting to the stage where we were all going to eat our dinner with this bubble hanging over us.

So my mother came in. Treasa came down. My brother Conor was there. I'm not sure where Victor was.

They all sat down and waited. Now, I've always been comfortable with who I am, but this wasn't easy. To them I was a son or brother, a hurler. I was a leader in a world of men's men. In Cloyne I had standing because I was a hurler, and hurling matters. Our house had produced three hurling sons and I had brought some serious medals through the lintel. I knew the pride that gave them. The room we were sitting in had its walls and shelves filled with the stories and mementos of hurling lives. Mainly mine.

So I sat facing them all and saying to myself, I have to do it, I have to do it. Yet I knew I just didn't want this shit. I longed to be in Lanzarote, training and thinking about three All-Irelands in a row and how sweet and uncomplicated that would be. I was in the condition of my life, I was eating almost perfectly, training well, Cork were going for history, I was playing well myself. This conversation we were about to have could scuttle a lot of things either side of our front door.

And selfishly, too, I knew it would all need more of my time to be dealing with this in a way that was never planned. To be honest, there was no plan, ever, but it was certainly never meant to be this way, telling my family the story before some internet gossips, newspapers or barflies confirmed it for them. Now I had to do what I felt was right, no matter how little it suited me.

So I told them the story pretty much exactly the way it had happened. The other, secret, story of this son they had reared in this house. I said, 'Look, I'm not into labels, I'm not this or I'm not that but this is what I've been doing, this is it, this is me, blah, blah, blah. If that makes me whatever, then I am what I am, but I refuse to go down the road of labels and stuff like that, I don't know what's ahead of me but that's where I am. That's me. Still Dónal Óg.'

There's no soft way to say hard things. My father began first, asking me questions. There was confusion in every line of the man's face. He said he was a man of the world, that he had lived and worked in London for ten years but he thought, well, if he had a son like this he thought he would dress differently and behave differently. 'They all have square jaws,' he said at one point, 'but you don't, you're into hurling.'

And in his love and his confusion he was annoying me as well. I wasn't ready for all this. 'What does it mean, I'm into hurling? That begins me and ends me?'

He said to me then, 'Right, you know the way we need to deal with this? You need to get fixed.'

For a second that pissed me off. Get me fixed! Not a nice thing to hear, but that's the way himself and myself would often talk about things. Right, we need to do this now, you know the drill, this needs to be fixed. And fuck it, we would fix it. Problem solved. Next thing.

I think my mother, in the way of things, always half knew or expected what she was hearing, but for Dad it was a big shock. Here was his son playing for Cork, his own young fella who had come in and played his part, sorting out the senior hurling team in the town, the young fella who was leading the whole thing, who took on a lot of tough characters about the place to get rid of them, so-called influential fellas, and now . . . Jesus Christ. This?

He had defended me and stuck up for me in every argument on every site he worked, on every terrace he stood on where some loud-mouth would have a go.

He couldn't sleep nights before games with the tension of going to watch me. And now he was lost.

He was sixty-three years old, sitting in the good living-room in his own home, hearing this. And before he could grasp it all, there was nothing really left to say. No mending it. No fixing it. Just getting on with it.

Treasa didn't say much, and the brother Conor? I remember Conor got up to leave, laid a hand on my father's shoulder and said, 'There you go now, that will broaden your mind.'

And the rest of us sat there in our room, filled with pictures of hurling teams and trophies and medals, and thought, Thanks for that, Conor, that's the perfect thing to say!

Then we went back out and had the dinner.

Dad said one more thing to me that I will never forget from that day, just something which told me the journey he was having to make in his brain. The whole thing was sinking in with him and instinctively again he was back by my side, ready for the world. He shook his head slowly and said, 'Like, Dónal Óg, the abuse you're going to get about this, I thought it was hard defending you from fellas giving out over your short puck-outs, but fuck it this one . . .'

I know what he was thinking. He was thinking, Right, I'll kill fellas if I have to. I don't know how I'm going to get my head around this one but I'll defend my son anyway.

Home was the worst of it and the best of it, I suppose. They needed to know and in the end it changed nothing, and if I had planned it I would only have wanted that, for nothing to change.

Some fellas were hard to tell. Since I came into the Cork team Ger Cunningham and I had been very close. He had passed on the famous jersey he had worn for eighteen years as Cork goalkeeper and then had the grace and patience to coach me and be my friend. He'd rung me in South Africa, full of concern, and I'd told Ger not to worry, we'd chat when I got back. I promised to ring him straight away when I got home.

Ger came down to the house and I said, 'Do you want a drink?' At the time I used to always have a bar fridge full up with drink in the house. It wouldn't be touched for months but then I'd go on a bender with my friends and the contents of the fridge would take a bad hammering.

Ger said, No thanks, that he was driving; so we started talking and I was telling him the story and he stopped me.

'You better get me one of those fucking drinks, Ógie.'

He was stone cold serious.

So I got him a bottle of Heineken to take the raw edge off the news. The man was worried for me, he was bothered and confused as well. This was new territory for a lot of people. But we had the conversation and, Ger being Ger, that was enough for him. He knew now and when he heard the talk about me he had a different line of attack when he went about defending me. They say a friend is the fella you ring when you have just killed somebody and they say, 'Don't move, I'll be over with two shovels.' I found I had a lot of those friends.

I remember Billy rang me and I knew he had heard. So I played him.

'How are things?'

'Blah, blah, blah, Billy!'

'OK so, yeah? Yeah?'

'Yeah, Billy.'

'OK, good luck so, I'll talk to you.'

All this kind of shit! Thirty seconds later, the phone rang again.

'Look, Ógie, I know you're in a bit of trouble at the moment, you know the story, I don't give a fuck what you do, I'm your friend. If you need any help or anything like that, I'm here for you always.'

Bang. He hung up the phone again. Just like that.

Jesus, that was repeated in some form or other loads of times. I'd be a feisty fucker who doesn't mind rubbing people the wrong way and it was more than I expected or hoped for in return. A feeling of closeness and support coming from people who mattered to me, people that you could never doubt ever again. They were there. Solid.

You'd be amazed what things will stick in your head from a time like that. Dinny O'Shea rang me up at that time.

'Ógie, I know there is stuff going on, but you know I'll back you whatever you're doing.'

There was a pause. I just didn't know what to say. This was such an awkward conversation for Dinny. He was one of the older fellas in Cloyne. Never in his life did he imagine making a call like this.

'It doesn't matter a fuck to me whether you are or not. I'm here for you.'

Another pause.

'And by the way, Ógie, there is a couple of Cloyne fellas working on the site with me. And they're of the same opinion.'

I'm tough, but there was so much emotion in so many of those conversations, it was wringing me out. Some of the conversations were earnest. Some emotional. Some make me laugh when I look back. Niall McCarthy absorbed the news and then got back to me with a handwritten sheet of eighteen questions.

And Dr Con. He has been looking after me since I was a kid and looking after Cork players for nearly four decades without a penny coming back.

I was convinced he knew, that he had to know, but the man nearly collapsed. We went for a coffee across from his surgery on the Western Road. He was telling me he was getting ready for war, wondering how we were going to fight the rumours and get it straightened out. Should I do an interview, a media thing?

I told Con. We have had so many good and deep discussions about it since, but he started off with a weak hand. He said to me that it would be easier to go the other way.

I knew why he said it. For me. But.

'Con, hold on a second, so it's easier for me to go the other way, so I'm going to get married, I'm maybe going to be resentful and pissed off with this poor girl who had married me or whatever and maybe there'll be kids and eventually I will have to pull the rug from everyone? That's not fucking me,' I said, 'no fucking way. If the other way means hassle or loneliness, I don't give a fuck, Con. You know that. I can't do or risk that. Who knows what will happen in time? I don't know what is around the corner, but what I do know is that I have to be true to myself, come what may.'

Con is a great friend to me and he was worried about the thing. So many people were. That was it. Nobody disappointed me. I told the people that needed to know and just got ready to get on with hurling.

21

After five meetings of stonewalling and filibustering with myself and John Gardiner, the Board decided late in October 2008 to ram through Gerald McCarthy's re-appointment. It was an act of aggression, a declaration of war. The only moment of comedy was when somebody even took that famous clip from *Downfall*, the movie about Hitler's last days, and subtitled it for YouTube so that Mick Dolan, the Chairman of the County Board, was one of the officers cringing before the demented Führer. The Führer had a comb-over. The clip got 30,000 hits in the space of a few weeks.

When we left that fifth meeting (even now my brain wants to shut down when I hear those two words, 'fifth meeting') I said to Gardiner, 'Listen, if the worst came to the very worst I could maybe live with Gerald, I could bear him.'

And John said, 'That's OK for you! You are a goalie, you're off doing your own stuff. We can't come down every session and put up with it. Three or four days of our week. That's how often we are dealing with it.'

And that was John. He'd gone from being the eighteen- or nineteen-year-old young fella he was back in 2002, unsure about what to do, having just broken into a team that was now heading out on strike, to being the leader of the group. He never ceased to surprise me in the weeks that followed.

From the start, too, I was surprised at how far the group was willing to go to resist the appointment of Gerald and his selectors. We held a meeting after we had sat with the County Board for that fifth time. When I was in players' meetings afterwards and we were contemplating a strike, I was thinking about what it meant for me also – immersion in a battle I didn't need or want. In the front line every day. I honestly didn't know if I would have the belly for more conflict, but the basic mood in the meeting was that something had to be done.

And if that was the case I was willing to do whatever it would take.

Why? Because what the boys in that room were willing to fight for is worth fighting for any time.

The Board had taken a gamble. They thought we would never go on strike again. We weren't so sure we would either. It was a needless battle. Gerald should never have been put in that position. Neither should we. In the end he went back to his natural instincts. So did we. Pity.

I remember, straight away after the fifth meeting, we said that we needed to go to Gerald and tell him what we had been saying about him. A meeting was set up for Donie Collins's house later that evening. A living-room. Myself and Gardiner sitting across from Gerald and Donie Collins. Gerald hadn't spoken at all till the end of the meeting and I had looked at him, fidgeting and taking it all in, and realized that this was one tough man who was going to face us down and do anything he could to salvage his pride. I knew it that night, and I spoke to John about the tragedy of what was likely to happen: the Board would drop Gerald – a legendary Cork hurler – and its top thirty players into a pit and let us fight it out, knowing our nature would ensure that only one would come back out, and they were betting that it would probably be Gerald.

It was a shame. We all did our best for two years to try to make it work. After the Kilkenny semi-final he could have walked. Everybody would have said, 'That was a bad experience, but we can shake hands and part.' Instead, if felt like the County Board dropped us into a pit and walked away. And what happened then? Ten thousand people marched in the streets. Families split. There was trouble in every club in the county.

'Have we the belly for this, John?' I knew, though, that there was only one way to preserve what we felt was right. Go to war and go for the long war. Half a job would be only codding ourselves. No point in trying to compromise; the best outcome would have been a patch-up job. We walked into it knowing certain things. We will be slaughtered by the media. We will be slaughtered by the public. It will be a long battle. Months and months. Jesus Christ. During the footballers' dispute with the County Board in the winter of 2007–8,

when we went on strike in support of them, we had signed a document with a mediator, Kieran Mulvey, to say we wouldn't do this
again. I remember saying to the lads when we signed that piece of
paper in January 2008, 'Well now it's ye will be breaking that. I won't
be around the place by the time of the next strike!'

The public reaction was normal. A natural thing. We look at stuff
about the Middle East and just say they must be all mad. Mindless.
That's us. Hamas hurlers.

And John Gardiner? He went to work in the bank every day and
he'd hear what people were saying. Lads know. They hear. 'Those
Cork fellas are gone again. Will they ever be happy?' His attitude was
defiant. He's a young man. There is a fierce toughness in him. At
times, because I have been through so much of it, I would have known
that some things needed to take their course, but he would be coming
at them like a ball of fire because that is his spirit.

One night he rang me at work. He was with his father. There had
been something in the paper. He said, 'We need to do something
about it.'

I said, 'John, we can't do anything about it. Leave it.'

He says, 'Where are ya?'

'Work, John.'

'Right, I'll be waiting outside.'

We always saw the strength in John. The same with Tom Kenny.
From an early stage we made it our business to include them in meetings with the Board or about team finances so they could see how
things operated. We always expected that we would be long gone by
the time another battle came around that demanded their leadership.

When Tom came into the panel at first he was a very quiet character. But in the Munster final of 2003 against Waterford he carried
us through the second half. There is great strength inside him. It
always bamboozled the Board that another generation of strong characters seemed to be coming along after the original troublemakers
had grown old.

We were all in that pit together. The County Board gambled that
the old warhorses would be jaded and wouldn't have the belly. They
didn't reckon on John Gardiner, Tom Kenny, et al.

At the start the lads felt that we had to go and explain to Gerald how strong the group was and that we had to do this before he was re-appointed. No man would insist on leaving his name on the table for re-appointment, knowing that the squad didn't want him, surely? It would be a chance for the County Board to thank Gerald for all that he had done, a sentiment we would have rowed in with, and Gerald would head off in the direction of the sunset with his dignity intact.

So nine fellas volunteered to go and talk with Gerald. John Gardiner, Kevin Hartnett, Shane O'Neill, John O'Callaghan, Joe Deane, Brian Corry, Seán Óg Ó hAilpín, Shane Murphy and Ronan Curran.

John rang Gerald and requested the meeting. Gerald agreed. In the morning Nially Mac, who had missed our own meeting, rang and asked, could he go too. The more the better, I said.

I couldn't attend, and probably that was no harm. I was on the road at 6 a.m. that morning, heading up the country to do some work at Intel. I had only just reached Intel's campus when I got lost. I looked for directions from a man who was out walking – I was on the phone to John Ga when I asked him – and he said to me, 'You're Cusack, aren't you, really pleased to meet you.'

It brought back that we are honoured to play for Cork and it is nice to be recognized sometimes and to have your hand shaken. The world isn't full of malice. He showed me exactly where to go and, I don't know, would he have been as helpful if he didn't know me? Myself and John had a philosophical moment on the phone after that!

During any breaks in the day's work I would be on the phone to the lads. My head was starting to throb. I hadn't got to bed till 2 a.m. the previous night and I wasn't as prepared for a day in Intel as I should have been.

The word from the meeting was worrying. Gerald said that basically he was going nowhere. End of story.

Nially Mac had reminded him of the fact that he had told Nially during the winter that if the players didn't want him then he would go. Gerald shrugged.

Joe, Seán Óg and John Ga did most of the talking, but some of the younger lads who were present said afterwards that they were now more determined than ever not to work with Gerald.

Driving home, I spoke in turn to John Ga, Timmy Mac, Joe Deane, Gatchy, Diarmaid Falvey and Seán Óg. Every one of them was worried about what was coming. So was I.

Suddenly the story was breaking every way. I got a call from a man very close to the centre. He said that Gerald was in cahoots with Frank Murphy all along and that Frank was relaying all that was going on in the meetings. I didn't know what to think. The source said that Gerald is gunning for me, number one.

After this conversation I spoke to Seán Óg at length. Seán Óg maintained that this would be a long battle but that we just had to hold hard. I spoke to Dessie Farrell. Dessie set about getting advice for us.

I met John Ga in Carrigtwohill Industrial Estate the next evening. We spoke to Seán Óg from the car. John looked tired, drained in fact.

As we sat there, the County Board voted by eighty to six to re-appoint Gerald. Cloyne abstained from the vote. The Blarney delegate, Alan White, said at the meeting that it was rumoured that the players had convened a meeting that went on till the early hours the previous night. He hoped that we wouldn't be heading into a winter similar to last year's.

The Board replied in classic County Board style. Everything was done by the book.

We held a meeting in the Sunset Ridge on the last Thursday in October. It was five minutes to two in the morning when I left for home. Shattered. Fraggy (Kieran Murphy of Sars), Neil Ronan and John O'Callaghan were missing. Everyone else was there.

We voted by secret ballot: a result of twenty-seven to two to never again play for Gerald McCarthy, whatever happened. All agreed he should go, but two lads were worried that it could be the end for them. It was made clear that if you voted yes you were out till Gerald McCarthy was gone. Ronan Curran made the point that anyone who wanted to leave the room should do so now. In two or three months we wouldn't accept a fella walking away and fracturing our unity, but at that moment nothing would be held against any player who wanted no more part in this. It was also stated to all that they could back out of the strike after the meeting if they didn't feel comfortable doing it in front of the group.

Six reps were elected, each of us with responsibility for communicating to a group of players. Some of the players had been receiving calls from a selector, outlining the consequences if they went with the main group. One of them had taped his call and he played it to us. This was bad form by men that should have known better, and it caused us to harden our views. It often crossed our minds to release the tape but, like Gerald's text, we never did – we knew it could harm the man too much.

In the early weeks we shipped some bad blows media-wise. We knew we would and we had agreed from the start that we would ride the unpopularity out and wait till the season approached. Hopefully then the tide would turn, and anyway if the onslaught on us from the County Board and Gerald was too slick, silence would be our best weapon.

Some things hurt. I had to give Dónal Lenihan, the former rugby player, a veiled warning one evening on Today FM after he made some unhelpful comments about the situation. If you want to fire off some shots, then be prepared for us to drag you into the pit; if you don't want to come in here, then mind your own business.

Seán Óg had given an interview during the 2007–8 footballers' dispute in which he laid the blame for a lot of Cork's ills at Frank's door. We were at a meeting with Frank the next morning when the paper was delivered. Coming from Seán Óg it was like a wrecking. So this time around Seán Óg drew fire. A priest verbally attacked himself and John Gardiner on the weekend of the Cork County convention. I don't know if it bothered Seán Óg at all, but I know that whenever things were getting tough I'd give him a call and his resolution and determination would inspire me. He sees things in such black-and-white terms, and when he is right it is an absolute duty for him to do the right thing too.

My first memory of him is back when we were kids, playing for the Cork under-14s, I remember his arm was in a cast, and obviously there weren't too many dark fellas around Cloyne or around Cork at that time. If you saw somebody with Seán Óg's complexion back then, people would be coming out the door to take a look, especially if he had a hurley in his hand. Anyway, he stood out. He was playing away with one hand, messing with the ball, and the word was that he was really good. I got on to the under-14 team and I played that year with him. We've known each other ever since.

Seems so long ago. We couldn't count the number of times we have trained together since then. It's a funny thing, but often when I get hate mail, the abuse ties myself and Seán Óg together. Gives certain people the chance to tie a couple of prejudices together. 'You and your South Sea Island friend', as one demented crank with a crayon put it.

I always think to myself that it's fair enough to be abusing me, but Seán Óg? Not on. Everywhere he goes the man leaves people feeling better about themselves with his genuine passion for life.

I'm thirty-two years old now, and independently minded, but if I was in a pub having a drink and Seán Óg came in, I wouldn't be comfortable drinking in front of him. He's a man I'd hate to disappoint. He's a friend and an inspiration and I'd do anything for him. I've known that for a while now. He has that effect on people. Just an inspiring man.

This last strike was the toughest and the meanest. The blows got personal and deliberate. The hate mail and crank calls came snowing in. We lost the Cork public and the clubs for the first few weeks and the rest of the country despised us. It was tough for Gerald. It was tough for us.

When it came to training, who kept us going? Seán Óg. His single-mindedness. His determination for Cork hurling, that it should be done right and with standards and honour. He's a man who could have sat back on his reputation a few years ago and uttered nothing but platitudes and clichés for the rest of his life. He will always be one of the great warriors and *laochs* of the game.

I was under a lot of pressure and had a lot of stuff going on off the field. I remember saying to myself, It's him keeping this together, it's Seán Óg. He said, 'We are going to go training and we are going to train properly and we are going to have proper attendance and we are going to act like a team.'

People see him speaking from the heart but not always speaking in a calculated way, and perhaps they wonder. Within our group, though, his strength and his single-mindedness and his presence as a man whose commitment can't be questioned inspired us all. Nobody works harder, trains harder or gives more back than Seán Óg does.

He set us on the road. He kept us there.

During the strike there was an event on at the Airport Hotel for the leukaemia ward at Cork Children's Hospital, and I'd promised a long time before that I would be there. There was a strike meeting in Alan Quirke's house earlier that day. I said to the boys after the meeting, Tom and Seán Óg, that I was going over to the hotel and asked them if they'd come.

The lads come with me, and Seán Óg of course leads the way in. He goes up on the stage, and the DJ recognizes Seán Óg, and now we are here the DJ doesn't really know what to do with us.

So he says to Seán Óg, 'Will you sing a song?' Now the obvious answer to that is, 'For fuck's sake, no.' But Seán Óg is unique and he really feels bad that he can't sing. He'd do anything for ya. And I'm looking at Seán Óg and saying, 'Jesus, Seán Óg, is this fella serious?' when the DJ pipes up, 'Well will ya dance so?'

Now there isn't a sports person in the country who wouldn't feel justified in laughing and saying, 'Eh, no thanks, I won't dance,' but Seán Óg is here in front of all these sick kids and he is the most genuine man I have ever met and if he can do anything for this room he will, so he says, 'All right so, I'll dance, what have you got?'

At this stage myself and TK are looking at Seán Óg, looking to the DJ, looking for the exits. Can't believe this is happening.

'What would you like?' asks the DJ.

'Ehm, well, have you got "YMCA"?' says Seán Óg to your man.

'God, I do,' says the DJ.

And by now even the DJ is looking at Seán Óg as much as to say, Is this really going to happen? And Tom and myself are looking at Seán Óg, waiting for him to say, 'For fuck's sake I'm only codding, will you cop yourself on, we're in the middle of a bitter strike here,' but Seán Óg is the wrong man for that.

So the DJ puts on bloody 'YMCA' and if I didn't know better I'd think Seán Óg is taking the piss out of me with this one now. The tune starts up and there's uproar as Seán Óg throws himself into the dancing. I'm saying to Tom, 'If this thing is on YouTube tomorrow in the middle of this strike we'll all be fucking hung.'

To make things worse, myself and Kenny and the footballers are there like a gang of wallflowers. And if it was anybody but Seán Óg we'd gladly stay that way, but now there's two thoughts running through the self-serving section of our brains. If we leave Seán Óg dancing on his own, then there's a good chance he's going to be disappointed in us, and that's bad. Second, there's also a good chance that the DJ will push his luck and ask each of us to do a turn individually.

So – there's – no – need – to-be – un-happy! And out we shuffle, trying to make a shape at doing the YMCA dance and in our agony we can't help noticing, what the hell, Seán Óg is really good at this, he's done it before! He must have.

That's Seán Óg. Any other person would have told the DJ to go and jump when they were asked to sing, but Seán Óg genuinely felt bad. So he danced. And the same old story, when we left it was Seán Óg who stayed behind with the kids.

I remember one morning, he had been in Kildare the previous night, presenting medals, and he was about first there at 9 a.m. on the Saturday for training. Another day I was presenting medals to the juvenile section in Russell Rovers. Beforehand, a guy at work had asked me to take his son to a hurley maker to get hurleys as a Christmas present. I asked the young fella on the way who was his favourite player and he said, 'Seán Óg,' so I rang Seán Óg and put him on loudspeaker so he could talk to him. Seán Óg is unreal. He'd still be talking to the lad if I hadn't cut it off after half an hour. Sometimes the man is too genuine for his own good.

These times when I look around the dressing-room and think to myself that Joe used to sit there and Sully was always there and Wayne Sherlock was there, I wonder how long I'll have a home for myself in the Cork dressing-room, and I think it is as long as Seán Óg is there. He brings such passion and inspiration to the whole place that everything is easier for me when he is around. We mightn't talk to each other every day and we mightn't even talk at a training session, but there's a silent thing that when Seán Óg picks it up and starts driving into it I'll respond and so will the lads.

(I know it might sound strange, but during one of the yoga sessions we've started doing we were to sit back to back and try to convey positive energy through intuition; I was paired with Seán Óg and afterwards the instructor singled out myself and Seán Óg as being the pair that she was getting the most energy from.)

I was away when Gerald McCarthy made his attack on Seán Óg. My father called. He was upset. He said Gerald had come out with desperate stuff about Seán Óg. He read out the highlights:

I accept that Seán Óg has a very busy life. His substantial commercial interests arising from his Cork hurling career, dealing with his agent, his membership of the GPA, his job with Ulster Bank and his on–off role with Cork, must make it difficult to find time to reflect. If he did find time, then perhaps he wouldn't be flip-flopping around the place and changing his mind about my abilities as a coach to suit the agenda of the day.

I don't know if the words came from Gerald himself or from a PR agency, but for a lot of people I think that was when the mood started to change. This attack on one of the great heroes of Irish sport and my friend gave me strength for the battle.

The weekend before I had gone away, I had asked Seán Óg to do something for me the next weekend when I'd be away – travel to County Down to do a favour I owed the Down goalkeeper, Graham Clarke – and he had agreed with his normal grace and enthusiasm. (The Down hurlers and fellas like Graham are the true unsung heroes of what we do.) Seán Óg had been working all week. It is a bad dose to have to drive to Down, a long haul and tough going. When Gerald's statement came out, Seán Óg was driving from Cork to Down to do that favour for me. If Seán Óg got €100 for that trip I'd be surprised, and I know the trouble they would have had making him take it. That was the irony of Gerald's attack.

I was so angry and disgusted. Seán Óg didn't deserve that. I've always said to people in Cork hurling that, instead of seeing Seán Óg as a threat, why not use him as much as possible for the good of the game? They saw him as a threat from early on, though.

Once, years ago, Seán Óg was supposed to start coaching on the north side of the city, where he is a god. There was a small budget set aside for it to pay Seán Óg. It was then decided that the budget for all the equipment Seán Óg would need to coach the kids of the north side should come out of Seán Óg's miserly wage too.

The insanity of it. To have had Seán Óg going into schools? To have him speak to kids with that passion and truth he brings to everything? Priceless. Pay him a fortune to do it! Cork hurling would be secure for a generation.

Gerald had crossed a line. He had said many times that there was no circumstance in which he would be moved or removed. I remember saying to myself that day, Gerald, I promise, you will be going and gone before Seán Óg goes.

22

I wonder what it is like coming into this team as a young fella. Regard-less of what you did during the strike it must be a tough enough set-up to join.

We were lucky, those of us who came in years ago together. We were successful underage players and we were drafted in as a block by one of our underage managers. And almost straight away we won ourselves an All-Ireland and felt comfortable in our skins. Too comfort-able, the County Board would say.

The young fellas who joined us for this season must feel like sappers sent to replace fallen veterans in a unit that has been fighting on the front line for a couple of years. We have been in the wars and that, I suppose, has made us close as a gang of fellas. We have our own stories and refer-ences. The group must seem almost impenetrable to newcomers. And if fellas read the papers or listen to some of the comments, they would imagine that half the team sits around discussing Marx and Engels and counter-insurgency techniques while the other half watches the stock exchange to be ready to cash in further when their earnest comrades finally bring the GAA into financial chaos and to the gates of that new dawn of rampant professionalism.

We were doing yoga last night. Denis has found us a great yoga instructor in Mallow and the sessions are of great benefit and at times good crack. Some of us couldn't stop laughing last evening, though, because Hoggy (Patrick Horgan) wore a T-shirt to the session with the numbers 5-0 written on it.

5-0! That was the score in a famous soccer game when the scrawny drug-addicted city fellows beat the fine country lads last year in La Manga. As long as I can remember, that is the way we have split the teams up. We've played city versus country games everywhere we have gone. Thailand. Vietnam. New Zealand. The USA. The Canaries. La Manga.

And La Manga was the first time that the city lads ever won. They all wrote the scoreline on their white T-shirts and came down to breakfast with them on next morning. Hoggy said he just wanted to bring it to show me.

I'll remember things like that as much as I will remember the strikes. It's the laughs that make us a team. I remember Jimmy McEvoy going over the edge of a glass platform on a high cliff in Nevis, New Zealand, in such a panic that he forgot to listen to the bungee-jump instructor telling him which cord to pull when he got to the lowest point. I'll remember elephant rides with Frank and nights when we were all so drunk we thought we'd never see again. Training weeks where they would push you to the limit on the training pitch and then let you push yourself to the limit in the bars. Until you copped on.

We work on everything in obsessive detail, trying to rub out the margin for error that might cost us the work of a season, but we're not doctrinaire. We screw up. We are human. Nobody is perfect. Even with all the systems and failsafes, we don't get it right all the time. That's what makes it entertaining.

For me, of course, humourless troublemaker that I am, it's got to be perfect. My hurleys, I dip the *bás* of them into marine varnish and rub in a mix of plaster, sand and ground glass to create a bit of friction there. I wear Nike Maxsight red-and-amber-tinted contact lenses in order to see the ball better, and special gloves which I tracked down to improve my grip in the rain. I tend to my core work, my reaction and speed work. I go to the gym and the alley on my own quite often. I prepare with respect for every eventuality and the ability it has to trip me up.

And yet and yet, you can't factor in the capacity for human error, the simple fact of being flesh and blood. Flashbacks. The All-Ireland semi-final of 2005 against Clare. We stayed in the Burlington Hotel. I wanted to do everything right. On the morning of the match I went down to the same curved wall in the car park that I have been beating a ball against since I came here as a minor years ago. Then I lay on the bed listening to music on the iPod.

And I lost track of time.

I'm lying there and next minute I realize, Oh Jesus Christ we're meant to be below for the bus to Croke Park. So I'm panicking and I get down and naturally aren't they all on the bus, tense and waiting to get to an All-Ireland semi-final.

When we got to Croke Park I had to spend a bit of time inside in the toilet, just getting it out of my head. I felt so guilty over it, which just shows you perhaps there is a danger in becoming too obsessive. I sat inside in the toilet, fighting that thought, getting it out of my head, but it kept coming back. If we get beaten today, me being late for the bus was a sign that we were slipping, that I was slipping.

Another one, over a year later. We are playing the 2006 All-Ireland final against Kilkenny. We are going for three in a row. The dream.

I have no problem saying I was and am maybe the best-prepared player on the field. On the Friday night before leaving, though, I came back down home to get my gear ready and found I had no boots from training. So I rang up Jimmy McEvoy and said, 'Jimmy, was there any Predator boots left inside in the training last night?' Jimmy said there was a pair of red-and-black ones left.

Result!

Jimmy said he'd give them to me the next day but I said no, I'd either go to him for the boots or he could bring them down to me, because what I'd do is I'd lay out all of my stuff on the floor, so I'd lay out my socks, my shorts, my under-armour, my other gear and my boots so I'd look at the 'man' then and see if anything was missing.

I still do it. I look at the man and see if there is anything obviously missing. It's a good habit for young kids to get into.

So Jimmy came down with my boots. Seán Óg got into the habit of washing his boots after training and I got into it too. A lot of the lads did – bring them to the shower and wash them. Anyway, Jimmy came out with the boots and gave me some peace in my head. Myself and all my gear would be ready for the train in the morning for the All-Ireland final. History crooking its finger at us.

In Croke Park we used to have a routine, where the keepers would go into the warm-up room and work away. If I had my way, we would be out working on the field an hour before throw-in, moving slowly up through the gears, but we had the warm-up room instead.

So we'd go into the warm-up room and we'd aim to give ourselves just under twenty minutes of doing mixed mobility work, getting the body going and things like that, so when we'd go on to the field we would be able to do our hurling stuff.

So the same precise routine, all the gear would be laid out. At that stage all your bottles and everything would be there, all done for you, your jersey would be in your position and I'd get my gear on, put my boots down ready on the floor and leave out my under-armour top. When I came back in from the warm-up room I'd put on my under-armour top and my jersey and my boots and that would be it.

We'd aim to come back in from the warm-up room about three minutes before John Allen would make his speech, then out on to the field. One of the lads would give us a shout on the three-minute mark.

This day it worked perfect. We came back in. Three in a row beckoning. I put on my boots and sat to listen and I'm thinking, Jesus Christ what's the story here with these boots? They are fucking huge. They feel like clown shoes.

Oh shit, something has gone wrong here. I have to check. I walk out into the middle of the floor and turn around. Might as well be wearing a big pair of clogs. Now it's about two minutes to go before John talks, and this is a three-in-a-row dressing-room, he is a man under serious pressure to get this right. Everyone is under pressure and the goalkeeper all of a sudden is saying, 'Here, John, we can't go on the field because I don't have my boots or maybe ye'll have to go out yourselves . . .'

Now it's like an under-12 dressing-room.

In the end I went over to our reserve goalie, Anthony Nash, and demanded to know what boot size he was. Wrong size. Over to the other keeper, Martin Coleman. Bingo!

'Marty, I need your fucking boots.'

I had other pairs of boots, of course, plenty of them, but not steel-studded Predators, which you need on the Croke Park surface. So I took Marty's Predators and Marty that day wore a different pair of boots and not the right ones at all because I wore his boots in the All-Ireland final. Mr Perfection.

Nobody ever reminds me of that, though. Not during the Tuesday night Dialectics of Feasible Socialism Lecture series, anyway.

*

Meanwhile, back at the yoga we are happy out. We have done yoga plenty of times before, but what we now like is our sympathetic instructor. She says that the best advice she can give us is to be where we are.

We all nod. (Except Cads, who was elsewhere.) I have been working on this yoga stuff for years and trying to learn as much about it as possible. I get there at times but then don't remain there, and there has always been some instructor pushing me to stretch just another bit, so that I feel as if a limb is going to fall off.

When I am finished hurling, one of the things I will take up is a martial art. Not for the combat side but for the spiritual side of it. And I'll explore yoga further.

Meanwhile I'll remember Hoggy in the T-shirt and the special guest at yoga tonight, the great Gatchy. There was so much moaning and groaning coming out of Gatch that whatever about him being where he was, a lot of lads wished they were somewhere else.

I got a back rub afterwards, had a nice meal and went home with Billy. We didn't discuss revolution all day.

23

Like a lot of things in life, it began with Niall McCarthy. Down the years Nially would never talk in the dressing-room. And that was grand. Each to their own. So it's the summer of 2008 and we're just going out to play Clare in Semple Stadium; next minute, Winston Churchill trapped in Nially Mac's body stands up and starts into an oration.

Nially starts off giving this epic fucking speech, which is great now because he has never spoken and he's passionate. But he has delayed us leaving the dressing-room.

Filled with the spirit of Nially Mac, we burst out the door and towards the light. I remember looking up the corridor and seeing that the Clare team had just burst out their door too, and thinking straight away, This is a bit dodgy.

Now I was as guilty as any fella in what happened afterwards, but I'd say it was half out of fear. We saw each other coming from different directions and hit the tunnel at almost the same time, with Clare slightly behind us. Two very wound-up teams.

It would have been grand if the Clare fellas had been in front of us, but they were coming in from behind. There was contact between myself and Frank Lohan; I gave him a butt of the hurley and then Frank gave me a fucking butt and then Sully was coming, and sure what happened happened. For a few seconds it got crazy, bodies all over the place and two lines of kids doing the guard of honour just to make it perfect. We got out and we went into a huddle and I remember I spoke. I said, 'Look, fuck that, whatever we do, concentrate on the scores, concentrate on the scores'; but in the back of my mind I knew there was going to be trouble.

At half-time I remember I was inside in the dressing-room and I was all covered in belts. I remember Con said, 'Are you all right?' and I said, 'I'm grand, nothing bad, just stinging from flakes.' Afterwards, when we watched it the boys got some laughs out of it because I only gave one belt and the Clare fellas were pulling on me like it was a training drill!

Next day, of course, the papers made out that it was Guernica. The *Examiner* carried a brutal picture of me with the hurley up over a fella's head as if I was going to execute him.

We got called in – Seán Óg, John, Sully and me – by the powers that be. As a Cork player this is when you look up and see a dark spot in the sky and ask, 'Is it a bird? Is it a plane? No, it's Superman. No wait, wait. It's Frank Murphy with the rule book.'

Frank rang me fierce late one night and said, 'Look, you're going to be cited,' or whatever. It was time for Frank to launch *CSI Semple*.

We went in and we met with Frank the following night, and for the next few days I spent a lot of time with Frank. He can be amazing. He had pictures and video grabs and timelines and witnesses. It's addictive stuff and I was in there and I was as bad as him. We were building a case. We were saying, 'Fuck it, maybe we are guilty but maybe it's not our fault that we are. Maybe we'll walk free! Maybe the GAA will compensate us for our traumas!'

When the time came we headed to Dublin on the train, all of us, and Dr Con came with us too, as a character witness. Contingent on not telling the truth! Probably, in hindsight, myself and Sully should have taken what was coming to us and let Seán Óg fight his corner. He was the most blameless of any of us and had never so much as been booked in a game before. He has such a sense of honour that he dropped his hurley when the fighting started.

There was a bit of debate as to whether or not Clare would come to the disciplinary hearing. We were shown into this room in Croke Park and told to wait, and of course we were giving out about the GAA as there was one plate of sandwiches there between the lot of us. So we were in the right form for the fight.

The Clare fellas hadn't turned up yet, so I went down to the room marked for them and took the Clare fellas' sandwiches and brought them back up for ourselves, imagining the fun there would be if they caught us red-handed! They're just arriving from Clare, and Frank Lohan is striding in, and hey! there's Cusack, the fucker who is after getting them in all the trouble and he is taking their sandwiches! Semplegate segues into Sandwichgate!

178 *Dónal Óg Cusack*

We brought the Clare sandwiches back up to the boys. I remember Con was pacing around the place anxiously and I remember saying to Con that he was making me nervous. Con was making speeches about how this has to be said and that had to be said. Then the word came back that I would be the first one in. I had to sit down beside this big fella, Danny Murphy from the Ulster Council. There were about fifteen suits around a table not big enough for ten; it reminded me of being back in primary school, sitting on these small seats, and this fella Danny Murphy beside me.

They are all dyed-in-the-wool GAA men. They obviously don't see me that way, and now they have me here where they want me. They adjust their glasses and try to get a better look.

Luckily, I had brought Perry Mason with me. Frank knew his way around this sort of procedure.

They had a big screen, and on the screen they had the scenes of violence that shocked a generation, etc. They had this fella hired that was playing the scenes on the big screen, and I remember this one fella with glasses kept having to ask, 'Show that again now? Where was that? Where was that again?'

Anyway, if I say so myself, I gave a fine performance from the dock. I know I did because the boys went in after me and when we had all done our stuff Frank came out and said, 'Mr Cusack, you gave a virtuoso performance! I think we'll be OK, fair play to you, boy!'

We have a good relationship, myself and Frank, when it comes to fighting for the same thing. I was saying, 'Fuck it, Frank, between the two of us we deserve an Oscar for that one.' We'd shown that the hurley which seemed to be about to execute Colin Lynch of Clare went down to the ground next. (If I'd hit him down on the head I wouldn't have cared too much because Lynch is a frightening enough fella anyway.) Frank gave such a wonderful performance that I half expected the GAA would give me a humanitarian prize there and then.

Frank is a great man to be in charge at times like this. He enjoys it. We'd missed the last train so Frank announced grandly, 'We'll have to get cars home now, boys.' So we hired cars.

I said, 'Frank, I'm starving.'

Hand straight up.

'You want food?'

He turned to the boys.

'Boys, do you want food?'

And he led us into this place, but they had stopped serving food, so he took out his mobile phone and dialled a number.

'Oliver! I'm with the boys and the boys are looking for food, where would we get it at this time of night?'

He was the leader of us and a great leader as well. He led us into a hotel and organized food for everybody. We got the dinner and we had a good old laugh. There was great banter between us all. I remember thinking, What a pity it was that we weren't all fighting together for the best for Cork hurling over the years.

It was a grand evening and at the end of it Frank said to me, 'What's your mobile number again there, Mr Cusack?' I'd said earlier for him to text me when he heard news of verdicts from the GAA. He'd said, 'Text? I can't operate that text at all!'

Anyway, like a lot of people, my own number is one that I'm not that familiar with calling out. I was so tired I accidentally gave Frank Diarmaid Falvey's number, which is very like my own.

Over the years Diarmaid's service to this team has gone way beyond the expectations of friendship. He is a friend to lots of players as individuals as much as he is to the team at this stage. I don't know why he does it or why he puts up with us, but now I had given Frank his mobile number.

Now, whatever about Frank disliking me, at least I'm a player. Falvey, this shaven-headed solicitor, this outsider who helps and advises us through so many things, I'd say Frank would put him down a hole and leave him there till he died!

It came to me the next morning. Oh Jesus, I gave Diarmaid Falvey's mobile number to Frank Murphy.

I rang Diarmaid, who'd be used to me thankfully, and said, 'Listen, if a fella who sounds like Frank rings you, don't tell him who you are because he'll think I'm taking the piss out him. Just say, "This isn't Dónal Óg at all," and then give him my number!'

As sure as Christ, anyway, Frank rings. Diarmuid knew straight.

He says, 'No, Frank, this isn't Dónal Óg at all. Dónal Óg's number is blah, blah, blah.'

Frank rang me then, all baffled.

'I rang some fella there, etc. etc.!'

'Oh Jesus, that's odd, I don't know what that's about, Frank!'

Semplegate went on for weeks, of course. We had a game looming against Waterford. There was a hearing in Portlaoise on the Friday evening before the game and a Cork man gave us a helicopter to travel up and back in because we were getting so close to the game and there was a chance we'd be playing. I remember Frank blessing himself as the helicopter was taking off and I said, 'Frank, if this helicopter went down it would sort a lot of problems in Cork!' He didn't laugh at that one at all, just looked at me for a couple of seconds.

So we flew to Portlaoise and gave our performance again and, my god, Frank was at his best. But no joy. Back down to Cork then that night, it was fierce late and Frank was talking, but some of the boys were fucked, they were gone, they were shattered.

Frank said to me, 'What do you want to do?'

I said, 'I'm clear in my head, I want to go to the death on this thing, I don't understand the thing fully but I'm not going to have any regrets in my mind, I want to fight this thing all the way.'

He actually said to us then that the thing was going to cost the County Board something like €20,000, some crazy figure; but he started listing out all that would have to be done, and we said, 'Right, we'll go for it.' In fairness to him, he said, 'Yeah, we'll go for it.'

So I set about emailing into the great black hole of the GAA's disciplinary structure at four in the morning. We went to Portlaoise again later that morning, a Saturday. I'd been up most of the night.

It was more like a courtroom setting this time. We were the boys, the very bold boys.

Frank. Jesus Christ, he was excellent. I watched and he destroyed the GAA solicitor. The poor guy had gotten the phone call at 4 a.m. to be here for this and he hadn't had much time for research. Frank had been doing nothing but research for weeks!

I watched the boys on the top table. They were the Tribunal Wing of the Disputes Resolution Authority, a group of lawyers and GAA greybeards that sits at the top of the complex GAA disciplinary structure. They were represented today by two fellas, including Eddie Keher from Kilkenny who has since had a lot of partisan things to say about Cork hurlers.

I thought that they were amused at Frank. Here was this mythical character of the GAA's back rooms, and he was now destroying this other fella, a bright young lawyer. I could even sense the boys were giving Frank a couple of breaks because they were enjoying the drama. And Frank was in his element.

We loved watching this. I would go up every now and then as if I was Junior Counsel on the case and whisper a couple of points to him. It was excellent courtroom drama and we were fighting for our lives because we had a match the next day. One of the boys had said that he wouldn't be capable of playing the next day, his head was so fried. I said, 'If I'm cleared I'm playing.' End of discussion.

So it went on till all hours again and then they read out a big proclamation of our guilt and that was it, it was over. Frank had put everything into it. That day we saw how capable he is and wondered at what might have been.

The next day in Thurles, Gerald asked, would the three of us walk out after the team had come on to the pitch. We were a bit reluctant, but we did. We got such a reception and I remember I put my fist up to the crowd and there was a massive roar. The word among the Cork supporters was: the boys were fighting till the early hours to try and get to play for the county – and of course the GAA did them!

Now we deserved the sanction, certainly Sully and myself did, but fuck, we nearly did it. The GAA's disciplinary system is like Vegas. It keeps inviting you to have another spin of the wheel.

Shane Murphy hit the crossbar with the last puck of the game that day. We lost by a goal. It would have been a famous victory.

Regrets? We released a brutal statement after Semplegate, absolutely terrible and embarrassing and self-righteous. When I think of that statement, I'm not proud.

I remember a funny thing which sums up the way it would be between myself and Frank. I have a habit of bringing a laptop to meetings and

keeping it open beside me; I'm not sure why, except that it gives you
a bit of an edge. At best I will have things on screen that I need to
remember and keep noting. At worst, if I need to buy a few seconds
of time, I can pretend to be consulting the thing.

Frank gets really spooked by the laptop. Gerald told me once that
he went to Frank looking for something for players and Frank said,
'Why not ask the man with the laptop!'

Around the time of Semplegate last summer we were at a meeting
with Frank about something else. It was known that Frank was keen
to conclude a deal on behalf of the Board with Coca-Cola for us to use
their Powerade drinks. This was an issue for us because Club Energise
have been very good to players and through the years of their sponsor-
ship of the GPA. For Cork players it would be a non-negotiable thing
that we take Club Energise bottles on to the field with us and we are
seen to drink Club Energise.

This meeting wasn't over the drinks issue, but we were sitting there
and I had the laptop open beside me and Frank was speaking and I
noticed on his desk there was a letter on Coca-Cola headed paper. All
I could see clearly was the letterhead; the smaller print was upside
down and I wouldn't have bionic eyesight at the best of times. Coca-
Cola weren't happy, from what I could make out, but I could read
only bits and pieces. I started bluffing Frank. I raised my eyebrows and
began pecking at the laptop keyboard and glancing back to the letter.

Frank looked at me and he saw what I was doing and I was happy
to let him see. We had already said that if one Powerade bottle appeared
on the field with the Cork team, we would be walking straight off,
even if it was an All-Ireland final.

So Frank says, 'Right. I think we need a little break, gentlemen.'

We got up and left the room. Five minutes later, when we recon-
vened, the letter was still there, but artfully Frank had it half covered
by something else. Just to let me know that he knew that I knew he
was dealing with Coca-Cola and had a letter on his table but . . .

On a Friday night, the week after Semplegate ended, Frank came to
us and asked us to cut a deal over the Club Energise/Powerade business.

Where Frank was coming from, I reckon, was the era of 'I do this

Born to hurl: my father has been at my shoulder at every step, including the eve of my first senior All-Ireland final in 1999 (*right*).

The Midleton CBS team that won the Harty Cup in 1995.

At the All-Stars with my parents, 2005.

I captained Cloyne in senior finals in 2004 (*above left*) and 2005 (*above right*). These two matches attracted an official combined attendance of over 40,000 in Páirc Uí Chaoimh.

Happy days: Ben
O'Connor lifts the
Liam McCarthy
Cup after we beat
Kilkenny in 2004.

We were back in Croke
Park for another final in
2005, beating Galway.

With two legends:
Ger Cunningham
and Sean McGrath.

Brothers forever: with Seán Óg on a team holiday.

On safari with Patsy Morrissey (*left*) and Frank Murphy in South Africa.

With the wizard: Joe Deane.

With Liam Walsh in his workshop, where we've spent many a happy hour.

The scoreboard read '*Fáilte go Staid Semple*' – but I don't think anyone expected this kind of welcome when we played Clare in a qualifier in 2008.

With Alan Kerins, Damian Joyce, Kevin Hartnett and a bunch of local kids in Zambia.

Barry Kelly sending me off for my second yellow card in the Galway game, in 2008.

It was a lonely walk to the dressing-room, just before half-time, and we were up against it . . .

. . . but our 14-man side went on to win an amazing match.

John Gardiner reading a statement at our first press conference during the strike: 'We would all, to a man, prefer to be labelled as difficult than as cowards; to be seen as fanatical rather than morally weak; to be seen as acting above our station rather than subservient and self-serving. We have no fear of the laws of the world; when there is a better player he must take our place; when there is a better team against us we will be defeated; when there is a better idea or ideal for Cork hurling, we will be irrelevant.'

Ten thousand people marched in support of us on 7 February 2009. I'm with Nicholas Murphy, Eoin Cadogan, Graham Canty, Brian Corcoran and John Gardiner.

Out in the cold in Mallow: our first day training on our own while on strike.

During the strike a certain element continuously put the word out that we didn't have the support of the people, and before we played Tipp the same people said that there wouldn't be people in Thurles to support us . . . wishful thinking on their part!

In the alley in Rochestown.

for you then you do this for me'. That was the way it always worked in Cork GAA.

Joe, Seán Óg, Tom Kenny, John Gardiner and I were there. We genuinely appreciated the way Frank had fought with us, but there was not a hope. The fellas sitting across from Frank didn't think like that at all.

We had to say to Frank that we really appreciated all he had done in Semplegate. And of course I couldn't help myself. I mentioned the letter.

Frank said, 'You know Coca-Cola aren't happy with me at all.'

I said, 'I know, Frank, I saw the all right.'

Anyway, we restated our position that, no matter what the match was, we would be heading back down the tunnel if we saw Powerade bottles out there on the pitch.

Gerald was with us that night. To be fair to him, he saw that this was a huge issue for us as players.

At one stage he said, 'Frank, we've had enough trouble now in tunnels for one year.'

Frank was looking at him in disgust.

It was a cul-de-sac. Frank insisted that we were playing with Cork, and the Board had a right to sign a deal. We said we didn't care what the Board signed, we had absolutely no contracts with the Cork County Board, we'd carry whatever bottles we wanted to carry when we went to play hurling.

We explained again. The GPA needed Club Energise just to survive. We believe in the GPA. So we're going to try to help Club Energise to survive and therefore help the GPA to survive.

I said that eventually the GPA would have nothing to do with that type of commercial stuff, that in the end it will only be doing what a players' organization should be doing: looking after players, making sure of proper coaching standards, insurance, maybe getting involved in making sure that rule changes work properly; all that type of stuff. By then the GPA should be part of the GAA and be funded by the GAA and be a positive influence on the Association. But to get to that stage it needs things like Club Energise.

Frank just sat silent for about a minute looking at us. The look on his face said, I'm stuck here, I'm caught in this one. They have no gratitude. They are stonewalling me.

And he was stumped. The times, they had a-changed.

24

Castletownroche, Co. Cork, 16 May

We played a challenge game against Limerick this evening in Castletownroche. Billy called for me at four o'clock and we struck off on our way to collect Nially Mac and Kevin. Geniuses that we are, we got a puncture straight away. A guy stopped in a Wexford car while we were changing the tyre. He said he was looking for directions to the airport, but it was as obvious as anything to Billy and myself that he just wanted to talk hurling. We did our best to be polite but we were in a rush and cut him short a little. Probably another black mark against the Cork hurlers!

It was shaping to be one of those nights. I cut my hand on the wheel when we were changing it and it started bleeding pretty heavily, which just added to the messing. I had to wrap insulation tape around it as we headed off. Perfect mental preparation.

There was a new field being opened in Castletownroche and we were there to do the honours with the inaugural match. All the players there at 5.15 and when I arrived there was an old man in the dressing-room who said that his job was to mind the place. I sat down beside him and he started talking.

Inevitably he brought up the strike. He said that he had been fully behind us but it was a small few that had been keeping us out.

It was one of those awkward 'don't mention the war' scenarios. The dressing-room wasn't exactly buzzing and I was conscious of the others in the room tuning in and out to what was being said. The man was in his seventies so I could hardly tell him to be careful about what he was saying!

The old man asked me about Joe Deane, how he was. He told me that he'd had testicular cancer himself. It was strange, sitting there in a Cork dressing-room, talking about the strike with these new faces all around and talking so frankly to this old man, talking about Joe who had been in dressing-rooms with me for so many years and now will never be again.

I got a proper dressing on my cut hand, a little scenario which amused Tom Kenny greatly.

'Is your finger all right, Ógie?'

I looked at him.

'Are you sure it's OK?'

I left my finger in the same upright position while pointing it in his direction to give him the message back.

Denis Walsh spoke really well again. Better, he told me I was captain for the night. I was proud. John Gardiner wasn't here so somebody needed to do the job, but after the winter we'd had, a time when I thought often that I might never get back to play for Cork again, this meant a lot to me.

All I said before we went on the field was that we needed to put our championship face on for the night. On the field after the warm-up Denis asked me to say a few more words to the lads to make sure that they were focused. I got them into a huddle and I said to them that last Tuesday night's training was the best session I had seen in years.

I meant it. It was the best because of the organization and purpose of it, but more importantly the sheer blazing intensity of it. I've been away for two weeks for the club championships, and the sessions which the lads have been doing meanwhile have been a pleasant surprise. At work I've been doing some projects that are out of my comfort zone, which is what I want, but it can be testing at times. One of these projects hadn't gone too great for me on Thursday evening. And having experienced the Tuesday session I was just really happy to get out on the field in the Páirc . . . That's how it should be. Denis Walsh's drills are excellent and his management of sessions is very good. Tuesday was great and Thursday was as good as I'd hoped for.

We played a game during the session on Thursday. I caught one ball and went to roll off The Hero, as Kieran Murphy from Erin's Own is known. As I turned away from him I felt a dart of pain to my back. I cleared the ball but dropped to my knees. Kevin Hartnett shouted at me to get up, so I did, but fuck it I was sore. The Hero must have clocked me! There was some slagging afterwards about it, but all good, and the whole thing was a sign of us pulling together and a sign of the intensity we are getting.

So in Castletownroche I told the lads that that intensity was what we needed to bring tonight. Intensity and teamwork. I told them what I meant by team, and I looked at Tadhg Óg Murphy as I spoke.

'If I'm in trouble, Tadhg Óg, you're coming to help me, and if you are in trouble, then I'm with you.'

There was an obvious reason to address this to Tadhg Óg. We have to mend the fences left by the strike.

At one of the open meetings we held during the strike, Tadhg Murphy, who is Tadhg Óg's father and who was a good player himself in the 1970s, came along to tackle us. He is a Sarsfields man and there would be bitterness towards us in Sarsfields at the best of times over the way Bertie Óg (who is Tadhg's brother) left the Cork management job in 2002. And Sars went and won the county championship last year for the first time since 1957, and our shenanigans were sort of taking away the pleasant aftertaste for them. There was one Sars man with us, Kieran 'Fraggy' Murphy, and quite a few with the rookie panel that Gerald put together. Tadhg Óg was one of them and his father had come along to stand up to us.

You'd have to say for the man that at least he had the balls to be standing up, but we saw him coming. We set up that meeting with a communications system between ourselves. If you looked at us as a group, we looked like thirty fellas in front of a meeting; but everyone was put in specific positions for specific reasons. I was sitting in the middle of the back row and over there was Joe Deane, where he could see everything that was going on and could relay anything that needed to be relayed. Joe's messages would come to me and I would pass them straight down to John Gardiner via Timmy Mac, who would be as safe as houses in that situation, nice and relaxed. (We changed it for the next meeting as we felt I would be better placed where Timmy was for the first meeting.)

As it happened, the meeting was far more positive towards us than we had anticipated. We got a standing ovation when we walked into the hall. Still, we knew Tadhg Murphy was going to come at us. We had to make sure he was seen to be allowed time to ask his question, but we didn't want it turning into the Tadhg Murphy show either. Gatchy was on duty with the microphone around the hall. Any word that needed to be passed to Gatchy would be texted from John Gardiner.

So Tadhg got his moment and he started to ask a couple of questions and he walked into the wrong fella. He was addressing the younger lads and spoke to Cathal Naughton, telling him that he should be worrying about his future. He finished with words of advice for Cathal: 'I'd just ask you to listen to your parents rather than listening to the older fellas on the panel.'

You had to admire him. This was a hard place to come to, and by saying what he was saying about parents he was taking the heat off his own son, making it clear that it was a family decision to take the Cork jersey while other players were striking to improve things. But Tadhg had directed the comments at the wrong young fella.

Naughton came straight back and said, 'First of all, I make my own decisions and I am here of my own accord, anyone who thinks I am being forced to be here is mistaken. And look, Tadhg, my parents would actually kill me if I went back with Gerald McCarthy.'

A massive cheer went up from the floor and Tadhg was a bit rattled by the whole thing as the microphone was whisked away from him, but for the rest of the meeting he was mad to get the mic back. Maybe he was coming at us with worse things.

We were watching him. I leaned over to Tom Kenny.

'Tom, what do you think, I don't think we should give that mic back to him at all.'

'Yeah yeah. Grand with me.'

Gardiner was OK with that too, so he got the message to Gatchy. 'Don't give the mic back to Tadhg!'

So for the rest of the meeting Gatchy was like Dora the Explorer, making the most convoluted journeys around the hall in order to avoid Tadhg, who was sitting right at the front. And people were giving out to Gatchy about the apparently stupid way he was going about getting the mic to fellas, and for us it was getting funnier and funnier watching him. Eventually, with the meeting going so well, we thought in fairness we should let Tadhg back in.

I leaned over to John Gardiner.

'John, what do you think, I think we should give that mic back to Tadhg – we are winning here by so much that whatever he'll say would be less effective than being able to say we wouldn't give him the mic.'

'Yeah yeah. Grand with me.'

So I said to Gardiner, 'Get the message to Gatchy.'

Gatchy made a beeline straight to Tadhg. He had his say and you had to respect him for it. He's a man of conviction and he came and said what he had to say to our faces.

So now I'm here with his son and the fences need mending, so I look at him and he nods back. Maybe things will never be perfect in this new team but we are working towards that.

We played well, very well to be honest, even though Limerick looked off the pace. We scored thirty-two points, and thirty-two points is good tipping any day. Last week, while I was playing for Cloyne, the lads scored twenty-two points on Dublin. We're moving well and we're pulling together.

After ten minutes I saw Kevin Hartnett down on his knees, holding his hand. The ref was putting pressure on me to take a puck-out but I pointed at Kevin.

'Ref, there is a man down there.'

He was taken off and replaced by Ray Ryan of all people. Bad enough to see Hartnett go, but seeing Ray Ryan come in? Ray was captain while we were out on strike and he had a lot to say for himself. He approached me one night in a nightclub and asked, could he talk to me. I couldn't. 'Ray, I've nothing to say to you.' Still. This has to be done. We have to drive on.

I had played well in the first half. I was seeing the ball well and was comfortable in my surroundings. Dr Con came up to me at half-time and told me that Kevin was in trouble with his finger. He said it was definitely broken and that it had been a dodgy pull. Of all the fucking luck. Kevin had been going well and had really taken on the attitude that he was going to fight tooth and nail to be kept on the panel.

I said to Con that I would say a few words about Kevin before we went back on to the field. A big angry part of me wanted to bury Limerick if it had been the case that he had been taken out. Con said, 'Not tonight, hold on to it, you can use it at a more appropriate time . . .' He was right. Big respect to the doc for that one.

After the game I met with lots of familiar faces. When I talk about the journey we have taken, I mean things like this. These were faces I wouldn't have known twelve months ago, but they have come to be friends of mine during the strike. Denis Withers, Secretary of the new club forum and a man who had helped us big-time during the strike. Bomber Roche and Pa the Piper. Noel. Eoin Cadogan's dad Jim and his brother Alan, all smiling. They know that we are going well.

We had a laugh together. I said it felt like we were back in Na Piarsaigh, training on our own on a Saturday morning in January.

The minute I got to the car I rang Kevin. He answered and said that he was just out of casualty. The finger had snapped in two. Poor bastard. I told him, 'Look, this is another test and a challenge; you know how to deal with it.'

He did say back to me that he thought he was being tested enough. No way I could argue that one with him.

We drove back. Nially Mac was in fine form. Nially is one of the characters of the team. Great company. The stories started to flow among us.

We used to go down, Nially and I, to the cryotherapy clinic in White's of Wexford. The temperature in the cryotherapy chamber is 110° below zero, dry cold. Nially, he has a fucking thing about cold. He loves it. Even in training he'd be inside in the ice baths, we'd be all finished and Nially would be still in there like a big polar bear with his head underneath the surface. That's Nially Mac. When Nially would be in the zone he would do everything perfectly, he'd do anything to improve.

On the morning of one All-Ireland final, Nially said to me, 'I think I'll go to the beach.'

'For fuck's sake, man, you can't go down to the beach this morning.'

'No, I'd love to go into the water.'

'For fuck's sake, Nially, we don't even know where the beach is. Do you know where it is? Is there even one?'

'I asked them down at reception and they told me.'

'No fucking way, Nially. It's not on. Really.'

So he went into the bath in the hotel room and filled it with cold water and got in there instead.

Down in the cold rooms in White's he is famous. You are only meant to stay in those chambers for three to four minutes max. Nially stayed in there for five and a half minutes. Regularly.

I used to go down with him sometimes. Corcoran said I was the ultimate inch fighter in his autobiography – I don't know about that but I know I am competitive, sometimes to the point of stupidity. After the four minutes I was saying, 'Right, Nially, let's go now, we've enough of it.'

No. Four minutes and thirty seconds would pass. And I'd be shuddering with the cold. 'C'mon Nially, we'll go.'

I stayed in there with him for five and a half minutes.

'C-c-c-c-mon N-n-n-n-niall-y!'

Even when I think back, it's not really funny because your body is so numb at that stage you can hardly think. The poor woman was getting panicky on the PA system. 'Come on, lads, you've to get out, you've to get out,' and I was thinking, Please, god, come and make him get out so I can get out too.

I thought I was going to have a heart attack over the lunatic, he nearly killed me in there and he'd come out then and be blowing his nose and roaring, thrilled with himself, and I was leant over a table, frozen solid. (This according to the version Nially was telling to Billy. And he wasn't far off the truth.)

To make it worse, that particular day, during the ten minutes you need to travel through Kilkenny on the way from Wexford to Cork I got a speeding ticket. In Kilkenny!!!

So we tell the old stories as we drive back in the car. We're long enough in the tooth for this now, old enough to be swapping old stories and the good memories we have built up over the last few years even though we have another season bearing down on us.

Myself and Billy went straight to the Alley Bar when we dropped Nially home. We were both down to work a shift. It was quiet when we got there, and I told Billy to drive on, that I would look after things, after all he has a wife and a couple of kids at home.

Billy wasn't gone ten minutes when the bar started to get busy.
Fucking typical. I got home at 2.30. Father stayed till the end with me
and was the last to leave the bar. He told me to call down the road to
home for a cup of tea and a chat. I called in to him all right and he put
on the kettle, but I told him I needed to hit the leaba. I couldn't stay
for the tea. I'm old enough to see the traps ahead on the road. The oul
fella with pints of Murphy's on board and Cork having played so well
tonight – that could have been a long one, with all due respect. We'd
have been talking till dawn.

A good day on the road to redemption. Sunday morning; text from
Hartnett:

> HEY BRO, JUST OUT OF SURGERY THERE. GOT A PLATE AND SOME
> PINS. WILL BE BACK HURLING IN 4WEEKS. B BACK IN TRAINING
> IN A FEW DAYS, I IMAGINE I CAN ATTEMPT ONE HANDED HURLING
> TOO. AIM IS TO BEAT YOU IN THE ALLEY. WIT ONE HAND ;-)

The anaesthetic obviously hadn't worn off yet.

25

One Thursday night soon after the whole South African business had
subsided and I had had earnest talks with about half the population of
Cork about my private life, we were down in Cloyne, watching some
match videos, when I got a phone call. Joe O'Leary, one of the county
selectors. Joe had worry in his voice. He'd gotten a call from a girl who
knew me, a solicitor in Dublin. There was a fella sharing the house
with her who was a reporter with *Ireland on Sunday* newspaper.

The reporter had been at an editorial meeting. I had been discussed
as a possible story. The paper had taken the view that they were going
to come to me and get me to do a story, and if I denied the story as
put to me, they would be letting me know that they would run with
it anyway.

For me, the people who needed to know knew. This new twist was
not part of the deal. I hadn't seen this girl in years but I trusted her if
the information was coming from her.

How was I going to deal with this now? If they were that confident
in the story, somebody must be feeding them stuff. I remember saying
to myself that this was going to be bad, something was going to break
this Sunday or the next or the one after, and it was going to be totally
uncontrolled and could set off a chain of stories. For everybody – the
family, the team, me – it needed to be controlled as well as possible.

I've often said that when I have the time I am going to find out who
was pushing this story harder and harder from Cork all the way to a
low-rent Dublin newspaper. Other times I have said, 'Do I really want
to know? It could be something I mightn't want to find out.' Back
then, though, with the walls closing in, I had no choices.

So I spoke to John Allen, one of the few men I know with no ego.
John's concern as manager and friend would always be for you. We
had spoken in South Africa; now I had to bring him up to speed on
what was coming down the chute.

The County Board had been on to John about things at this stage and they'd been saying they'd deal with it. John, sensing the lads in the blazers coming on stage with their blunderbusses, said, 'No thanks, this is very sensitive.' The boys kind of twigged then. Oh Jesus Christ, there is some truth to it! And straight away the County Board boys wanted to wash their hands of it. They couldn't handle it.

I said to John that if it came out, all I cared about was that we handle it properly within the team. John agreed.

So as usual when I'm in trouble I went to Diarmaid Falvey and asked him to type up a standard answer to any media questions. We weren't training till the following night, so we decided we should have this standard answer if any of the boys were rung by a paper or radio station.

Diarmaid wrote it. It was texted out to every player. 'If you get a call about any one of the other players, this is your answer.'

The answer they were to give was short and sweet and twofold: I don't know what you're talking about. I don't think it's a proper thing for you or your paper to be investigating.

I was rattled. I was in Dublin that day for a meeting between the GPA and John O'Donoghue, the Minister for Sport. I came out of the house and noticed the car had a flat tyre. I went to fix it but the nut lock wouldn't fit the nuts on my car's wheel. I left it there. Got a taxi to the airport. Shaken. I'll never fucking forget, we went in to John O'Donoghue, and I wasn't prepared. John O'Donoghue said something and I got tongue-tied. I hadn't a clue what my answer should be. I turned to Dessie Farrell and more or less said, Dessie, help me here.

I flew home and asked one of the boys to collect me. I had a juvenile coaching thing to do for the club, and there was a hurry on. I did the coaching thing with the boys, went in home, ate my dinner with the family, came out again and called Billy. Told him about the car problem. Asked if he could get the right size nut lock. He collected me the next day and we went to my car. He asked to see what I had got. I showed him. He tried it. Turned the nut first time. I'm a qualified tradesman. Things like that are a piece of cake. The little caps over the bolts – I never took them off. My mind was elsewhere.

Billy looked at me and said, 'You're not thinking right at all, what's the story?'

What was the story? When would it appear? At the next Cork training session some of the lads who had received texts and who hadn't been involved in chats with me in South Africa or since needed a little clarification.

Seán Óg was the captain and he made a speech. Straight to the point. 'Look,' he said, 'this is the story. One of our fellas is in trouble, bang, bang, bang.' Straight down the line.

I sat there before Seán Óg even started, wondering how would the fellas handle this, who knew it was me, would I start becoming more trouble than I was worth within the group? Brian Corcoran had come over, though. He sat down beside me for the team meeting and put his arm on my shoulder. Just like that.

And I knew that was a message to allcomers that maybe they would have seen a bit of weakness in me at the time, but that Corcoran was behind me anyway. And having Corcoran with you was good enough. Whatever about anybody taking me on for some reason, they sure as fuck weren't going after the both of us. Not Corcoran. That arm, the arm of one of the great heroes, it meant a lot.

It wouldn't have happened anyway. There would be no fracture, no cracking. Not with those boys. That was how we dealt with it.

As sure as eggs are eggs, of course, one of the lads got the media phone call, and the lad who got the call was Sully! Sully being Sully, he had the official version written down beside him both in his office and in his car, imagine that. So he got the phone call, says to himself, 'Fuck it, we're off to the races here,' picks up the card, blah, blah, blah. Hangs up straight away. Fair play to him.

And *Ireland on Sunday* newspaper?

I spoke to Dessie about it, and his view was that we need to do something about it as an issue that could affect any amateur player. Dessie had had intrusions into his own life, but I wasn't too worried at this stage about making a big issue of it. I said, 'Look, I don't want to make a fuss,' but Dessie was strong on it. His point was that if it was anyone else, we'd be doing it for them. So he spoke to Seán Kelly, then the President of the GAA.

The difference between Kelly and the Cork County Board was striking. Seán Kelly got on to *Ireland on Sunday* and spoke to them about the issue and put serious pressure on them not to go with it if they knew what was good for their GAA coverage.

I always remember that about him, he was always a brave man anyway, but that was a small private thing he went on the line for.

That should have been the end of it, but it wasn't. I was in work one evening and a security guard, a fella called Denis Allen, came down to me. Denis and I would have had plenty of rows through the years. He would be strong on the old trinity of Irish life – GAA, church, Fianna Fáil – and I would be in trouble with all three at any given time!

Where I work in DePuy, a medical devices manufacturer, we are in a controlled environment. This day I was heading down the corridor, and Denis came running after me. I knew right away something was up. There was no running allowed in the building (and Denis is the security man) but he had been in reception and somebody had been buzzed up through the barriers and in. She had said she was looking for Dónal Óg Cusack. Sharp enough he knew, just by the way the question was framed or pitched. There was something up. He put two and two together and wheeled around before the receptionist could say anything.

'Have you an appointment with Dónal Óg?'

'No. I haven't.'

'Where are you from?'

'I'm a journalist from *Ireland on Sunday*.'

'Oh. Sorry, but Dónal Óg is not here at all today.'

It was an unreal bit of luck that Denis was there. I would have been doorstepped in my own workplace otherwise.

As it happened, I was on the phone to Dessie when Denis came down and told me. I said to Dessie, 'They're here now in my work. I've got to go.'

Next I got a phone call from my father, saying that there had been a letter handed in at home and there was another letter which had been handed in across the road to another family of Cusacks. And then my brother Conor rang. Conor said to me that Dad was at home looking at the unopened letter like it was a ticking bomb. He was going insane over all this pressure and the helplessness of being at the centre of it, waiting for something to break. The brother said to get home quick, to open up the letter fast and put Dad out of his misery because he was going to crack and open it himself at any second.

I did. The letter inside was so slimy that you wouldn't pick it up with a pair of tongs. 'Delighted to hear about my news. Would love to do a story. Blah, blah, blah.'

And you wonder about these people sometimes and their justification that they are just doing their job. *Ireland on Sunday* impacted on a lot of lives just with the threat of going to print about the private life of an amateur sportsperson.

The family were under strain, an entire team was under pressure. Even my employer changed the process for people coming to visit employees as a result of the intrusion.

And of course I had to open a second round of talks with other guys on the team, fellas who hadn't been told but who would have had a right to feel, if they read this in a newspaper first, that they should have been told.

It was draining and for another while it sucked away what energy I had left. Again they were tough, earnest conversations where you had to be genuine with everybody and address their concerns.

When finally it was all done and everybody knew all there was to know about the private life of the fella in the hooped Cork jersey, we turned our eyes back to the three-in-a-row.

26

Maybe it is a harsh thing to say, but the Galway win in Gerald's last season belonged to Dónal and to John Allen more than it would ever belong to Gerald. We had limped towards the game, looking for a way to function around him if we couldn't function with him. Cathal O'Reilly had lifted us a little, but we were struggling and the Cork public's patience was wearing thin.

Gerald was leading us shuffling like a chain gang into oblivion. Beaten by Tipp in the Páirc. Almost beaten by Dublin in the Páirc. By the time we were to face the Galway of Ger Loughnane and Joe Canning we were dead men walking. We were discounted goods. Irrelevant before death. The worst way for men to go.

On the day, Galway exploded on us. Well, Joe Canning exploded on Sully and myself anyway. All summer the pressure had been mounting on Sully and when Canning caught a ball after ten minutes and moved across the square, dragging Sully off with one hand and then batting the ball past me using the other, it looked like the worst kind of trouble. Sully and myself were in for an afternoon of drama.

We didn't know that the worst was yet to come. We got into injury time in the first half. Alan Kerins, Galway forward, old friend of mine, etc., came bearing down on us, swapping passes with Damien Hayes. The last pass put Alan through on the edge of the square.

Two choices: let him score or bring him down. I brought him down. He scored anyway. I was on a very harsh yellow card for running into Niall Healy just after Canning had taken his goal when fending off Sully earlier. A couple of minutes later one of the umpires had stepped into the goal and confiscated my batch of sliotars like a teacher taking away your chewing gum. And then the referee, Barry Kelly, was into me for a little chiding session about my quick puck-outs. So now he had his moment. Barry Kelly was nearly beside himself with pleasure, showing me a second yellow and then a red.

So we were at the edge of the precipice. The County Board boys must have sensed blood in the water. Sully in trouble. Me taking the long walk. Galway suddenly rampant. They put away their penalty just before the break. They celebrated and began sharpening the knives for the second half.

It was bad. Marty Coleman came in and his first job was to face a penalty from Joe Canning. Could have blown Marty's head off. I just felt bad, leaving Marty in that sort of situation. Bad enough going in cold, but facing a penalty straight off? Ah fuck. I remember walking off and, in fairness to Dr Con, he knew that I was getting fierce stick and he walked along with me. Small little things like that make a difference.

Half-time came as a mercy. I was in the dressing-rooms and I remember that Deccie O'Sullivan the physio, Gatchy and Dr Con were on to me. They said, 'You'll have to talk.' That was the last thing I wanted, but I did speak because fuck there was fierce spirit sitting in that dressing-room and if me speaking was going to make a difference, I'd do it.

I said, 'Right, lads, here we were, we are dying here, this is it, is it all over for us?'

The fellas, they knew we were in trouble. Sometimes you want direction. On a day like that, maybe the emotion was what we needed.

I just said to them that it couldn't end like this, I said that someday we'd be gone but we couldn't go down like this, and I said we were brothers and this couldn't be the end. Not like this.

And I remember saying, 'Look, boys, I never fucking asked for anything, never did, off any fella here, but lads I don't want it to finish like this for us and please don't let it finish like this.' I said that we were still alive and we could do something about it. And told them something that my grandfather (who is eighty-four and goes up for a few pints every day and smokes heavily) always says to me: 'Live while you can, Dónal Óg, and die when you can't help it.'

And I knew the tears were rolling down my cheeks and I looked around and there were other fellas crying, with madness or love or whatever it was that held us. I don't know if anything in life will ever be so raw and intense again.

But we were going to get put to the knife. Teams know that. They know when fellas are going to knife them. Out on the field it's different from the way we pretend it is on *The Sunday Game* in those harmless interviews. We can all be some kind of gentleman off the pitch, but out on the field on a championship afternoon, especially at that level, most of the fellas have that killer inside them, some bit of badness in them. And if they don't have it in them, they have to have the capability of doing it through their skill anyway.

We were going out to be buried by a younger, hungrier, meaner team. Our last hope was to remember what we meant to each other.

Die when you can't help it. There was strength enough and unity enough in us to save this one.

The selectors did make some good changes that day. We'd shuffled predictably enough to make up for my loss. Cathal Naughton had come off to let Marty Coleman replace me, but as soon as half-time came Sully was called ashore and Naughton was back on.

We were playing two men in the full-forward line in front of the Galway goal. For Cloyne against Midleton a couple of years before, we had a man sent off and at half-time I made the same call tactically: two men in front of the goal and just get the ball in. Afterwards I remember thinking about it and how it could work better.

When you leave two players in the full-forward line, leaving them in front of the goals is the wrong thing to do. It means that almost every ball that goes in there will be fought three against two. So what we should have done was put the two men in the two corners and played all the ball up the wings, literally every ball up the wings, and then get our runners to come through the middle. What you actually find then is that it will take the extra man out of the game because you have the bodies coming in anyway when you run at him.

So when the second half began I said to myself that the boys were setting up wrong because I'd made the same mistake myself. I went to the selectors and I said, 'Lads, you can tell me to fuck off out of here now if you want, but I think we need to look at how we're set up,' and in fairness to the boys they told me to sit down on the bench with them, and they listened.

I said to them, 'This is what we should do, we should play Joe and

Hoggie out in the two corners and get the word to all our fellas to play the balls up the wings and then go and support.'

It sounded good to them so they said, 'Yeah, that's it.' So the message then had to be sent on to the boys that this was what we were doing, but the reality was that things had got so bad in the dressing-room that the fella that was running the message was sometimes telling the boys that Dónal Óg had said to do this. The boys would half believe in it if they thought it was coming from one of their own. If they thought that it was Gerald that was saying it, there was a chance of them just shaking their heads.

So for a while we just dropped balls in to Ollie Canning, who was the extra man. He swept them up and gave them back to us. But then we started hitting the corners and the ball stuck like darts in one corner especially. Joe Deane's.

Joe terrorized them.

We knew that was the game then, and the boys cut loose. Joe was Joe, tidy and perfect, and soon Ollie Canning had to be switched to mark him full-time. Conor Dervan sweeping up wasn't nearly as worrying.

Cathal Naughton ran everywhere, ripping them apart with his speed. And Benjy got on more and more ball as everything just unfolded perfectly for us. John Gardiner came back to the square to wrestle with the mighty Joe Canning.

Jesus, it was stunning. Benjy landed a sideline cut with just under twenty minutes left to put us two ahead. He was forty-five metres out and that's some feat. Two minutes later, Canning landed a sideline from nearly twenty metres further away to pull it back to one point. Fuck.

The intensity burned your face but you couldn't look away. After Canning's sideline we got the next three points. The pace and the thunder of the game never fell. This was one of those rare afternoons. For Loughnane as the manager of Galway it was a last stand. For some of our team it was the same.

We were pulling away when the whistle went and the scenes that followed were unreal, 'The Banks' being sung in the Thurles sun as we struggled to get back to the dressing-room. We looked at one

another in that cool half-lit dressing-room and we knew. This was a
win that came from what we were, from the battles we had fought
and the journey we had taken; it was a win for each other and for
ourselves as brothers, a win for what we stood for. We embraced and
we smiled. No medals but a win had never been sweeter.

Gerald headed out to tell the media how it had been done.

27

Clarecastle, Co. Clare, Saturday 23 May

I'm starting to feel good about the boys.

We are away for a training weekend a week before we play Tipperary. We had an all-hurling session this morning. Denis Walsh said that it would be good for the keepers to join in, and he explained why. He was right. What the session was focusing on was totally applicable to us: no overhead pulling! We three goalies were happy to be part of it.

As a group we are starting to blend. Maybe teams are inclined that way. Maybe it's a reflex, like knowing you have to be fit. We know if we don't become a team, all our journeys to get here will have been pointless.

Pa Finn, a selector, came out with a classic during one of the drills. Denis Walsh was setting it up, putting us in pairs, and said that one person was to dictate and the other was to follow . . . As I stepped up Finn says, 'Well, Cusack you are the dictator anyway.'

Maybe you had to be there, but in terms of where we were coming from as a group that is progress. We can joke about all that stuff at this stage.

Towards the end of one session the lads took a number of penalties – Hoggy, Curran, John Ga . . . We talked about Brendan Cummins, the Tipperary keeper, and there was a bit of debate. I told some of the guys who I didn't think needed to be involved in the debate that if I was a coach I would have a buzzer and every time they came on to the field it would go off and I could hunt them out over the side-lines again.

One of them made a funny comment that I didn't quite catch but was told afterwards to a good laugh what he'd said. 'Ger Mac was right. That fucker is uncoachable!'

This making-jokes business is grand, but enough is enough. Respect!

After the session we went back to the hotel for a bit of grub and then I asked Gatch to bring a couple of us into town. I wanted to get some bread and fruit for the night. Some other lads asked if they could come along. Aisake and Kevin had to go in the back of the van. Gatchy and myself got out at a shop and went inside, leaving the pair of them locked in back. We could hear them knocking – 'Let us out!' We were intent on leaving them there and bringing them back to the hotel without saying a word, but while we were in the shop they busted free.

It was a small thing, a little laugh among a few fellas on a team, but we need moments like that, we need a laugh like we had at what Pa said this morning. That's what oils teams and keeps them going. This team has been in the coal mine too long, bent over and in the dark. We need the moments of lightness.

We play an As versus Bs game in the evening. Good tempo. I do my best to communicate as much as possible with Cads and Conor O'Sullivan, as I think they are both going to start for next week. Cads is a friend and we work together and go to the alley together. Conor was one of the players in Gerald's replacement squad.

At one stage Conor makes a mistake and Cads, who is pumped, fucks him out of it. When we are done, I tell Cads that it wasn't on and if anything like that happens next week we need to act in a controlled manner. No fucks thrown at each other in front of the opposition. I tell Conor O'Sullivan not to worry about it as Cads means well and to trust himself next week as he is well good enough.

After the game we went back and had a meal and a meeting. By chance I ended up sitting with Denis Walsh. He's a good thoughtful guy and I really enjoyed talking tactics and coaching with him.

Before he came to us as manager, Denis was a bit of an unknown quantity. He'd had a brief stint at the start of the season with Carrigtwohill but all I knew about him was from my friend Thomas O'Brien, saying to me that he thought they had found the manager they needed. Next thing, he was Cork manager and I was recalling something that somebody else said about him. Damien Irwin, a former player himself with Cork and Killeagh, said to me that if he gets as much out of a team as he got out of himself, he will be a great manager.

A board was produced with a list of names on it. My name was down for a rub at midnight! My back is always a concern because of the scoliosis. There is not much you can do about scoliosis unless you go down the brace route like Forrest Gump, but the more rubs I get in it, the better. I keep it at bay and ease the muscles that are affected by it.

The physios were up until one in the morning doing the rubs. It's some dedication. In 2006 I remember Richie Mooney, one of our masseurs, was instructed to stay in the team room all night, and anything a player would want, he was to look after it. Fair play. I hope they know how much a part of it they are and how we depend on them.

I had my rub and headed back to the room. I'm in with Marty and, as always, I enjoy his company. We are in competition but we are friends. People would have the impression that between us three goal-keepers there would be resentment and jockeying and one-upmanship. Not so.

Marty and Nashy are both good enough to play now. I know that and they know it. But I hope that whenever I am gone, they'll know I tried to create as good an environment for them as for myself and never, ever did I try to steal a march on them with anything. Every-thing that we ever got for the goalies was got for three.

Yeah, there's also a selfish side to me as well in that, because I know that if the boys are good (and they are), then they are pushing me on as well. If I can stay pushing on, I'm going to keep on trying to have the little edge, keep training on Christmas Day, etc.

It goes back to why I like to work with fellas like Hartnett or Seán Óg, apart from friendship. There is that selfish part of me that knows training with those fellas who have a savage hunger for training just drags me along. I get on well with the two goalkeepers and the day that I'm dropped or retired I'll be happy to see one of them play, but I don't want it to happen for a while yet, and meanwhile the best compliment I can pay Marty and Anthony is to work like a demon to keep my place.

Last summer, when I got sent off against Galway, it was Marty who came in (as his dad had done when Paddy Barry was sent off in his last game in goals for Cork in 1974). Marty did great. Afterwards he came into the dressing-room and he came over to me and he hugged me and I know this, I swear to Christ, I'd say we were holding on to each other for about two minutes and Marty was crying like mad because it was a great day for him and I was crying also. It was a pressure thing for him, coming in like that, and for fuck's sake he'd know I'd be close to him and I have great time for him. Rooming with Marty just increases my good feeling about the team this weekend.

Sunday 24 May

The alarm wakes us at 8.20 a.m. and we head down for breakfast.

The team has a 9 a.m. meeting with Denis Walsh to review and prepare for the week ahead. Training has been cancelled this morning; there is a pool session instead, as the management feels that the guys have done enough for the week.

The outfield lads are on a different preparation curve from ourselves, though, so I ask Denis, would he be all right with it if we did our own session. He is OK with that, so the three of us go down to the Clare-castle club with Eddie Jackman, one of the physical trainers, to do our own session at 10.15.

It's an excellent session. Work with the medicine ball, plenty of hurling. It's on one of those lovely mornings when you just feel alive and appreciate what it is to be a player.

Nashy is not in great form, though. He tells me later that he has been told he is all right to play with the intermediates next Sunday; that means he is number 3. We all have our own battles.

Johnny Callinan, one of Clare's greatest players, calls down to the field and I have a good chat with him after. He's a part of the mytho-logy of this place. Talking to him, I realize Clarecastle was a good choice as a place to come to a week before the championship.

As we are training, a lot of the local lads watch on. Then they start a game of backs and forwards themselves. There are some places you go and you can feel that hurling is in the soul of the place. I can feel hurling here, it reminds me of home.

Anthony Daly is from here, from down on Madden's Terrace in the village. He was a bit of a bogeyman to us in the mid-1990s when Clare were strong, but I always liked Daly. I always could identify Clare's struggle as being like our own in Cloyne. Johnny Callinan could have hurled anywhere, he was that good, but he played fourteen years for Clare without winning a Munster championship medal. Sitting in Cloyne, where the struggle seems endless, something like that makes you think. Clare became unpopular very quickly in the 1990s but I always took a bit of inspiration from them and understood why they had to do certain things in order to compete.

Daly was managing Clare when we beat them in the All-Ireland semi-final in 2005. What I saw in the Clare jerseys that day was a well-motivated and well-organized group. You could tell their brains and their heart came from Daly. After the game I wanted to write to him, and I actually got his address from my friend Christy O'Connor, the goalkeeper and writer. In the end I didn't write the letter as I was afraid it might sound patronizing and Daly wouldn't appreciate it, but in his home place this morning you can get a sense of that madness and love for hurling which makes him what he is. Dublin hurling is lucky to have him. I hope he succeeds there.

With the session over we head back to the hotel for a meal and then pile on to the bus to head back to Cork. I brought some work documents with me to review and get as much of that work done on the bus home as possible. Must be getting old.

On the way home, myself, Nially and Billy go for an ice cream. Coincidentally we meet Tom Kenny, Kevin and Shane Murphy in the same place. The sun is shining and we have a little extension of the weekend. A good week's work and a weekend of excellent training done. Tipp in Thurles next week. Nice ice cream. And the lads for company.

Again I tell myself to appreciate and live in the moment, but one thought comes into my brain. In four of the last five championship games that we have lost, going back to the All-Ireland final of 2006, Barry Kelly has been the referee. He is down to ref us on Sunday.

As a player you want consistency in terms of what a referee will look for. Kelly always comes down to me before games and often he will give me messages which contradict what he said the previous day. Against Tipperary last summer he came in and said, 'Don't come outside the square for your puck-outs; you can take them quick, I don't care how fast you puck out the ball, but don't come outside the square.' Then, before the game against Galway, not long after, he says, 'Don't be pucking the ball out fast.'

I said, 'For fuck's sake, Barry, you're after making fierce bad calls against me over the last couple of years, a couple of weeks ago you were telling me the opposite.'

And he just said, 'I'm the boss,' and showed me the whistle like a cop flashing his badge.

To me it seems as if he likes the idea of coming down to me and laying down the law.

Some of the decisions still bug me. He gave a 65 against me for coming out of the square with the puck-out against Tipp in 2007. Fine, but do it to every goalie, every time it happens.

In the 2006 All-Ireland final he gave Kilkenny a handy point from a free at a vital stage of the game, claiming that I had thrown the ball instead of hand-passing it. I hadn't.

Against Waterford in the league semi-final two years ago, his umpires called a ball over the line that wasn't. Dan Shanahan hit the ball across and it hit Sully's leg. I was in the ready position when it came off Sully and I made the save. The boys thought it was a goal because they had made their minds up before I got there; in their mind's eye it was a goal and they reached for the flag. But I actually saved it on the line and it rolled out. They had just assumed I wouldn't get to the save. It was a brutal, appalling decision. Genuinely the save was one of the best I had ever made.

And then the business of sending me off against Galway. I brought my friend Alan Kerins down as he came through. He put the sliotar in the net anyway.

Alan said to Kelly that his goal should stand. Kelly said to Alan, 'I can't send him off if I give you the goal.'

Technically he was correct, but in my reckoning he took a fair bit of pleasure out of showing me his red card. Referees need the establishment, and some of them play to the establishment because of that. Needless to say, I am not part of the establishment. I am a high-profile target.

So I have decided that if he comes up to me before the game on

Sunday I will tell him what I think of him. If he leaves me alone, then I am better off staying away from him.

Jesus. Enjoy the sun. Eat the ice cream. Barry Kelly is a problem to which you have no solution.

28

We've been back training for a while now and I love just being back in the rhythm of it. Pushing hard. Recovering. Feeling like we are moving somewhere.

Funny thing is, although I look forward to training every day, a couple of guys around the team have been on to me about how quiet I am these times. You'd think they would be grateful.

Joe O'Leary said to me that if anyone asked the new lads what kind of fella I was, they'd say that I was a crank. Joe reckoned I was gone fierce fucking quiet. He's concerned.

'You're a quiet fellow always, Ógie – probably way quieter than your reputation portrays you – but right now you're gone too fucking quiet.'

I know people will find it hard to believe, but I am often genuinely quiet. John Allen used to give out awads at training occasionally. I have a sugar bowl on my table right now for my quietness. The Silent Pig Award! It has the words 'It is the quiet pig that eats the most' written on the side.

Then Dr Con said it to me a couple of days later. Con would know a lot of what's going on around the team, fellas would be saying stuff to him. Con advised me that I needed to start smiling and talking around the place.

Here's the thing. When we went back there, I just wanted to get back playing, just wanted to enjoy going into the dressing-room, getting ready, going out to do the stuff and getting away home. I made a decision to try to enjoy and appreciate this thing we fought so hard for – but fellas pick me up wrong there sometimes. That's the only thing bothering me. I actually love the idea of just going in, not talking to anyone if I don't want to talk to them, doing my training and just have my own little zone of peace and tranquillity.

In one of Gerald's early statements, before the deluge of them arrived, he said that he reckoned there was a predisposition to conflict among an element in the Cork dressing-room.

Ah, Gerald boy.

Take a slice of the strike. Just a couple of weeks. Without mentioning all the abuse, the hate mail, the immediate sense you get even in work situations of somebody being for you or being against you, all those little things that wear you out. Take the season of goodwill.

Christmas was a low-energy time but there was no chance of the two armies coming out of the trenches and meeting on no-man's-land for a puck-around and a few Club Energises. On the day before Christmas Eve I trained at 7 a.m., worked, went home and headed back to work later for the Christmas shutdown. I spoke with Kevin and organized training for over the holidays. John Ga called. Poor man was having serious difficulty with Derry Gowan, his liaison with the County Board. John said that Derry always sounded as if someone was with him. Once he answered the phone with the words, 'Yes, Frank.'

John was getting fed up with the entire farce. Just before Christmas, Gowan was due to get more information on the structure of the proposed talks – we had gotten burnt once already in the strike, and the next time we were heading into talks we wanted to know exactly what we were getting into. Gowan delayed and eventually couldn't give the clarification. Any time he was pressed he would tell John that he would have to come back to him. In fairness to him, Derry is old and was in and out of hospitals a lot during this period. Another man who should never have been put in that position. Of course the organ grinder himself was lying low so we had to put up with this.

Finally and incredibly he gave John one hour to come back to him with a suggested name of a person to mediate talks or he would appoint someone himself. John said, 'Sure you can't do that as we don't know what is meant to be happening.' He went ahead and did so anyway, naming Olann Kelleher as Chair of any forthcoming talks.

We hadn't agreed to these talks as we didn't know what the structure would be. And delegates who had been party to the original Board motion all agreed that it had been stated that all three parties to the talks had to be agreed on the Chair. Having been set up so badly, the thing was destined to failure from the start. It had to be played out, though.

To celebrate the great triumph of appointing Kelleher, the Board sent out a release to all media outlets in the country, a statement designed to create the impression that things were getting better and that they were in control. The statement also had the effect of putting more pressure on us. It would look bad if we were to reject a neutral man even though he'd been appointed by the Board.

We had to scramble again to get our story out and regain lost ground. We got limited stuff in the *Examiner* and couldn't get the *Echo* (we were still very Cork-centric in our media dealings). Next morning, travelling early to the ball alley with Kevin, I rang John Ga and we decided on the route to take. We got a hold of the *Echo* late on, but along with the other outlets in the country the back page read 'Players move closer to agreement'.

Derry Gowan had got us on that one.

Good news? Any? The footballers announced that they were not going to a medal-presentation ceremony over Christmas. (We still haven't received our 2006 medals, by the way!) My brother Conor's only inter-county medals came that year, but the Board still haven't given them to us.

We trained on the last Saturday morning before Christmas. There were twenty-four of us there, cold but grimly determined. We were feeling a little besieged and the training sessions every week reminded us of what we had been.

(We moved the sessions around a lot. Clubs would come under pressure not to host us. Calls would be made 'in a private capacity', just letting the club know that the Board was aware that we had been training there. Mallow were good to us. Clyda Rovers were good to us. We ended up towards the end in Na Piarsaigh most Saturday mornings; the club were wonderful to us and the women who came in to make us hot food Saturday after Saturday will always have our gratitude. They did it at a time when people would have been urging them to poison us and not feed us. And they did it with such humour and warmth, it touched me and will remain with me.)

On this last session before Christmas we had homework to catch up on. Gerald had previously sent an open letter to all of us. We felt it was a PR stunt. After training we worked through a response and all agreed that we would sign it.

Later Gerald would accuse me of sending the letter to him at Christmas, as if the letter was designed to ruin his holidays. Ah for fuck's sake, Ger. You and the PR boys fire off all this rubbish and you think that we'll hold off till well after Christmas in case your lobster bisque turns rancid?

That night, the 2008 panel headed into town on a night out. We started at Ger Cunningham's pub, then went on to Mulligan's and to Rearden's. Good night – good session. Made a change from all the doom and gloom. I heard the next day that some of the younger lads got a bit of stick off some lads from the St Finbarr's club that night. The Barrs are Gerald's club.

I hated hearing that – one of the younger lads had been in tears with temper over what was said and not being able to fight, but we had agreed among ourselves that, whatever happened, we couldn't get into any trouble. To be fair to the lads in question, even though they would be well able to look after themselves they just headed off home. Must have been hard, though. Everything was happening together.

I was drained. During Christmas week I had work in Dublin. Meetings with the club in Cloyne. Training. Everything was happening together. One night I got home to the parents' house in Cloyne at 2.30 a.m. I will never forget this, my mother came down and asked me, did I want some food. I said that I was OK, thanks, I just needed to polish my shoes as I was going to Dublin on the 6 a.m. train. She took the shoes from me and polished and shined them and gave me a lecture about taking it easy. No irony there from a woman up in the early hours polishing her grown son's shoes!

On the 23rd, when I shut down the plant for the Christmas break, I got a sad feeling over me. The end of another year – I spent a bit of time thinking about all the Christmases I had spent there, and I hoped people would say that I was as positive an influence on the place as it has been on me. I really appreciate what DePuy and the people down there in the Ringaskiddy plant have done for me.

I have always appreciated being able to go to work. I started picking fruit in Ballymaloe, moved on to making windows for the Cahills in Cloyne, served my time in Cork City with Seán Ahern. Seán is a legendary figure in the electrical game in Cork. At one stage he had up to 150 men working for him. I started working for him back in 1995 in the Mercy Hospital. The DePuy site in Ringaskiddy was being constructed and I was sent down to work for a guy called Mick Noonan. I've been there ever since. My job title is Electrical Engineer for the site.

Mick was a great character and had a big influence on my thinking about life. He would send me off to do jobs by myself around Europe and the States, in part because he knew it would be good for my development. He was that type of man. He is now engineering manager in GE Healthcare.

Mick had a lot of tragedy in his family life and one thing he always said to me was that death didn't put sport into a less significant perspective; it reminded us instead of how important sport is, and how much it brings to our lives. 'People would be giving out about you taking hurling too seriously, Dónal Óg. When you are alive and well you can't take it seriously enough.'

About eighteen months ago I nearly made a bad mistake. I had a lot of involvement in stuff outside of DePuy and it was pulling me apart and I felt that I wasn't giving DePuy the time they deserved. I had a number of other offers and I made up my mind that I would leave. I went to my manager, Gary Clerkin, about it and gave him the option that I could work out my notice or that I would work until the end of the next quarter in order to give him time to get a replacement. (I imagined a worldwide head-hunting operation would have to be cranked up!)

Having a wise head, he told me to take my time. He sat me down and listened to my reasons for wanting to leave and said not to do anything until he came back. And he came back with a plan and some advice, and he saved me from making a big mistake in my life. You always need help like that along the way, and I was lucky I got it there. I work for himself and a man called Dan Donovan, and between them I could have no better people to work for. They are demanding, but they want to see you develop and get on and will help you to do so.

Kevin and I trained on Christmas Eve morning. On Christmas Day, Seán Óg and his brother Teu joined us in the gym and in the alley. Some Christmas Days you train and wonder if any of your rivals are pushing themselves this way. That morning we wondered if we would be anybody's rival, come the summer.

Afterwards the two Ó hAilpíns came back to the house and showered and had food. It was Christmas Day and we just enjoyed each other's company. I hope that friendship and respect never deserts us.

(I remember once, myself and Seán Óg were invited to a dinner party out in Falvey's place. We were the only ones there without PhDs – Diarmaid will kill me for saying that but he'll know what I mean – so after a while we struck off into Cork, where we met Aisake and Teu. To make a long story short, we ended up in Instinct, a gay club. The lads caused some stir in there. Seán Óg still gets a great kick out of telling the story of Aisake getting chatted up and put in a bit of a corner. One of the lads' old schoolmates came up to them and he was cross-dressed. Quite a night out for the lads.)

The holidays were short and sweet. Unrest never sleeps. We had a teleconference with the player reps on 28 December and decided that we wouldn't enter into talks that involved Gerald McCarthy. In our eyes there was no point in sitting down with him, and the group was strong in saying that. One message now: we will never stand in the same dressing-room as him again.

Full of festive goodwill, though, we decided that we would meet with the Board as there would obviously always be a Board needed somewhere in the equation. And we would meet with Ollan Kelleher.

By now John Ga was starting to realize the truth of something I'd said to him back at the start. If this went on for any length of time, he would feel as fatigued and tired as a soldier at war. The whole thing would take up all his thoughts, keep him awake at night, make him feel unhealthy and drained. And when he felt that way, that's when he'd have to be strongest.

With that in mind, I think myself and John had a heavy heart about the whole Ollan Kelleher adventure. We met him first in his offices in Cork City, just John and myself. We started the game off pulling hard.

We said that we were sports people but that we were capable of playing any game that was necessary. We told him that we hadn't agreed to him but we had no objection to him either. We told him we had no notes, or paper for taking down notes, as we were very clear in our position. We let him know that position. And we let him know our position on not meeting with Gerald McCarthy.

He told us how he had been appointed and said that he was used to dealing with sports people. I knew where the connection had come from as I had gotten a tip-off. I never like walking into a room not knowing where the exits are and not knowing about who I'm meeting.

One thing I will never forget was that he had a book open on the table with the heading 'mediation' on it. I don't know what effect was intended. If an electrician came to my house and had a book open about rewiring it would give me cause to go back to the Yellow Pages.

He kept implying that a couple of guys were about the size of the problem, and we had to make it clear that this was not just about a couple of guys. At one stage during the discussions he asked, did myself and John need five minutes to think about what he had said. Now by this stage myself and John had been together enough and involved in so much that there was hardly the width of a cigarette paper between our views. We told him there wasn't any point. He said he felt we should! We said no point! For some reason he still left us to think about it. Maybe it was written in his book somewhere . . .

Curiouser and curiouser. Later on that night, Ollan sent John a text asking John to get me to ring him. John and I weren't keen on that. We had agreed that John was Ollan's contact. When I rang him, he asked if he could come straight to me in future. I considered telling him to fuck off but I let him at it.

Next contact was when he rang me to tell me that the Board were disappointed that we wouldn't meet with Gerald McCarthy. He again asked us to meet with the Board and also with Gerald. I again reiterated our position: we will not meet with Gerald.

On 4 January, a Sunday, we found ourselves in a familiar spot, an engineering company out in an industrial complex in Mahon. We had meetings out here with Kieran Mulvey during the 2007–8 strike. There should be a blue plaque outside the door of the place by now: The OK Corral.

I don't know what it said about catering in Ollan's mediation book, but the amount of food there was unreal. Mainly sweet things. They must have been trying to change the mood through sugar rushes. We were given our own room and told by Ollan that the Board had their room and that there was a common room into which he would bring us in a few minutes, after he had spoken to the Board. In the meantime he wanted us to prepare an opening few words. So a few minutes later we went in and met with Gerry O'Sullivan and Bob Ryan, the two Board men who were there.

Gerry set out their position. I set out ours. To be honest, I was nearly too sick to repeat our position yet again, I'd said everything so many times at this stage. Our position was still having the same effect on Bob Ryan. We had a few heated exchanges, mainly with Bob. We told him that we didn't trust him. Bob said that that was bolloxology. I hadn't heard that term in years. Bolloxology! Anyway, after some lively debate and some give and take of bolloxology we left them in the room.

After a few minutes Ollan came in.

'Fair play, ye gave yer opinions anyway.'

After a few minutes he came back and he said that, surprise, surprise, Gerald had just arrived.

We were shocked. Then for the next few minutes it was Ollan's turn to be shocked. I said that we were very disappointed. Ollan said that he must have misread the situation, or we must have misread it.

John said that that was it, we were off.

We went from zero to sixty in the blink of an eye, we travelled to a world beyond bolloxology. Walking out on the talks was going to play badly in the media. Murdering the mediator who had brought us so many sweet things to eat would definitely leave us with a PR problem. We knew this was an ideal scenario for the Board. We felt we had been manipulated.

We needed to get a story out. Our story. We organized a teleconference. A text went out. Eight out of the ten reps dialled in. We decided quickly that we would just get the story out that the talks had finished without resolution due to Gerald McCarthy having been parachuted in. Then we went out and sold it to the papers as fast as we could.

We probably got a draw out of the whole episode. That was just one meeting in an endless line. The account above is just a slice drawn from our diaries. There was enough during that time to make a book. This is not that book.

It felt like months of walking across a minefield. Some days we lost. Some days we won. Some days we made mistakes. Some days our calls were good. Some days things just blew up in our faces.

It went on that way for months, from early October 2008, when we started meeting with the Board, until 10 March 2009, when Gerald resigned.

Some things we never saw coming. One night, the County Board met behind closed doors. We were trying to figure that out when word broke that Gerald's mother had died. After the initial sympathy you would feel for anybody in that position, we had to work out how we would deal with the following few days. If we all went to the funeral it would be inflammatory and would appear cynical. We would be accused of being seen to be there for show. If we didn't go, then we would be described as heartless. No win.

We had a teleconference. We were due to have a meeting that night. As a sign of respect we called off that meeting and decided to send a Mass card from the team. Some players expressed a wish to pay their respects at the funeral, so we decided that any player who wished to do so should go as an individual.

Gerald hammered us for that anyway, in the statement released when he finally resigned. Falsely and unfairly.

The story went out that we, the ruling junta of senior players, had ordered players not to go. Absolutely false. As if we would begin instructing each other about whose funeral it was OK to attend and whose it wasn't.

The Cork replacement squad were fulfilling the league fixtures meanwhile. They'd each been given gym memberships (how fucking hard we had to fight for that right) and promised a holiday in

La Manga. They played Waterford at that time and lost by just two points. Waterford had a weak team out but Ken McGrath was playing. Cork were fierce fired up and we were told that Ray Ryan had made a speech, saying that they were the ones in possession of the Cork jersey and it was up to others to come and take it from them.

It's summer now. The Championship is looming for us next week. Ray is fine; we just don't think so much any more about what Ray said while we were away. Our war seems so long ago.

29

The strike follows us around. It followed me to Africa.

Paddy Barry, who hurled with Cork in the 1970s, is based in Lusaka in Zambia. He's a priest, a missionary there; and last November, with the strike still young, he was to meet myself and Kevin Hartnett off an overnight bus.

We asked how we would recognize Paddy Barry. The only other white man in the place, we were told. Fair enough.

So myself and Hartnett arrived in the mayhem of Lusaka bus station and went looking for the only white man in the place. Two Cork men looking for a Cork man in Lusaka. Typical. We couldn't find him. Just as typical, I suppose, I went away for a walk and left Hartnett on lookout duty. And of course I bumped into Paddy Barry while I was walking.

We'd been travelling all night and Paddy brought us back to the priests' house and showed us to our rooms and let us sleep a while. He called us at lunchtime. On the way to eat he took me aside.

'There'll be a fella at lunch and he has no time for you.'

'What? OK, so . . .'

'Just marking your cards. A priest from home. A northerner. No time for you at all.'

And I could tell that Paddy was dreading lunch because he assumed I was a certain kind of fiery character and he obviously knew that this fella might rear up and Zambia, having achieved independence without a shot being fired, was about to sink into war-torn chaos over the issue of the Cork hurlers.

So we sat down to lunch anyway and next minute, as soon as he was introduced, our man from the North says it straight out: 'Is it off limits to speak about the Cork situation? Can we talk about it?'

I looked at Paddy. He was dying a death, poor man. So I said, 'We've no problem about it. The only thing now is, if you ask my opinion on something, I'll be giving you my opinion as to what I think. It mightn't exactly suit your own opinion. OK?'

'Yeah, OK, well I just want to start off with saying that I don't like Dessie Farrell. And also I might as well tell you that I thought some of Ben O'Connor's statements were right out of line.'

Stad na saoirse! We are in Lusaka. In Zambia. I'm nodding and taking all this in. I'm saying right, grand, grand, grand and just waiting for my turn to reply and I'm thinking he might have got off lightly if he'd left it with his GPA views, but having a go at Benjy and Dessie personally? I'm sorry he has to get a full half-hour of my fucking Charles Stewart Parnell impression now.

Still. Is there no escape from this? Anywhere?

The Great West Road is the longest, straightest road you could imagine. It runs from Lusaka to Kaoma in the Western Province. Six hundred kilometres of road. You couldn't imagine it, really, till you have seen it. You stand there and you look down this way and then look back that way and there is nothing there but the road stretching for ever.

Kaoma is a dusty town of 12,000 people but it makes the middle of nowhere seem like Manhattan.

Last summer in Semple Stadium against Galway I got sent off for jumping on and bringing down Alan Kerins. Or, as I put it when I'm talking to him, for him falling over as I brushed against him.

Kerins is a remarkable fella. I've known him since minor days. He first went to Zambia in 2005, working for three months as a volunteer physiotherapist in a home for physically disabled children in Mongu, not far from Kaoma. At the time the Western Province was enduring one of the worst droughts in living memory.

Having seen what he saw, Alan started a campaign that has raised over a quarter of a million euro for AIDS orphans, water schemes, food aid, school-building, housing development, childcare and re-habilitation in Zambia.

For me he has been just one of those fellas that you strike up a friend-ship with and have good time for over the years. For a while he had been on to me about going out to Zambia, and for just as long I had been dodging him. I wasn't sure. I was busy.

In the end I said, 'Look, I'll go and I'll bring another Cork fella for company as well,' so I said it to Hartnett and Hartnett just said, 'Yeah, no problem.'

So Kerins suggested a project and we said, 'Grand, we'll take that on.' We were to install solar panels on a kitchen block and to wire up shower units.

Being from Cork we didn't need any instruction or supervision.

Before he left, Kerins showed us what they wanted us to wire up.

'By the way, is there any gear around the place? Ladders?'

'No!'

'Oh.'

Anyway, Kaoma. Dust and a road and not a lot else. There is an orphanage there which was started up by an Irish nun, Sister Molly. So there we were, and first thing I wanted to figure out, being as I am, was what the structure was, who was in charge, who did you see to get things done? Who is the Frank Murphy of Kaoma?

So indeed it turned out that there was a fella there already who seemed to have the answers, if not a ladder. A man called Matt who was an old fella who had been burnt to a shrivel by the African sun. This was the man who was looking after things and the man we needed to talk to, to find out what was really going on about the place. Most people wouldn't need to know the sort of stuff I had to ask Matt, but I was certain I couldn't stay there for two weeks without knowing the lay of the land.

So while all the other GAA boys who had made the trip went away off up to the children, who greeted them like heroes every day, I found Matt and I stayed with him and burst his brain with questions. He was vague enough, bit like a Kerryman answering a Corkman's questions. Yerra . . . I was asking him about solar panels because one of our jobs was to fit the roof of a kitchen with these panels. 'Right,' said Matt and he began pulling stuff out from underneath his bed.

Jesus, I said to myself, this is going to be a disaster.

That was our first day. When we got down to work, Harnett and myself set about making a ladder as a priority. We cobbled together a simple ladder that we could climb up, but when it was done we realized that what we really needed was a stepladder. That would require hinges and another half to the ladder again. We could spend our two weeks making the perfect stepladder. Or we could improvise.

So Kevin Hartnett, Cork hurler and PhD student in electronic engineering, stepped into the breach. I don't know, would any other man do it, but in the heat of Africa, Hartnett became the second side of the ladder! And of course, grateful as I was that my mate would do this, soon I was taking the piss. This is an extraordinarily intelligent fella and he's come around the world to act as one half of a stepladder while I'm up, working away above him. Pretty soon, seeing how far I could push it, I was getting him to hold screwdrivers in his mouth while I was up the ladder, and then I'd start dropping stuff, bits of stones and debris, on top of his head.

Fine way for a man to end up, somewhere in Africa, holding a ladder and maybe he's got a hammer in his mouth and he's trying to curse this latest bit of dust and dirt to fall on him.

'Grrrr, fuck.'

'Sorry, Hartnett boy.'

One day I burst out laughing. Too much.

'I think you're doing that on purpose, Cusack.'

The man is as tough as fucking nails, though. It was entertaining to see how long this man would stay and do this without freaking. He did it and stuck with it, though, because it had to be done. It was like training, some fellas are wired like that. The only other person I know who would do that would be Seán Óg.

Another day we needed to go up into an attic to sort out the connections for the solar panels. The kitchen kept suffering power cuts but hopefully *now* the solar panels would keep the lights going all night.

We nearly did a thesis working it all out, Hartnett and myself. I'm an electrician by trade and I'd have a good interest in it, but he's an electrical engineer, he's doing a PhD in the field, so he knows things way, way beyond my expertise.

It came time to go up into the attic to explore the kitchen lighting system. Now one of the worst jobs when you're an electrician is going up into an attic. It's bad having to do it in Cork, but in Africa in the heat and with absolutely no lighting up there? That's a different story!

Right from when we were starting the job I saw it coming, I was saying to myself, I'm not going up in that fucking attic. Bob Geldof wouldn't go into the attic. Bono wouldn't go into the attic. They'd organize a suitable person to go in there.

And then I'm thinking, If I'm not going to go up I have the terrible responsibility of organizing a suitable person. It has to be Hartnett, he'll have to go up. Maybe it won't have struck him because he's a bit more academic than I am. Or maybe he has been saying to himself that having acted as half a ladder, there would be no way he would have to go into the attic when the time came. Cusack would be morally obliged to go in.

It doesn't work like that.

I've had enough of the mice and the rats you get in attics back home. Up here in this Zambian attic space there might be something that could kill you stone dead. It's best if a man called Udi is the test case for this!

I'm aware now that I'm not even going to come out of a story about working on a humanitarian project in Africa looking remotely good, but the other part of the deal, the sustainability bit, was that there was a local electrician called Udi whom we were meant to train up. Udi used to be with us most days, but Udi was no more an electrician than I am an astronaut. It had, for instance, taken a long time to explain to our mate Udi why we needed earthed fuses for the shower block, that everybody would be electrocuted otherwise. Udi had a lot to learn.

So, brave Cork men that we are, we sent Udi up to the attic first, and even Udi was grumbling and giving out. He wasn't too inclined to go up but we were giving him a few quid every day, which delighted him because he liked a drink. Between the money and our anxious prodding we got him up the ladder and through the trapdoor.

Trouble was, once Udi was up there, he didn't know what he was looking for. Hartnett, who had stood as the other half of a stepladder, and Udi, who had gone up into the darkest attic in Africa, had done their bit. I'd been Blackadder to their Baldrick for long enough. Shit. Nothing for it. I took the torch and climbed up.

No exaggeration. I was terrified.

The heat up there was shocking, for a start. It was like climbing into a furnace. And in my imagination there could have been anything waiting in the darkness, from a dozing snake to a man-eating spider to a paid-up member of the Cork County Board. Anything!

In fact it was surprisingly clean up there, so I went over to where we needed to work. I was convinced I could hear something moving around so I shone the torch around one more time and, shit, there was a huge spider sitting there watching me.

They say about moments like this that the spider is probably more scared of you than you are of the spider. In this case, though, the spider was playing at home. I was thinking, If this fella is more scared of me, he'd have died of a heart attack thirty seconds ago. Either way I'm looking at him and he's looking at me and I reckon we are both thinking that even a skinny fella like me would keep him alive for a long time up there in the attic. Because I'm sure by now that this is no ordinary spider. This is a flesh-eater. Probably from Kilkenny or somewhere.

I came down quickly.

'Hartnett, you're not going to believe it, there is this fucking huge spider up there.'

'Oh Jesus Christ.'

'Fuh-king huge! I think this is the fair side of the deal, Hartnett. If the two of us go up there now – it's only right – then there is a fifty–fifty chance one of us will survive!'

Fair play to Hartnett – he has a sense of honour! The two of us went up. Of course by now the spider had shrunk to the size of a normal spider, but to see the fear in Hartnett at that start of the climb into the darkness was worth anything. As he was going through into the attic he thought he was going to have to go *mano a mano* with the world's biggest tarantula.

I'll never forget another day: Hartnett and I were down in Kaoma with Brian Carroll, the Offaly forward, who had to go to the bank for some reason. So himself and Hartnett went in and I remember I was sitting outside the bank and I realized that there were no other white men to be seen. Anywhere. Thousands of people in the street but just one white face. It got me thinking. Jesus Christ, I'm the only white man here and I'm sitting outside the bank! How does that look? And then I noticed something even more odd. Lots of people on the street, I mean lots, had mobile phones. There were people starving and dying around them, AIDS orphans everywhere, but mobile phones had found their way to Kaoma.

Another day, some of the other guys came back and they were fierce upset. They had been out the road and had seen this family out there in dire straits. They were distressed over it now, and myself and Hartnett for some reason felt we had to go out the road too, just to see if there was anything could be done.

It was bad. There was a mother, a daughter and a son of the daughter, three generations, and they were picking the roots out of the ground for food. They were dying. The young mother had AIDS, so the kid possibly had AIDS too, and it was the most fucking brutal and depressing thing I had ever seen.

So we went away and bought mattresses for them and we bought some kind of grain-like food. We asked how long what we were buying would keep the family going for. The man said till Christmas. If we gave them another batch it would keep them alive till spring. He said that there was no point in getting them more than that. If they got their strength up they would find their feet. So we bought them enough to keep them going till March and walked away, thinking how fucked up the world is and how we never wanted to have to make such a grisly calculation again.

Back in Cork the next March we sat and wondered how the family were getting on and just hoped to Christ they were all right. When we brought out those small few bits of stuff that day, they'd just started weeping and crying like mad. I'll never forget it, the comfort they got from a few skinny mattresses and some grain.

We stayed on, Hartnett and myself, a few days longer than the others. We were going home by ourselves. Kerins was staying on even longer, so we had to get a bus back to Lusaka, where Paddy Barry was to meet us.

The bus was leaving at midnight. It was mayhem getting on to the vehicle because it had driven to Kaoma from somewhere else and it was almost full by the time it got to us. We had tickets booked and we had a good bit of gear so, as you can imagine, we were vastly popular when we struggled towards the overstuffed bus. There was nowhere to put the gear. Anything we tried started a shouting match.

They wanted to put the gear down underneath. We were thinking, It goes down underneath and we never see it again!

Now while we had been waiting at the bus station, there were a couple of boys playing pool inside, and I had said to Hartnett to come on over and we'd see what the story was with the boys. They were playing and drinking so I got my money down and took one of them on. There is that bit of a bollow in me. I beat him on his own table. He didn't like it and he was getting a bit smart with me and I was getting a bit smart with him because I didn't think he was any danger. He and the other fella had sachets of vodka which they were drinking constantly. They'd squeeze the sachets up into the mouth.

Anyway, by the time I was on the bus the fella who I had beaten in pool was sitting down on an aisle seat and still a bit sore. He says to me, 'Sit down, you farmer!'

Farmer! Worse than Frank Murphy calling Alan Cummins a tennis player all those years ago!

In the end I remember I sat in beside this big huge lad who had a leather jacket on him – I couldn't believe it, it was roasting and the man was so hot he was making me warmer just sitting beside him – and a small little fella squeezed in on the other side of me. So I was sandwiched in between them and Hartnett was up across the way in a two-seater and we were supposed to be watching out for each other just in case but, typical Hartnett, he ended up talking to this fella, telling him the whole life story, where he was from and everything.

About halfway through the journey the bus stopped and everyone got off. So, like a pair of sheep, we got off as well. There was some sort of checkpoint and everyone was walking towards it. Hartnett went away because he had to go to the toilet, so I started walking and then when everyone stopped they formed a loose queue. I thought they were queuing to get drinks of water but I had water with me, so I walked past them. Next minute the fellas start shouting and yelling at me, but I have my water so I shout back in my thick Cork accent: 'Ah no, I'm all right boy! It's all right, I have de water.'

And I kept walking till, the next minute, a soldier appeared in front of me with his gun pointed at me. Oh Jesus Christ, what's going on here? So I went back to the queue, wondering where the hell was Hartnett. He was probably going to come running past everyone now and get shot.

So he came out and I said, 'Hartnett, whatever you do, I don't know what's going on here, but go into the queue, just go into the queue.' So anyway we got up close and saw that an official was spraying stuff on to everybody's hand. So I gladly took whatever it was and walked past the checkpoint, where we had to wait till the bus came along after another ten or fifteen minutes. Such a strange feeling. Somewhere in the middle of Zambia, in the early hours of the morning, hands desanitized, and waiting on a bus. Just two Cork hurlers waiting to move on to Lusaka where they will be met by another Cork hurler, Paddy Barry.

At lunch that day I buried the northern priest over the space of half an hour and I enjoyed doing it. All his arguments were old and threadbare and clichéd and it was easy to knock them down. I'd been doing that for ten years.

I remember Father Paddy looked stricken. He was sure there was going to be a fight. Afterwards, though, he seemed quite pleased with it all.

'Do you know we never had anything like that out here. Quite entertaining to have a row.'

We all went out for a meal and our friend from the North was very gracious. He spoke to me in front of everybody.

'You're after changing my mind on a lot of things. I was delighted to meet with you and talk with you today, and you are after changing my opinion on a lot of topics.'

Now I was surprised at how easy he gave in, but it was a nice, decent thing for the man to say. Before we had arrived in Lusaka I imagine he'd had to forgive himself in advance for even meeting with us.

Hartnett and myself flew home and vowed that we would bring twenty fellas from Cork back in 2009. And it is coming to pass. We are going out in November again, when the hurling is done. We're going to build a school ourselves, a proper school with two classrooms and an office.

We'll start from scratch and we'll leave a little piece of Cork pride and cockiness behind us there. And, with any luck, a generation of Zambian troublemakers and strikers will pour out of that place with a mission to afflict the comfortable and comfort the afflicted.

30

Things people abuse me about from behind the goal. An incomplete list.

Being from Cork.
The GPA.
My personal life.
Goals that Waterford have scored against me.
Short puck-outs.
Strikes.
Sliotars.
Sendings off.
My personal life.

Mostly it's just the same fucking thing. The fellas that want to hurt you will go for the personal stuff. Calling you queer, ingenious stuff like that. What I try to do, in my own preparation, is to develop trigger points so that when I hear the abuse, something else comes into my head. Something positive.

It's human nature for thousands of years that this abuse is coming from. It's not going to change. So I have a trigger that I've developed through meditation and visualization, and when I'd hear the abuse then in my head I trigger a good image that I've already thought about. I'm always outnumbered, never outgunned! It's my only way of dealing with it. Otherwise I would hear it and think about it and I don't want to be wasting my time that way.

I feel the experience teaches me and I can play games with it. I read this analogy in *The Seven Habits of Highly Effective People* by Stephen R. Covey. Suppose now that you are on a train and you aren't in good form and a fella comes up and sits a bit too close to you and he has a load of kids with him. It's Sunday morning and you've had hassle getting to the train at the last minute and found this grand seat and you have your cup of coffee and your papers and you're there on your train, you're after having a busy week and now you are going away to watch a match or whatever, but this guy is sitting too close, with half the train to choose from, and his kids are running around the fucking place like mad. They're bumping off you and screaming and your man is sitting there and he is doing nothing.

So finally you say to yourself, Well fuck this anyway, and you say it to him, 'Jesus look would you ever look after the kids there, they're annoying everyone.'

And he looks at you and says, 'I'm sorry, Jesus, I'm so sorry about that. To be honest I'm in another world. I'd say the kids are just on a big high, we're just after leaving the hospital, my wife's there and she has only days to live and I don't think they know how to deal with it and they're just so happy to be out of that atmosphere. To be honest I'm struggling to deal with it all myself . . .'

So straight away you are sorry to have gone there. You can't be angry with him any more, not with what is going on in his life, and now you have brought all sorts of new dark thoughts into your head.

So instead of confronting it, I put myself in a frame of mind to deal with it.

Most days it works!

I have worked on skills like that. I remember when I was a young fella, I was doing visualization even though I didn't know that I was. Before every game I'd love just sitting in my father's car with a Prodigy tape in there and I'd be just dreaming about the match that day. I'd be dreaming about it. Even my father, I swear to Christ, my father, the poor man got to like some of the Prodigy stuff, I'd have it on so much. *Music for the Jilted Generation* got us to a good few big games. The father would listen to the end of 'One Love' and say, 'Do you know what that's like now, me banging the table before the match!'

My first few years with Cork, I wasn't as comfortable as I should have been on the field. I was in kind of a survival mode, which is a very natural thing for a goalkeeper as well.

I can't put my finger on when the abuse about my personal life started, funnily enough. I hear it all the time, though – Ballygunner in a challenge game this year, Kilkenny this year, when I walked on to the field in Clarecastle for a training session . . .

I remember a Waterford Crystal Cup match a couple of years ago. These fellas behind the goals were saying stupid shit to me. Anyway, I pucked a ball out and my brother Conor was playing and he was only back from injury. He went down in a tussle. It was obvious he was hurt and one of my men behind the goal said to me, 'That's your fault now that he got hurt.'

Now I could take the other stuff, but that was the most stupid thing I'd ever heard so I turned around and I went over to the wire and I said, 'Look, are you a tough guy?' I pointed up along the wire on the terracing and I said, 'The gate is open there now if you want to come in to me, if you're feeling that tough.'

And I went back into the goals.

But of course his friends were thinking, He won't go in there and like we'll put him under pressure now because this is a classic for us, this is a result!

So after a while he says, 'I fucking will come in to you so.'

And then he actually started making a shape at coming down the terrace and I'm thinking to myself, Oh Jesus Christ, he is coming in to me, what's fucking going to happen next? The pair of us could get arrested or whatever.

So I called Gatchy and I asked him to get Billy for me. So Billy comes over and says, 'What's up?' – this is all in the middle of a match – and I explained the situation.

So the minute the whistle blew, Billy was straight in and ready to fight your man if he came through the gate. And the pair of us walked away with one eye on your man, and his mates still at him to go in and fight.

Billy was laughing. He says, 'You're always in fucking trouble!'

And then later the unfairness of it struck him.

'All right so, Ógie, let's get this straight. You couldn't be seen to be clocking your man but what you were doing was, you were bringing me over to fucking do it for you. I would have to lay him out and then I'd get the fucking big suspension! It was all right for me to be getting into trouble, but not you! I'm expendable?'

It was funny afterwards but you need to learn to deal with it properly. Obviously that day I would have failed in my own thing and I would have thought about it all and responded and let it weaken me. And if that weakens you, it does affect your performance, and if you let it affect your performance you are letting the fellas in front of you down. So you deal with it.

Some days it would have a worse effect on others, Sully for example, than it would have on me. He'd be conscious of it, standing at full-back. After a game he'd often say it.

'Fuck it, Ógie, you were getting some abuse.'

Other days, you just wonder. There were these young fellas behind the goals in the first half of a game and they were spewing out this stupid shit at me. And I'm thinking my positive thoughts and pulling the triggers, but at half-time I remember saying to myself, 'At least those fuckers will be gone in the second half.' And I swear to God, they fucking followed me down the other side for the second half so they could continue abusing me. And then you'd be saying to yourself, 'Do I draw them on me or what?'

That was a league match in Waterford in 2007. At the end, a Waterford guy came up to me and said to me, 'Look, Dónal Óg, I'm delighted to see you back in here.'

I thought, Jesus, wasn't that nice, but I knew as well why he did it: it was a reaction to what he was listening to behind the goals. I know it was. He was an older fella but it was a nice gesture by him.

I hurt my leg that day and I should have come off and there were ten minutes to go and the abuse was still going on and on. Dr Con came in, looked at the leg and said, 'You're coming off.'

I refused. 'Con, I'm not going. Fuck it, I'm not, I'm telling you now. There is ten minutes to go, if I was a sub goalkeeper I wouldn't want to come on here at all, you're putting the boys out there in a desperate position. If I was sub goalkeeper it would be the worst time to be coming on.'

And Con was savage over it and so was Deccie O'Sullivan but I remember staying on and I remember afterwards saying to myself, 'The boys that were abusing me aren't going to get the satisfaction of thinking I walked away.'

I made one good save, from Eoin McGrath, in those last ten minutes. Standing hurt and being abused in the lashing rain, knowing that I'd only stayed out of stubbornness, and the abuse making me more stubborn, making that save was a big plus.

There's a hundred other incidents. Or perhaps there are none. To me they don't exist. I'm not the first goalkeeper to get abuse. Davy Fitz took it for a long time. I'm sure other lads do, too. The fellas shouting at you matter and they don't matter at all. In other words, the abuse and the shouting and the shards of hatred matter as much as you let them matter. On the list at the top of this chapter there's nothing I'm ashamed of at all. Most of that list, apart from the goals that have gone whickering past me, I'm proud about. So it's all somebody else's problem.

That malice will be in the air in Semple Stadium next Sunday when we play Tipperary.

In the early years, playing in goal for Cork, I wanted to just survive every game. Since 2003 or so, I have pushed on and when I prepare now it is to be a creative part of the team. Dealing with the atmosphere and pushing on is part of my contribution to the team.

31

I'm like a child when it comes to new hurleys. It's probably a crime against the environment, the number of sticks I have, but a few times a year – and especially just before the championship – I go to Liam Walsh's workshop and just enjoy myself.

Hurleys have always been part of my life. I love the touch, the smell, the feel, the weight, the balance, the possibilities of a good new hurley. I love to look at a hurley, to admire its lines and all the craft that has gone into it. I like talking to hurlers about hurleys, hearing people's theories on what makes a good stick, what to do to keep a good stick. All that. Everybody remembers their first stick and their first visit to a genuine hurley maker.

When I was younger Maurice Cahill from Cloyne, who is a few years older than me but still a close friend of mine, took me to a hurley maker over in Midleton. You're getting serious about the game when you know what sort of hurley you want and like.

Sometimes we used to go and get the hurleys made, but more often we'd be dropping in sticks to be mended. One day we dropped off a few hurleys and next time I saw Maurice he said to me, 'You're not going to believe this, that poor man in Midleton hung himself up above in the workshop.'

And to my shame I said straight back, 'Maurice, what about my hurleys?'

Maurice still tells that story to illustrate to people what a charming man I am deep down. I can only say that I was young and didn't fully understand the world.

(Come to think of it, Maurice has a bit of form in this regard. When I was young I used to work for the Cahills in their window factory in an old school building down the road outside the town. From the age of thirteen or fourteen I'd be down there every summer, and after school on Monday, Tuesday and Thursday evenings.

I'd be down there by myself. The work was easy, but it would be creepy enough at night, being in there alone. I had to work at three different stations to do the job and I always kept a weapon at each station! I had sprays, a knife and a small hatchet. Just in case.

Maurice used to bring me to school in Cloyne. He said to me once that I looked fierce jumpy sometimes if one of them would call in to the factory. I explained to him how creepy it was and told him about the weapons. For fuck's sake, he told all the lads about it!)

Anyway, I remember that we got the hurleys back. Back then, Liam Walsh was a young fella who worked for the man. Liam bought some of the gear from there and started making the hurleys himself, and he became renowned all over the place really for making excellent sticks.

Liam has been very good to me over the years. He'll always have a couple of planks with the characteristics that I like. The wider the gap between the lines of the grain, the healthier the ground that the ash tree was grown in; a hurley is a living organic thing and I like at least half an inch between the lines of the grain. The grain needs to run in uniform lines all the way from the handle to the top of the *bás*. I think that sort of spread in the grain absorbs the shock better. Liam has a great *grá* for the thing and I enjoy that about him. He'll experiment. He'll try to do different shapes of hurleys and do radical things with them.

It was Liam who changed the shape of the hurleys. The Cork hurley with the big *bás*, that came from Welshy. He and I tried other things for goalkeeper hurleys. We wondered why, for instance, the shaft of the hurley ran down towards the bottom of the *bás*; surely the shaft could go down the centre of the *bás*? With an equal amount of *bás* on both sides of the shaft, maybe you would have a greater chance of stopping a ball? Those sticks never balanced, though. The striking wasn't right and the weight felt off. It was an interesting experiment and it just made you respect the game more. The perfection of a good hurley isn't something to be tampered with lightly.

The main thing is the balance: I love a fierce straight hurley. I generally wouldn't give a fella a lend of a hurley belonging to me because if he bent it I would go mad. I don't understand how anybody can persist if a hurley is bent. When you strike the ball with a bent hurley you're dragging the ball one way or the other.

We were down in the alley there last week, myself, Gardiner and Hartnett and a couple of other lads, and we were talking about sticks. I was saying how I used to love my hurley so much when I was a young fella that I'd be able to jab-lift the ball without the hurley touching the ground. It took me months to teach myself to do that, but I developed that skill to stop myself scratching me hurleys. That's obsession.

I should have kept my mouth shut, of course. By the time we were leaving, Gardiner had been practising and could do it. Not sure how useful a skill it will be for him, but he'll always know where he got it from.

Every hurler knows that bit of sadness when you break a favourite hurley. Even in the middle of a game it registers with you when a good stick breaks. We went through a desperate period of breaking hurleys a few years back, and it was fierce frustrating. You could break three or four hurleys a game.

We played Kilkenny in a National League game in 2003, Dónal O'Grady's first year, and I broke two hurleys in the first half. When I came out after half-time I made a beeline for the sub goalkeeper, Paul Morrissey, because he used to look after sticks.

He said, 'You're not going to believe this, I'm fierce sorry, but I broke one of your hurleys pucking around at half-time.'

In the second half Eddie Brennan came flying through with ten minutes to go and I broke my hurley off him. The next week we were watching the tape with O'Grady, and it was typical of O'Grady, if he believed in you, to back you to the hilt. So the pull came on the video and the boys were full of anticipation. Good craic going around, everyone waiting to see if Cusack would be hung.

And O'Grady says, 'You were going for the ball there, weren't you, Ógie.'

And I said, 'I was, yeah.'

The boys were savage to see me getting away with it.

Around that time we decided to address this problem of breaking hurleys. My cousin Vincent works a lot with timber, so I started working with him, trying to find something that would protect a hurley against damage. In the end we came up with marine varnish with some plaster sand and other dirt in it to coarsen the surface a little and give it a little grip. The father mixes up this stuff, puts it on, hangs the sticks up and then he'd file away the bits of stuff where the varnish has formed into a cone or whatever. What we're trying to do is form a seal around the hurley that will stop it from breaking. So far it has been successful.

Sometimes the sticks can cause a bit of panic. During the summer of 1999, when we were on our way to the All-Ireland, poor Welshy was having incredible problems with his back. He literally had to lie on the floor on the flat of his back for six months. All very well, but in the week of the All-Ireland I was in the horrors, worrying about sticks. Myself and Maurice had been plaguing the poor man all summer. We would call up to him and cajole and beg him, and in fairness he'd get stuff ready for me. It probably set his recovery back weeks, but he did it.

Come the week of the All-Ireland final, though, I was having problems with my hurleys and Maurice and myself decided that there was nothing for it but to bother Welshy again. So we called up and he was in a bad way, but we laid it on thick about the game and the county and what it meant, and finally he got up and mended a couple of hurleys for me.

Welshy would always talk about it since. He's laid out and in pain and the lunatics from Cloyne are saying, 'Welshy come on to fuck, we need a help here, get up.'

And of course come Sunday, the morning of the All-Ireland final in 1999, I went out, pucking around with Bernard Rochford, and broke my hurley. The morning of the match! Poor Welshy on the flat of his back for six months except when I'd force him up to work, and now this. Broke his hurley in a puck-around.

Welshy played and he has a feel for what he is doing. He loves the game and would never go down the mass-production route. He would be too interested in getting the right balance and keeping the hurley straight; I remember that Paddy Joe Ring used to be amazed that the hurleys Welshy made could be so straight.

A couple of years ago, for my thirtieth birthday, the lads in the village threw a surprise party and took me off to Rome for the weekend. And Welshy gave me ten sticks. Perfect specimens of his art. We had a brilliant weekend in Rome, but every now and then I'd allow myself to look forward to getting home and examining and treating those perfect implements of the hurling art.

Like a kid, I was. And that's how I feel now, heading out for Welshy's place, knowing that he'll have sticks and planks with my name on them and conversation to make the day die easy.

32

Cloyne, Sunday 31 May

The sun is shining. Championship weather.

Start the day by eating a bit of fruit and a bit of bread. Then to something I always do before big games. I wander down to the grave-yard in Cloyne.

I was brought up as a Catholic and I can remember evenings when my mother would have all the family kneeling and praying in our sitting-room. I've drifted from that but always when I go to the grave-yard I say a prayer at each grave. Until I got to my mid-twenties I would say a prayer every night even if I was too drunk to see the bed in front of me. There had been a priest in our parish called Father Cronin – he was big into his hurling and was a selector on the county-winning team in '87 – and before he left Cloyne he asked me to say an Our Father, a Hail Mary and a Glory Be To God each night before I went to sleep. And I did. I'd say I didn't miss a night for over ten years, no matter what else I did before I slept.

I have lost that, though – maybe it will come back to me someday.

Graves. Christy Ring first. Sixty thousand people lined the way from Cork when he made the journey to this plot. I ask him to lend me the courage that he used to have.

And Paddy Joe Ring – Christy's brother – since I was twelve years old Paddy Joe would say to me and to anybody that would listen that I would play in goals for Cork one day. I can still hear and see him saying it to me, and I would be so proud when he would do so. Proud out.

Also, *mol an óige*, his words would make me want to practise. Every day I played hurling when I was younger. Every day I took the hurley in my hand and worked. I would puck the ball off of the gable wall for ever. My parents keep our house in Cloyne very well, but my father never painted the gable end as that was my practice wall. When I left home he painted it.

Then there was the field. Every day after school, even if it was nearly dark, I would run up and down the field, trying to hit all the posts that held up the wire around the pitch. I genuinely loved that feeling. The more I practised the better I got.

The round tower in Cloyne was built to protect the people from Viking invasions. You can see the tower from the field. Cloyne people have been looking at that tower for over 1,000 years now. I wanted to be in touch with my place and would visualize the people racing with their kids and their belongings into the sanctuary of the tower. They'd get inside and pull the ladder up. I loved that image. I could feel it then and can still feel it now, the history in the place, the tower, the churches, the caves, the tunnels which ran from Cloyne House to the graveyard; there is a thread that ties us here and keeps us belonging.

There is a famous picture of Ring pucking in the field with his own son Christy, and the tower in the background. When we would play with Cloyne I would always say to the lads to remember the tower. We would use that as a symbol of what we wanted to be . . .

I can remember when I was thirteen not being picked for the Cork under-14s after going for loads of trials, and crying my eyes out, thinking that I had missed out and that this would stop me playing for Cork ever in the future. My father tells me that when I was younger they would debate whether I should stay out of goals and they'd try to make a forward of me. Paddy Joe was adamant – he'll play in goals for Cork if he's put in there.

Probably that sounds romantic, but it's true. I remember a great story Paddy Joe used to tell me. Once it was commonplace that lads in Cloyne would have a few pints, the morning of a game. One morning Paddy Joe had one too many and it was obvious when the game was on. At half-time Tom Shea gave him a couple of hits of whiskey in order to 'straighten him out'.

Needless to say, it didn't have the effect that Tom wanted.

*

Graves. Willie John Ring. The last of the three boys in Christy's family. He was in hospital for a long time at the end of last year before he died. He was the President of the club and as such he called me to the hospital to give me a few orders before he died. Willie John told me that they were orders and I knew they were orders. He used to know exactly what was happening with the field and in the club. Everything.

His mind never lost its sharpness for hurling. He was one of the few hurling minds that Christy would sit and listen to. It was a privilege to have the same experience. I spent hours and hours of my life listening and talking to him about the game – sometimes just the two of us in his sitting-room, a hurley by his side and a hurley by mine. I remember one day when he was ill he went through the entire Kilkenny team and their positions, analysing and parsing them. I will never forget that because I could hardly do it myself.

He gave me so many memories that I value. He would always tell me that the furthest distance I would ever have to travel was the distance between my two ears.

You were right there, Willie John.

We would talk often about the old days, and Willie John gave me a very good insight into the darker sides of being a Cork player in a small place like Cloyne. In 1939, for instance, there had been a split in the club over Christy. Willie John had ended up playing with Ballina-curra. Paddy Joe went away and hurled with Russell Rovers for five years. And Christy himself had no club when he played for Cork the next summer.

Willie John had seen it all with Christy and told me a lot of things that happened which would never be spoken about in Cloyne. Some of what Willie John told me helped my natural scepticism about certain matters when I was involved in taking a stand over things, and it gave me some understanding of what was happening when bitter things did happen. It helped me cope better with the bad stuff that came along.

I remember Willie John called me down to him before we played the All-Ireland minor final in 1995. He told me that when I got to Croke Park I would think that the stands were falling down on me but not to worry about that. He was right there, too. There was something about the old stands in Croke Park that made them look as if they were tilting towards the field.

Willie John would also call at home once a week, up to last year when he got sick. Sometimes all the family, except the mother who used to provide the tea, cake and biscuits, would be in the room listening and talking to him – even my sister Treasa – nothing else would be discussed except hurling. I mean that. Nothing else.

He spoke to me a lot too about fighting death. Resisting. I couldn't get over it, the guts and the will of the man. He spoke about the pain of nearly being dead but refusing to let go. We were in the Midleton Hospital Conservatory and there were old men all over the place in their last days, old men whose race was run and now they were shuffling towards death.

Willie John wouldn't have any of it. He fought till the final breath.

His wife came in to see him on the last day I talked with him. We were speaking about hurling and he hunted her out impatiently and told her he needed to talk to me. He wanted to talk hurling. The orders he gave me were like three commandments: that I have a pint with his son when he died (Willie Ring was a County Board officer and there was many a public and private argument between himself and myself); that the field wasn't to be sold and I was to do whatever it took to make sure it didn't happen; and that Cloyne were to win the Senior County Championship.

I never spoke to him after that. It was the last time I saw Willie John.

Two of Willie John's orders came to be. Some day I will close out on his third order. I will. A senior county title. The old yearning we all share. Don't worry, Willie John, I will. We will. Come what may.

Graves. Bryan Ahern. A neighbour of mine who loved the game. Bryan's house was a real traditional house in Cloyne, and for me he represented all that was good about the place. He loved his hurling. A pint. A chat. Roy Keane. Christy Ring.

Bryan left behind five girls and a boy, each of them blessed with as big and as kind a heart as he had himself. Mickey O'Connell married one of his daughters, Patricia.

A story. One night, a Sunday night at elevenish in Cloyne, I got a text from a person who was very close to me.

'Dónal Óg, I am after swallowing fifty Ponstan. Will that do any harm to me?'

My heart stopped. I called her. She wouldn't answer the phone. Called again. Same. Then the phone got turned off.

For some reason I just knew that the person wasn't messing about. I had been talking to her earlier in the day and I can still remember the darkness that I felt coming from her then. Even now, when I am thinking of it my back is starting to shiver as I feel that darkness. I had an idea that she would be in a certain place. I went to my father and asked him to get out of bed. I told him the story. We got the torches and went down the field. No sign.

I have always been calm in pressure situations but this was as close to pure blind panic as I can ever remember feeling. We crossed the street to another possible location, and as we crossed I saw one of Bryan Ahern's daughters outside their house in a distressed state. We went up there and saw my friend, lying on the floor unconscious. There was a nurse – Ann Marie Motherway, wife of our club Secretary, Seán Motherway – tending to her. And we waited. I will never forget that feeling, waiting for the ambulance.

That night is never talked about among us, but I know in my heart that my friend was drawn to the Ahern house in her distress because Bryan and his wife had made such a beautiful welcoming home there. Without them being there she might have felt there was nowhere else to go and that death and the unknown would have been a nicer place.

It was touch and go for a few days, but she pulled through. I was in the hospital most of that night. I remember I still got up and went to work a few hours later. For some reason I always went to work. Lots of faults, but I have always wanted to work.

Anyway, Bryan, you were one of the good ones . . .

Graves. Along to Tom O'Shea, the father of the O'Sheas. I never knew him but still I feel that he is a big part of Cloyne, and if it does happen that the dead watch over us I know he would be doing so today. One of his sons, Dinny, has become very close to me and would be a hurling mentor to me. Dinny has had some tough times, his wife has been very ill, but the two of them have battled on bravely. When I was in trouble with the lads in the club last year, Dinny was the first guy I went to, as I knew he would tell me straight what the story was. A trusted friend of mine and of my father.

And now to Paddy Cusack. My grandfather. Tom O'Shea and himself are buried directly across from each other, just like where they used to live in the little ring of houses when they fathered twenty-six kids between them.

Paddy was one of the first people in Cloyne to have a TV. He made batteries during the war and made hurleys for a long time for Cloyne. Older people would tell you that he was one of three people who kept the club going when times were tough.

My grandmother used to tell a story to me that one night the GAA club ran a dance but didn't get enough money to be able to afford to pay the band. Paddy came home and took money out of their very limited savings and paid for the band.

When Cloyne were playing in the East Cork final in 1976, a problem arose with a lack of hurleys. Paddy got some ash on the Saturday, the day before the final, making the hurleys in the kitchen. The next day the majority of the hurleys were broken!

On to Francis Cusack, my father's mother, and to Joanne Costine, my grandmother on the Costine side. Joanne was my first 'best friend'. I used to visit her every day of my life. She would 'stand' to me every day, but besides that I loved her. She had an unreal nature, fourteen kids in the house but it was always full of food, people said. And that's how I remember it when I came along. I remember one occasion especially when she was in the kitchen giving sugar, butter and tea to a lady. I was young but I understood and had a feeling for what I was seeing. The lady looked at me and was embarrassed, and my grandmother said to her, 'Don't worry about Dónal Óg, he knows that he shouldn't talk about certain things.'

She was my friend. I still have dreams where I think she is alive.

Graves. Smurf. For fuck's sake, you shouldn't be here, but wherever you are I hope things are OK with you, bro.

It says on the cross of Smurf's grave, 'A true Bhoys fan'. I was in Glasgow with him on so many occasions, so many great and mad weekends. He was a Celtic fan and a Bhoy, but to me he was part of Cloyne, part of us, part of me. He shouldn't fucking be here today but so it goes, I suppose. Even the *laochs* fall.

I would like to call home but I don't have time now. This graveyard visit is taking longer each year.

33

Sometimes I wonder if, when you retire and it's gone, will the hurling and what you were involved in seem the time of your life, the period when you felt most alive and most open and closest to your potential as a human being? Is there life after the game, life after hurling? And will it be as raw and as thrilling?

I stand in Cloyne at the door of my parents' house and a hurling life seems to have passed in a flash since I first went over the back wall to the field.

One day I am hitching in to Cork to train for underage teams. The next day it is a Saturday morning in September 1999 and I am getting ready to leave for Dublin to play in my first All-Ireland senior final.

Word must have gotten around about what time I was leaving. I'll never forget the crowd on the street outside the house that morning – I'm emotional just to think about it. I said a few words before I left, mentioned some people of Cloyne and especially the ones who had passed away from the village.

It was the same in '03, '04, '05 and '06: every time people would come and I would speak before I left. Family friends and neighbours tight together. It would be elevenish when I would leave but already there would be brandy and whiskey being consumed – my parents are fierce good people for hospitality and there would be plenty of everything there on that morning. The town would be decked in red and white – bunting and flags everywhere.

There is a ditch in front of a house on the way out of Cloyne at a place where a guy called Shakey Mickey lives. When we are playing, Mickey always has a big Cloyne or Cork flag coming up from behind that ditch. It's a sight. Because the front is elevated you can never see the pole, just the flag. Shakey is a real fiery character around the town but a guy that I like and somebody I always feel I can connect with. I don't know why, but when I see that flag I always imagine that Mickey is behind there, inside in the ditch, holding it tight as the wind is trying its best to blow our flag away. I picture Mickey holding it there, almost in defiance for the people passing. I don't know why – maybe it is just an image I connect with – but it definitely triggers happiness in my head, especially when I am heading to a match.

On those mornings too, a number of people would give me cards with gifts. Paddy Joe gave me a few quid before the '99 final – to think of it now – fair play to him.

Rituals. I would bring brown bread with me that Billy's wife, Siobhan, would have baked that morning. I'd call down to her in her deli before I left for games in Dublin and she would slice it up and wrap it for me to have it perfect for that night. I would eat it before I went to bed. I would also bring some Cloyne honey with me to be used in my porridge the next morning. What I am saying is, you need your head clear and if your head is clear it gives you more time to get things right that you mightn't get right if you are under pressure outside the game.

In 1999 they had the reception in Cloyne for us, the Friday night after the All-Ireland. The team comes home on the Monday night to Cork and up through the city centre. Tradition has it that on the Tuesday night the cup would go to the home of the club captain. In 1946 Christy Ring was given a reception in Cloyne when he brought the cup to the village after captaining Cork to the All-Ireland. Five thousand people showed and Christy was given a wallet stuffed with notes collected in the parish. I left Cloyne in 1999 with notes in my pocket from Christy's brother, and with due respect to the great Ringy he was a Glen player in 1946 when he brought the cup. When Sully and I brought it back, we brought it back as Cloyne men true and true!

What can I remember now of that Friday night? About as much as is recalled about 1946! Crowd barriers being put up (not a common sight in Cloyne!), speeches, songs, pictures, autographs, rakes of drink. It passed in a happy blur.

Maybe you remember the bad days more keenly. We lost those three county finals together, and every time afterwards it would be dark by the time we got to Cloyne. Every year at the cross you'd have maybe

200 people waiting and you'd be getting off the bus with such incredible pain in your heart.

The first two years I spoke as captain; the third year, to be honest, I hadn't the will for it, but Sully was captain and he spoke. It was picturesque and poignant there at the crossroads. We fucking dream of winning the county in Cloyne, and there we were, getting off the bus for the third year in a row, beaten, and there were children crying and men all upset and bothered and the whole balance of the place not right.

Jesus, to do it once, fucking twice, and I swear to God a third time, I thought I was going fucking insane.

One of the mornings after those finals, it was 2005, I remember going off into my parents' bedroom and my parents were still in bed and I remember sitting on the bottom of the bed and bawling me eyes out crying, with my parents there with me.

Is there something wrong with a fella that would carry on like that over hurling? Or will life ever be that vivid again?

I remember I couldn't sleep and I had been down in the field that morning from the break of dawn, and one of Smurf's brothers, the one we call Bomber, was down there as well, and I remember saying to him, 'Either it's the fucking drink is driving us mad or the hurling but this is having such an effect on us we might not recover.' And my mother gave out to me that morning about taking it all so fucking seriously; but if you knew what went into those years, what it meant to the group of us . . .

What will it all look like when we have retired? I know the memories we will carry will partly be of saves made and scores taken, but they will also be of each other.

Did it all end in 2006? In Cloyne we lost our third county final in a row. With Cork, we were beaten by Kilkenny and they went on to claim our decade as we lumbered along under Gerald's stuttering reign.

Yet I have great memories of that year. In September there was hope of it being a great year, and for Cloyne perhaps the year of all years. I remember leaving the village that morning as something so special – not because we were going for three-in-a-row but because there were three Cloyne lads leaving from my house: my brother Conor, who was on the panel, Billy and myself. Kevin Hartnett came with us (he is from the parish but his club, Russell Rovers, are out the road in a different townland) and obviously he had his own leave-taking done at home, but I know that meant a lot to people in the town – three lads from the four streets involved and the great Sully, all of us heading to Dublin and going for three-in-a-row.

It is vital to have everything right when you are going into big games – even though you might not think it, what is going on with you off the field does affect you. From time to time you will get away with it, but as a rule you won't. In 2006 I was right: all I had been doing was hurling and looking after myself. No loose ends. Everything else was under control – relationships, business, work, health, etc.

I was an All-Star that year (and still think that I should have been the year before, too). During 2006, when skipping rope and visualizing to myself, I used to think about Davy Fitzgerald, who had the 2005 All-Star, and say to myself: 'I don't think you will go as far as me today! I am better than you!'

I can still remember the night before the All-Ireland semi-final. I knew I was in good form. I was happy and in the best condition of my life. My mother rang me that night. She said to me that she had never seen me looking so well and so healthy and that she just wanted to let me know how proud she was of me. Back then John Allen had the ability to make me think that I could fly, and I would have done anything for him or my friends on that team, but my mother's words that night – I can still remember the good feeling I had after the call. I was listening to my iPod – dance tracks all the way – gripping all my hurleys and going through my notes. I have never felt better.

When hurling finishes, will there ever be times so perfect and still?

The next day in my locker space I had words printed on a sheet and hanging where I was togging off:

Today you must do more than is required of you. Never think your job is finished. There's always something that can be done – something that can help to ensure victory. You must be a self-starter. You must possess that spark of individual initiative that sets a leader apart from the led. Self-Motivation is the key to being one step ahead of everyone else and standing head and shoulders above the crowd. Once you get going don't stop. Always be on the lookout for the chance to do something better. Never stop trying. Fill yourself with the warrior Spirit – and send that Warrior into action.

I won Man of the Match that day. I was twenty-nine years old and hurling still held a world full of possibilities.

Five weeks or so later we came home to Cloyne from our third county final, empty-handed again, and, desperate as that night was, in our heads it wasn't over and in our hearts we weren't giving up.

That was then. I'm thirty-two now and we play Tipperary this afternoon as a Cork team which would show stress fractures if you could X-ray us.

The whole paradigm changes when you come on to the Cork panel. Keeps changing. First you are just glad to be there. Then you just want to be playing. And then you win an All-Ireland medal, and next thing you want to win another one. And fuck it, you want to win an All-Star, just to show that nobody is carrying you. You are no passenger here.

Then all of a sudden it's not good enough, not the medals or the awards. You just want to keep going on your own internal journey. You feel right at the centre of it and you want to be the best you can, the best there is, the best there has ever been, and you want the same for the team around you, and if enough of you have arrived at that point there is a bond there and a will there which is incredible.

Cork becomes so big. If Cork are losing you are beaten. It becomes who you are and opponents like Kilkenny become the enemy.

And then the strange thing about GAA – you get dropped and that's it. You are out of the equation. It's just not your war any more. War isn't the right word, maybe, but it's the same adrenalin rush, the same dependency on those around you, the same feeling in your head all day long. And then it's over. They pull you out.

I write loads of things on my walls, words that I will see first thing in the morning to put me in the right place for the day. The paradigm is one of the things that is up there. You know when you get up in the morning, it's all about the way you look at things, it's all about you being a Cork hurler.

Since I went out to the field behind our house in Cloyne this has been the central thread of my life. People label me this and label me that but in my head I have been a hurler. From the time I could walk and hold a stick until now, the way I've really expressed myself and lived my life is through the game.

And I don't know now how much longer that will be the case. It will change. If we lose, if we lose badly and I make mistakes, Marty or Nasher will take the jersey which I once took from Ger Cunningham. And I hope I will be ready enough and gracious enough to do as Ger did and pass on best wishes to the Number 1.

I think about Ger walking away that Friday night of the week I made my debut. The first time in eighteen years he hadn't a championship Sunday to worry about. It was somebody else's war now.

An epic sports career like Ger's keeps you young, the dressing-room and the distraction of the games keeps you nearly in a state of happy adolescence. And when it ends there is a cruel tug of the carpet from underneath your feet and you land on your arse in the world of middle age, wondering how you got there. And on a field somewhere somebody else is fighting your war and the paradigm is changing for them.

Will you be jealous? Bitter? Can you watch? Can you live without the rushes of adrenalin and the brotherhood of the dressing-room? I've been thinking about it, but I don't want to think about it. There is life in me yet, though.

We need a win, and if not a win a good performance that reminds us of what we can be. And we need to drive on from there. I've a feeling there is a life beyond hurling but I'm not ready to find out about it yet.

No way.

34

I'm driving back to the house in Midleton, fiddling with the radio. Marty Morrissey is hosting the *SportsBag* show this morning. Three guests. Some hack, Babs Keating, and (ta da!) Sully. On the morning of a big game I wouldn't normally listen to this stuff, but I stay tuned as Sully is on. Speaking to the nation.

On the first big Sunday of his retirement Sully has been drawn back to the limelight. Whether we admit it or not, we'll all miss that a little bit when we walk out the door.

Billy's car pulls in behind me as I come into my estate. I have all my gear ready and waiting since the night before, and we're on the road quickly, collecting Nially Mac and off to meet the team bus at the Silver Springs Hotel.

Usual seats on the bus. Creature of habit. Seán Óg, Dr Con *agus mé féin* at the back of the bus. Con is reading, Seán Óg and I listening to iPods. MGMT is big with me today.

At the hotel in Tipperary, the Dundrum House, there are Cork flags hanging over the railings at the entrance. Some years we mightn't have noticed a thing like that, but today it cheers us. I grab all my gear and shove it into the team room and head back for food. While we eat I sit at a table with Con, Seán Óg and Aisake. We are tense and edgy but Con is doing his best to lighten our mood. He keeps the conversation going and throws some of his humour into the mix.

Con comes out with a minor classic at one stage, but for his troubles I snap at him and tell him to fuck off. He tells Aisake that if he scores a goal today he should imitate his brother Setanta's celebration style from six years ago. Poor Aisake may be six foot seven inches tall but he doesn't need to be drawing comparisons down on himself about his big brothers. Not on the day he is making his championship debut.

Myself and Seán Óg aren't impressed, but to be fair to Con it was a funny one to think about afterwards, the thought of us with another

Ó hAilpín in the full-forward line, more than half a decade on, and him grabbing a goal and continuing exactly where Setanta left off, making this funny celebration gesture for calm on the terraces and the pitch.

It's funny, but not now. I snap at Con and Seán Óg growls, but Con has known us since we were kids and he knows what we are like, so he gets a great kick out of the fact that he has gotten a rise out of the pair of us. Con's work here is done. He has kept us from overthinking things.

I go for a rub from John the masseur and then get my gear on, put the grips on the hurleys and go through the warm-up with Marty again. Denis Walsh comes over and talks through the puck-outs with me. I check that my understanding of today's strategy is the same as his. It is. We are 100 per cent on the same wavelength. Perfect. When the abuse starts coming down from the terraces from those who want to see every puck-out driven into oblivion, it's a reassurance to know that this is how we planned things.

I go through my final visualization and breathing routines while listening to my music on the earphones. Denis speaks to us and he speaks beautifully. Just right. He is a quiet and earnest man, Denis, and in a short space of time he has understood the heart of our team. Everything today and in our preparation has been perfect.

So Denis speaks and there's a phrase he uses today which catches in my head: 'freedom in the heart'.

That's what we need. After all the stresses, the strikes, the meetings and the troubles, we are hurling again. This is a place we love and a game that we love. This is the essence of it. We have nothing to lose here today in Semple Stadium, and what we have to regain is the love and the enjoyment. Freedom in the heart. Perfect words for where we stand.

We take the bus to the stadium now. Excellent video clips on the bus, great music to match. All positive stuff created by Joe O'Leary and given to us in this environment Denis is creating. On the way to the dressing-room at Semple Stadium there is a great reception from the Cork fans. It's been a long cold winter, and we feel the warm applause like sun on our backs.

Everything in the dressing-room has been made ready to perfection by Gatchy. What a man to have in our corner. My after-match wear is hanging up, along with two jerseys and my under-armour. Here are the sliotars, a bottle with my mix in it. Not a thing out of place for any of us, nothing which could even cause a ripple in our focus.

We walk out to the field and look at the ground. Hard and hot, but this is Thurles on a sunny day. The field of dreams. I meet Micheál Ó Muircheartaigh and we pause for a chat. Strange, but I used to always see Micheál as a pillar of the establishment and thought he would have little time for me and I would have little time for him. So before I met him I had little interest in him or the myths around him. A couple of years ago, though, we were on a tour in the States and I met him and enjoyed his company greatly. He surprised me with the understanding he had regarding coaching. I remember one day sitting down to eat some food with him and the bus was ready to leave outside, but the pair of us were feeling under no pressure to get on board as we were enjoying the chat. Since then I always have a few words with him. It's good to be here and it's good to see you, Micheál. I mean it.

In the old Thurles set-up, under the stand here the dressing-rooms had huge walls that gave us plenty of space to puck in. These new dressing-rooms are very good from a player's point of view but they don't have those walls, so I go to the corridor and start pucking against the wall by myself.

The curtain-raiser game is over and the intermediate teams are coming back in. Most of them wish me the best of luck as they pass and I reply to all of them but never look – the ball is my priority. Every single ball. *Gach uile liathród*.

Nasher, Marty and myself go through our dynamic stretching next. We always do our stretches at this stage so that when we go on to the field we can concentrate on hurling. Frank Murphy passes by. I look at him. He has few words these days.

'Good luck, gents.'

And he keeps moving. The County Board are seriously low-profile this season and today is no different.

Five minutes before the team are due out on the pitch we three goalies head back into the dressing-room. I have a final word with Eoin Cadogan. Big day for my young friend. I tell him that the first major thing he needs to remember is to be positive and the second major thing is to listen to what I say and to do what I tell him. Then he'll be grand!

We grin at each other. He has been working with me in recent times out in DePuy and between work and the ball alley we have gotten to know each other well over this winter. Cads is a strong-minded guy. Today, though, he knows who is in charge!

We grin because it's not really that I would enjoy bossing him (though I do) but because I know that for things to run well in the square today this is the way it has to be. I have been here many times before, and bossing the full-back line is just part of the job.

I put on the under-armour and my Cork jersey. There is something very special about that famous red-and-white hooped keeper's jersey. John Ga is togging off beside me. We embrace before we go into the huddle and I say, 'Gardiner, well done! We got here.'

He smiles at me and I smile back. We know the struggle we shared and there's a thousand unsaid words within those few seconds. Then into the huddle. Denis Walsh speaks with passion again and all I remember is, when he strikes that chord again about freedom, the way he says it affects me greatly.

John Ga speaks and we burst out towards the light. There is a long tunnel in Thurles – when you get to the end and turn the corner you see the brilliant white light of Semple Stadium on a championship Sunday. That draws you on. Words can't define this place. We are hurlers. This is hurling. We are in our Mecca.

Today Mecca is a place of work. This is down in my head as a busy day. We have two debutants in the full-back line, and when we watched the league final a few weeks ago John O'Brien burst through and rapped a shot at goal from distance early on. Lots of players would have been happy with the point that early in the game, but it showed that this summer the Tipp forwards will go for goal, whatever chance they get.

The heat out here is serious today and I'm conscious during the warm-up to not overdo it. For some reason we are warming up in front of the Tipp crowd at the Killinan End. Why?

I am getting some stick right from the time I jog down to the goals.

When they announce the teams and my name is called out over the intercom there is huge booing from behind the goal. It won't affect my performance, I know that, but maybe I need to develop my mindset even further so that I actually don't hear them. I'm not there yet – I'm a long way, but not yet at the point where I can't hear thousands of people booing the mention of my name.

I hear it but drive on. Playing well is the best revenge. My touch feels perfect. Fuck ye all!

Con comes down to me and says that the lads want to know which way we should play. I say to go against the wind. It normally takes teams time to settle down in big games like this, and playing against the wind doesn't really bother us, due to our style. If we are coming at them in the second half, though, the wind will add to the momentum. We win the toss and face the breeze. A good start.

Barry Kelly comes down and wishes me the best of luck. No lecture today. Just, 'The best of luck.'

Yeah, yeah. I bite the tongue. 'Best of luck to you too, Barry.'

Then the pre-match parade. We walk in line and I go through my breathing. Controlling your breathing is critical if you want to be calm in goals. Inhale for three seconds. Hold it for three seconds. Exhale for three seconds. By the time I am around to the other side of the field I am at ten, ten, ten.

It's steaming hot and there is pressure. This is very important. This is it. I feel in control now, though. I'm ready.

At our last session on Friday night at home in the Páirc we could feel the winter of trouble resolving itself and the game taking hold of us again. We had a lovely night, just training lightly and feeling the old urgency of the championship pushing us on. There was a good attitude and spirit in the group, and for some of us who thought that we'd never again train a couple of nights before a big game it was a night to enjoy.

Over the last few years it has become usual at the end of the final session for the players to go away and have their own few words together. John had asked me to speak after he did, but when he spoke it was with more passion than I have ever heard from him. He has grown so much since he was the young fella on the panel in 2002. Still in his mid-twenties, he has put himself on the line and led us through this really bitter strike, and when we go on to the field behind him he will be an even better leader for it.

On Friday he said to us, 'The last time we had all stood together like this was before we went in to meet the clubs in the Maryborough House Hotel.' He said that on the night we felt that we were going into the unknown, but we came through and we got the result. He said, 'Nobody knew what we would be heading into on Sunday, but if we face up to what we have to do again, if we stand up and be counted, we can win.'

It was a great speech and it closed off lots of things. For weeks we have been walking on eggshells around the issue of the strike as we struggled to make a team of ourselves. As John spoke there were lads in the circle who weren't part of the strike and lads there who were on the team who replaced us during the strike. As a group, though, the history of the team runs through that strike and, like any group joining a team, the new faces have to accommodate the history.

By talking about the strike John freed us all from it. Everybody did whatever they felt they had to do. Now we are together in the same jersey in this same circle and, as in any team, all our histories will have to blend. That's the only way we can drive on.

John finished and there was nothing left to say. He turned to me. I said there was no need for more talk.

The game begins. When the ball is thrown in I try to see what way they are lined up, who is on who. At the start Michael Webster, their big awkward forward, is on Conor O'Sullivan. Not good. Needs to be changed quick or we will be cleaned out under high balls. Eoin Kelly starts well. He's been injured for ever and I thought he would be slower.

I want to slow this game down in the first half, so any chance I get I do just that. Against Kilkenny in the league final, Tipp got success using the fire-and-brimstone method. They will try to do the same thing to us today and we don't want them getting that momentum going against us. So I follow the ball out to collect it from near the wire when they score or hit a wide. I take as long as possible with the puck-outs, take my time going out to frees and taking them.

Shane O'Neill gets injured early on, gets a bad bang – I know when I go out to where he is lying that he is in trouble. He is bleeding heavily after a collision with Webster. When Con comes out to tend to him it's obvious Shane's day is over, but I tell Con to drag it out as long as possible. Shane has to be taken off and Shane Murphy comes in. Now we have a full-back line, all three of whom have not been regulars. Not a time to be thinking about that, though.

The abuse continues from behind the goal. 'We're on strike, we're on strike, we're on strike.' That's the most harmless stuff. There's worse. 'Seán Óg is a refugee,' they chant, 'Seán Óg is a refugee.' There is a guy with a megaphone who is leading the choir.

About twenty minutes into the game we win a free, deep in our own half, out in the corner to my left. Barry Kelly is having a word with somebody and as I'm in no hurry to take the free I stand and wait. It's one of those natural breaks in the rhythm and the stadium goes quiet.

Next thing the megaphone starts behind me in the Killinan End. 'He's gay, he's bent, his arse is up for rent, Dónal Óg, Dónal Óg. He's gay, he's bent, his arse is up for rent, Dónal Óg, Dónal Óg.'

Only a few voices join in, but the silence in the stadium is so perfect that almost everybody hears the megaphone. Sully, who is in the stand, tells me later that he went down to the guards and asked them to throw the guy out. Denis Walsh, who was on the other side of the field, hears it and later wrote me a letter because of the effect it had on him.

And that's what gets to you. Other people. I leaned over the free and took it and struck it well. I have trained myself for this, but my father is in the back of my mind. I know how tough he is, though, he'll get through it. My mother doesn't go to games any more. The stress is too much. My sister Treasa has been deeply upset a few times by what she has heard. Teammates get bothered and hurt. I hate what it does to those around me, especially when it doesn't hurt me at all.

Standing there, though, down on the field in this stadium that I love, letting the words fly past me, I get the feeling that something good should come of this, from all the abuse shouted from behind the wire at games, from little knots of people on the street, from the chatroom bigots, from the one inter-county player who has ever abused me for being what I am. (A Tipp man, as it happened. He ended up getting taken off that day. I remember thinking, You should be concentrating on the fucking game. That would be a real Cork one, wouldn't it – You didn't concentrate on the game, boy!)

The advice is always to ignore these people, to never give them the satisfaction of knowing that you have even heard them; but I'm thinking that in a large stadium like this, almost filled today with hurling people, there must be so many men and women who are standing silent, knowing that their own sexuality or that of some-body they love isn't to the liking of the man with the megaphone; so many people are feeling the little arrows of poison raining down from the Killinan End.

So it's here in this book, between these covers, come what may. It's all here, what I am and how I am; and it makes no difference to me if you call me bent or you call me brokeback or if it amuses you to think that my arse is up for rent.

And if there are a hundred or a thousand hurlers or rugby players or camogie players out there in their teens, struggling with the idea of what they are, I hope they'll know that fools with megaphones or runny mouths just don't count. Sully going down to the guards counts. Denis Walsh putting a pen to paper, he counts. Dinny O'Shea telling me that there are men on his site, men from Cloyne, that agree with him that it doesn't matter what Ógie is – he's one of them. That counts.

Nially Mac and his questions. Dr Con. Falv. Seán Óg. Corcoran. Every fella or woman who said to me along the way that they are there for me. My family. My club. My friends.

You have your journey and you weigh up the goodness and love in all that against a bit of doggerel from the terrace from a poor loser who has paid in to see us play and has brought his little megaphone and his own little problems along. Why bother with him ever?

Fuck, I just played on and there wasn't a fragment of my game or my life that I felt he had influenced. He didn't steal a moment of my happiness at being in Semple Stadium in the red and white of Cork with my teammates and friends, playing the greatest game on earth.

It was harder than usual to let go of thoughts about the family, but

some dangerous balls come out of the sky to deal with. I was happy
with every bit of handling and footwork except one moment from a
long-range free from Cummins. It depends on the way you look at
things, I suppose – Cads and Kevin said to me after that it was a great
save, but I'm not happy as I should have grabbed it.

By half-time we are going OK. We've weathered their storm. We
are only three points down. In the dressing-room Denis speaks. Once
he is finished, I say a few words. I believe Tipp are there for the taking
today. And I say it. We need to go flat out for the start of the second
half, though. If a guy gets hurt or can't go any more, another man will
come on, as Shane Murphy has done for Shane O'Neill. Let's not pace
ourselves. Go flat out.

Thirty-five minutes.

35

We come out for the second half and the sun is in my eyes. No point in grabbing a hat – a hat only puts you off further, I think, and you have to look up at the sun anyway.

Fuck. The ball is hardly in when we mess about with a clearance, and next thing there is a man in behind. He has it. I need to go early as he is so close. I'm going to my left but, as I go there, the ball gets deflected to the other side. I can't shift my momentum. Goal.

Bad start. Focus on the next ball. I look up to see if there is anything on from the puck-out. As a goalkeeper the moments after a goal goes past you are the ones when you should look to see if there is anything on, as everyone on the field seems to lose concentration for a few moments. That includes officials. Watch. Some of the most experienced defenders in the game, when they want to do a guy off the ball, they do it at this stage of the game.

There is nothing on, so I take my time. You will get away with taking your time more after conceding a goal.

Bit by bit now we work our way into this game – even when we are missing chances I feel that we are on our way back and we will get there. I just keep saying to the lads in front of me, 'Keep it tight here, the boys will get the scores, don't let them down.'

Now is the time to push on. We can bury Tipperary.

Cadogan is going great guns in front of me. At the start of the game I wanted to keep him going and up for it. Now in the second half I need to tell him to box clever. He is pumped and on the edge – that's fine, but he needs to be reminded of that in case he doesn't see it. I have experienced this with Sully so many times over the years.

The game starts to open up and I hit a good few well-targeted puck-outs. They'll be forgotten. It's the bad puck-outs people recall.

I need to look for Cathal Naughton, who has come on and who is

shockingly quick. He will be good for us if I can get him on the ball.
It doesn't work out that well for him or for us, though.

Denis Walsh comes around to the goals at one stage and we speak
about the set-up of the full-back line. He says, 'Leave it the way it is
for now, but if you think it should change then change it.' Trust.

Cads is having a Punch-and-Judy battle with Webster. At one stage
Webster's hurley falls in the square. I'm pumped up and, well, I
shouldn't have done what I did next and I'm not proud that I did it,
but maybe, as in that story of the scorpion carrying the frog across
the river, it is just my nature. We are in a combat situation with
Webster. When his weapon falls to the floor, I stand on it and pull the
other half up in my hand. It breaks handily and I throw it away as if
I have just discarded a broken stick.

Massive roars come from the stands – some abuse, some support.
So it goes.

In the end we run out of time. We have performed well and we
have rediscovered ourselves. We could and should have taken a famous
victory here, but we have enough. We have the soul of a team back.

I turn and I applaud the fans who slope upwards in a long red-and-
white bank behind the goal. I appreciated their support and their
presence and want to show it. A couple of kids come on to the field
and look for autographs. I sign a couple, but I need to get out of here.
I want to see Brendan Cummins on the way out – congratulate him
and tell him what a great keeper he is. He saved a penalty from Hoggy
in the second half. Funny, we had debated penalties and Cummins for
so long. At the end of our last session I stood for a few penalties from
Hoggy. He has a great shot but he wasn't naturally striking the ball to
the keeper's left, which is where he should strike it. I told him, for
what it's worth, to hit it wherever he wants but not at Cummins'
right-hand side. He did the right thing this afternoon but Cummins,
man that he is, got his head (of all things) in the way anyhow.

Barry Kelly is in the tunnel. He puts out his hand. It is shaking,
from the nerves and pressure, I suppose. You're a tough man, I think
to myself. I shake his hand anyway.

And I go back to the room.

John Ga is beside me. The room is silent. Denis Walsh makes one of the most inspiring post-match speeches I have ever heard. I can't sit still, though, my mind is racing at the lost opportunity.

There is a raw genuineness about a place like this that is hard to describe. Liam Sheedy, the Tipp boss, comes in and speaks after Denis has done. He says that he has watched and admired us greatly over the last few years, the way we have done our business and that it was us that raised the standard for all else to follow.

Gatchy tells me afterwards that the County Board boys were cringing in the corner during this.

John Ga beside me is devastated. He has the head in the knees. I feel for him. He has been through a hell of a lot this winter and stood up to every bit of it. I also think of his dad, John also – he was there beside him shoulder to shoulder, every step. And beside us, too, every inch of the way. Two great men.

I shower, get on the gear. I thank Pat Buckley for helping to get us back to where we are.

Gatch – the Sancho Panza to this team – takes everything from me. All I want is my money and my iPod. I know where I am going and I want my music to ease it.

I ask John, is he coming for a drink, and he says, 'Yeah, fuck, let's do it.'

We walk out into the sunlight. All of the loyal supporters we had during the strike are there waiting for us.

We lost some friends but we gained more. We are followed by a more passionate animal now, one who feels more part of it and has a right to feel that way.

We walk down the town. At certain pubs with the Cork support spilling out on to the street we stop for autographs and pictures. At other pubs I get stick. A lot of it. Beery abuse from the crowds spilling on to the street from the pubs in Liberty Square. I'm thinking to myself that if I wanted a fight I would get into one, no problem, right now. And then John says something to me which just makes me laugh out loud.

He says to me that he should catch me by the hand and the pair of us – Cusack and Gardiner, hurling's most despised agitators – should walk down the road hand in hand. That would sort them. And now

I'm deaf and immune to them all as we walk on by, getting a great laugh just from the thought of it.

Billy is outside The Castle, waiting for us. We go in and have a few cold beers. We meet Michael Webster's brother and share a joke and a chat. That's the GAA. Tipp is a hurling county. I have always felt Tipperary people are hurling people. Myself, John and Billy are a lot of things, but we are definitely hurling people too. Among real hurling people there is a kind of communion of minds.

We go back to the team hotel in a mellow state, get on to our bus. I sit in the back beside Seán Óg. He is listening to his music and I am listening to mine. Some of the lads venture up and down the bus. We have been defeated but the atmosphere says that we are down today but definitely not out. We have a pulse. A heart beating strongly.

There is an appreciation of music in the group. We share headphones and I mess with the likes of Hoggy and Cads about how it was my generation who had all the real dance tunes.

When we hit Cork, Seán Óg drops me to Mulligan's. I meet Ray there and we have a few pints. Then to the Catwalk with Cads and Billy.

(Now the Catwalk is a place that you mightn't see too many Cork hurlers in, but myself and Caddy love the music; Billy isn't entirely sold on it but he goes along. Myself and Cads have a fantasy which we often talk about which involves the Catwalk – thirty-six hours – Frank and Ger Mac with a DJ in a dance-off. There's a rifle too somewhere, but I'd better not go into it!)

Down to Rearden's in Washington Street. I hook up with Ben O'Connor. Myself and Ben are always happy in each other's company, even after all these years on teams together. Things get a bit blurred from there. I have a good chat with Roy O'Donovan the soccer player. I think it was a good chat and I think it was about life in Sunderland. I'm fairly sure it was Roy O'Donovan. Who knows?

I leave in the early hours with Kevin and his girlfriend Keara and with Gatch and Billy. The last three head home. Myself and Kevin keep on going into the night. No sleep or stop. This team of ours that we thought was dead, it's up and about and walking, and soon we hope it will be kicking ass.

Many times last winter I thought I would never play championship hurling for Cork again. Today was a good day. And Kevin. With his busted finger he has been training up and down the terraces of Páirc Uí Chaoimh with Deccie our physio. Pushing himself as only he can. That experience will only make him stronger. His time is near.

Days like today are a gift.

The night that follows is a long story. Sunrise finds us sitting on Union Bridge, talking *raméis* to each other. Looking at the reflections of our city in our own beautiful Lee.

Did we invent him with our mad Cork imaginations or did the man in the long trenchcoat who joined us next really exist? He opened the coat and it was lined with small green bottles of beer which he shared among us.

A red County Council van bumped past and a minute later cruised by again for a better look. Third time it stopped.

'Lads? Unlucky to lose it. Well done, boys.'

And now a taxi driver pulls up on the path and the sun hasn't yet found its heat and the early houses are still locked, but we drink our beers and sit on this bridge in Cork and talk hurling and it feels as if we are Cork hurlers again. Cork's hurlers and Cork's people are glad to see us.

Cars blow their horns and the odd fist waves. Billy Morgan sends me a text: 'Ogie I was proud to be a Cork man yesterday.' Winter and its discontent is gone and there is some warmth now on our shoulders. We are as alive as alive can be.

Come what may – *Ceannarach abú!*

Picture Credits

Index